ETHICAL
ESP

by Ann Ree Colton

ARC PUBLISHING COMPANY
Post Office Box 1138
Glendale, California 91209

9|0²

Second Printing, 1984

ISBN: 0-917187-03-2

Library of Congress catalog card number: 78-149600

Printed in the United States of America
DeVorss & Co., Marina del Rey, California 90294

This book is written to render a
service to those who would awaken
in themselves the unspeakable riches
to be gained through spiritual illumination.

CONTENTS

INTRODUCTION

The searchlight of science is beginning to place its attention upon ESP and related subjects. Scientific research in this fascinating field is disclosing knowledge of little-known energies — thereby bringing mankind closer to a mighty Energy Age.

The timely scientific breakthroughs in certain areas of ESP have introduced new questions to the modern mind. These questions revolve around the need for clear-cut answers related to the ethical use of ESP. For over forty years Ann Ree Colton has pondered the questions now being asked. Her logical and illuminating answers are the basis for this important book.

The unique ESP abilities of Ann Ree Colton have provided her with first-hand knowledge pertaining to the little-known energies and invisible worlds beginning to be tapped by scientific researchers. From the time of childhood, she has had remarkable extrasensory powers that over the years have become highly sensitized instruments of perception. However, rather than exploit these powers for personal gain, she dedicated to use her gifts "to give hope to others."

As modern man gradually removes the mystery from ESP, Biblical truths will become more meaningful. The scribes of all ancient Scriptures and the enlightened scientists of today are joining hands across the barriers of time — and the facets of truth related to the supernatural are being polished and presented for modern-day understanding.

The wonder that is man is only beginning to be comprehended. Sages over the ages have known the basic truths of life and extrasensory life. Now men of science with vast technological resources at their command are beginning to tap the secrets of man's inner universe.

In the year of 1952 Ann Ree Colton began to write about the *inner life* that is so real to her. Her first books contain numerous prophecies; among these are predictions about science discovering new worlds of energy, including the energy field around the human body. She also tells of science eventually harnessing the energies from the planets. In other writings she defines the different levels of telepathy and describes man's *etheric anatomy* and soul-faculties. Her knowledge of the etheric anatomy provides the foundation for a brilliant system of spiritual healing. Among her many perceptive revelations is the fascinating "genesis story," which discloses the various geneses states of the earth's creation and mankind's evolvement. She sees man as now entering the age of *self-genesis* — a great new scientific-spiritual age.

Prophets have come — and have shown the way. New prophets are still appearing and telling of the coming wonders of God — wonders that never cease. Ann Ree Colton has been a prophet for over forty years. Her unique revelations are perfect adjuncts to present-day scientific breakthroughs in ESP. She sees for man a spiritually liberated future — after all the wars have been fought, es-

pecially the inevitable war each individual must fight—
the war between his lower nature and his higher nature.
The weapons of his higher nature are ethics — the Biblical
code of ethics fortified by new ethics required for each era.

For the approaching Energy Age to avoid becoming a disaster, it will be necessary that it also be an Age of Ethics
— ethics in the use of powerful cosmic energies and ethics
in the use of telepathic and other extrasensory energies. Even
now, on the dawn of the Energy Age, the ethics related to
ESP need to be defined by those who are aware of its dangers
and its blessings. These ethics will be invaluable to all who
would like to know how to avoid misusing their innate
psychic powers and how such powers may be used as spiritual
instruments to glorify God—the Giver of all extrasensory
gifts. For such inquiring souls this book will prove a priceless
guide in their quest for knowledge and truth — and especially
for their desire to fulfill their full creative, psychic, and
spiritual potential in the present life.

My work with Ann Ree Colton began in 1952 when I
made tape recordings of her meditative visions. These first
recordings resulted in three prophetic books, *Islands of
Light*, *Vision for the Future*, and *The Lively Oracles*. The
remarkable clairvoyance with which Ann Ree was endowed
from early childhood had become over the years a refined
spiritual gift. Every day new prophetic visions and remarkable revelations came to her mind during her meditations and
also during other times of the day, especially in answer to my
numerous questions. Her dictation to me became so voluminous that we knew we had to fulfill the Biblical injunction to
"sell all" and to place ourselves entirely in the hands of God.
Our only assurance through spiritual guidance was that
there would be "water plenty and food enough."

As the years progressed Ann Ree was able to place in books
and correspondence lessons her many thought-provoking

ideas, inspired insights, brilliant revelations, perceptive prophecies, and beautiful mantramic prayers. Her creative output was enormous, and the diverse subjects she discussed required a rare versatility. This she was able to fulfill.

Several years ago, as public interest in ESP began to mount, we knew that a number of persons were confused as to psychic gifts and their use. Many persons received their answers from Ann Ree's lectures on "The Difference Between the Psychical and the Spiritual." The new ideas she introduced on this important subject may now be found in the pages of this book.

The governments of Russia and other communistic countries are seriously interested in probing the depths of ESP. They are approaching these subjects through the efforts of qualified scientists. Whether communistic countries use their knowledge of ESP in an ethical manner remains to be seen, especially the use of telepathy for espionage or for controlling the minds of the masses. Russian scientists have proved that telepathy is a reality. Some of them have expressed concern over how the government will use such information. Russian astronauts are taught telepathy as part of their training program.

Certain American universities are beginning to research telepathy, ESP, and reincarnation. There is a growing new interest in all aspects of these subjects. The forthcoming knowledge will surely bless the world in surprising ways, even as knowledge of the atom introduced mankind to a great new age.

Religions rigidly adhering for centuries to certain precepts and dogma are gradually softening their positions and becoming more flexible and open-minded.

Ann Ree Colton has prophesied these changes in science and religion. What she has predicted over the past twenty years is now coming to pass—but there are many other prophecies that are yet to be fulfilled.

Scientific photographs of the "aura" are a remarkable accomplishment. According to Ann Ree, science will one day have the equipment sensitive enough to photograph "certain types of angels using more dense atoms." This achievement will certainly be a *breakthrough* and will influence the thinking of countless minds.

Another prediction now drawing close to the realm of believability is Ann Ree's prophecy that men will be able to fly without need of an airplane. She states: "The solar and planetary energies in man's body will be harnessed to give him a levitation and locomotion power over gravity. With a simple compass-like directing apparatus attached to certain portions of his body, he will draw upon the solar fire of his etheric energy body. He will glide and move above the ground or earth by mechanically drawing upon the solar energy stored in the atoms of his own body."

In 1952 Ann Ree Colton wrote: "Men will reach the time in the coming 30 years when things they hear will neither surprise them, startle them, nor dismay them. So shall the world take such a pace in the swiftness of change, of science, of inventions, that man shall receive one thing upon another as of science, and think of them not as the miracle of the mind or the miracle of that which is given, but will take them as he has taken all else within his world, and include them within his actions.

"When science has matured, men shall enter into the noiseless age. Men will no longer depend upon the mineral kingdom for their energies within mechanics and industry; but they shall discover the secrets of other energies within the earth. The earth has groaned and suffered in that men have bled the earth of the oils so needed in the equilibrium of the axis of the earth. The energies from the oil and ores of the earth shall be replaced by five energies: (1) the energy from every type of atom; (2) the solar energy from within the earth's atmosphere; (3) the energy from the ocean water and ocean depths; (4) the energy from the planets; (5) the energy from a sub-electronic force within the earth.

"Men of the earth will begin to enter a noiseless age from the years of 1973 to 1980. The neon, the combustions, the poisonous atmospheres from industrial fumes, and the mechanical sound irritants will become a thing of the past. Much of the sickness of a neurotic nature has been caused by the noise accompanying scientific progress. In the latter part of the 20th century the greater percentage of strident noise will be overcome.

"Before men chart the sea of space, and master the astronomical revelation of God, they must yet make tillable the earth. Science will make the 'desert . . . blossom as the rose'. Science will conserve the forest, discover new ores, discover the true nutritional balances for men, and will revolutionize the sciences of medicine, chemistry, physics. Within 3,000 years the earth will become a garden of productivity.

"Science will discover the eternal atoms of man, simultaneously with an unknown layer of minerals in the earth. And science also will reveal, through gauges and instruments, that each eternal atom in man's body correlates to a star in the universe. Science will term this body to be immortal, and will call it the 'counterpart body' of man. When this occurs, men will no longer doubt or disbelieve that they are eternal.

"In the year of 1976 men will express science through Uranus and the spiritual Jupiter to come; and with the benefic sun, the era and time of benevolence will touch the earth. This benevolence will be the approaching of brotherhood to men.

"Science will discover a means of controlling weather through knowledge of the moon.

"Men, searching for the Light and for the higher spiral on which to stand, seek the answers. Where 100 years ago a few priceless minds and strong ones sought the answers, today thousands are seeking the answers. The force of the seeking is beginning to bring evolvement unto man, and he shall face reality as he is in earth and as he is to God.

"In the next 3,000 years the true rituals of heaven will purge away the crystallizations gathered from the physical concepts in religious ritual. The age of science will introduce new symbologies which will free the true rituals of the Heavenly Sacraments.

"Within 300 years the minds of men shall open to one another through the simple laws of telepathy. Men shall, out of the upheavals of oppression, begin their way upward, mind to mind, and heart to heart.

"Astronomy and astrology shall blend in the coming years of 2000 onto 2053. Men will come more intimately to know the world of astronomy as of star and planet. The world of astrology, as revealing men's temperaments and the portraying influences in their lives, shall blend into the things which are affected by the sun.

"Charlatanism and exploitation shall receive a great blow in the year of 1973. Men shall no longer receive in earth the part, but in their heart's consciousness shall ask, and receive the whole. That of the part as in error given to men in system as of astrology shall be void and cast out.

"The true system of astrology as blending with astronomy will come into earth through science and shall bring a new blending. Men shall use that of the stars and planets even as they use the signals at railroad crossings and even as they use the great radar which is coming into the earth as men have never dreamed.

"Science within the next 70 years shall prove to mankind the life which extends beyond human consciousness onto a higher thing explained as of the soul's light.

"In the year of 1978 men in earth will begin a new type of navigation and will discover new means and methods by which air is commanded in a particular stratum of space. Men will use instruments which work in an eccentric and peculiar way, overcoming that between force, gravity, and space.

"In the next 300 years, men shall see in earth men of acute knowledge who carry — which is rare in the physical world unto this time — the equal faculty of body with the faculty of mind, and with the equal faculty of body a justice and a soul balance in light and love."

A teacher of teachers, Ann Ree Colton is known by many to be an advanced philosophical thinker as well as clairvoyant and prophet. Her philosophy of life is compatible with all great Scriptures that teach of the vast potential within man and the spiritual rewards that await the sincere aspirant. She envisions an era when the higher aspects of ESP will be a natural part of human life. However, before this time of peace, goodwill and creative fulfillment, the world must first come to grips with each physical and spiritual problem — including the known and unknown aspects of ESP. This book is a step in that direction.

JONATHAN MURRO

I

THE DIFFERENCE BETWEEN
LOWER ESP AND HIGHER ESP*

All persons have ESP. In the pure, ESP is as a moving river of light pointing the way to godly things for man. In the selfishly motivated, ESP is as a fork of lightning—blasting and damaging. Some persons having ESP look upon it as a burden, while others look upon ESP as a gift-blessing from God.

In an undisciplined mind and will, ESP is an enigma. In the untrained and unaware, an inhibited ESP produces a fearful manifestation and a superstitious mentality. To the materialistic mind, incidents stemming from ESP are looked upon as chance, luck, or coincidence.

---

* At the conclusion of this book may be found a glossary defining unfamiliar terminology and words.

Spiritual ESP, having a sacred milieu and function of its own, defies and masters the barriers between matter and spirit. There are levels or degrees of ESP that can be perceived only with the eye and power of the spirit. In lower energy aspects of ESP there are mischievous, intelligible, psychical forces that challenge the naive expectancy of one who has yet to open the spiritual eye.

ESP is clearly defined in both the Old and New Testaments. In the Bible, men are warned to avoid persons using the lower aspects of ESP. Today men learned in all fields of knowledge are yet confused as to the difference between spiritual ESP and the crude phases of psychical ESP.

As one spiritually evolves, he learns that there is a fixed supernal ethic governing the use of ESP. As ethic advances in the use of ESP, it will be ascertained that using the magnified aspect of ESP to dominate the will of another abuses and disastrously reverses the sacred power of ESP.

ESP is the periscope of the subconscious. ESP rises up as a periscope, extending the range of the insight beyond the energy frequency waves and reach of the senses. ESP, when used with ethic, becomes the master soul-faculty. ESP, when used to gratify sensuality, leads one to lust and degeneration. Men fearing ESP have in some former era or time either used ESP in its lower aspects or have been the victims of lower ESP.

ESP is a pre-perceiving side of knowing activated by *extrasensory willing*. ESP gives the knower the power to extend the consciousness into events yet to be physically manifested. ESP is a will instrument. All persons having strong wills have a greater capacity to call forth ESP powers. If the will is forceful or selfishly designed, ESP becomes an instrument for destruction. If the will is spiritually exalted, the result is blessedness. When one has a burning desire to make union with universal cause and to know God, the higher ESP power will enable him to rise to illimitable heights of illumination and revealment.

In the soul of every man is the memory of other times and ages. The ages least impressed upon man's mind, emotions and thoughts are the ages in which knowledge of the psychic nature was least active. The most effervescent and progressive periods of man's rise occur in a psychic era or time. *In greater psychic eras men rise.* All of the salient history, philosophy and creative records are written when men in mass are engaged in the enlargement of, and dependency upon, their higher extrasensory powers.

There are several ways in which the ESP powers are presently expressed: some use the psychical powers knowing not that they use them; some experiment with ESP powers, using them blindly, ignoring discipline and ethic; some, having used ESP powers ethically in former lives, use them now in the present life for good and for service to mankind; and some use psychic powers inadvertently as an unexplained forewarning during a period of danger or crisis.

The use of psychic powers for financial gain and exploitation will in this age become obsolete, as the understanding of the psychic arts will be incorporated into the scientific way of life. Man will understand his psychic nature technically. Teachers related to higher ESP will encourage the mastering of the ESP powers in connection with the spiritual life.

The higher ESP power is a soul power. It cannot be bought, purchased or sold. It is available only to those who approach its thresholds with the perfect payment of a devoted and dedicated heart.

In the present time, there is much excitation concerning the evidence and validity of ESP. Men of this age being of a scientific trend in thought and action seek to dissect and define with physical gauges the powers of ESP in man. An external approach to the inward complexities of man results only in external verifications. Regardless of how many psychic subjects or persons one may observe in his scientific dissecting or evaluating, no one, by outer observation, can totally determine the full or complete functions of ESP.

Science is presently proving the validity of ESP. Science will confirm that man is a conglomerate of atoms, light, forces, and energies. Science also will show that the psychical nature of man is the result of an intelligible force compelling man to achieve more and beyond the range of his ordinary senses. The greater scientific contributions in this field of research will be made by highly evolved individualistic scientists who will explore within themselves through their own psychical powers the true working of ESP.

Lower ESP uses the lower mind; higher ESP uses the higher mind. Energized and mechanized analysis will touch only the lower aspect of ESP. However, this analysis by science will contribute to man's great breakthrough into the spiritual life.

When man finally learns that he is authorized by scientific acceptance of the psychic forces in his nature, he will of himself be compelled to move forward progressively into the greater precincts and powers of the soul.

Energized psychic analysis by a materialistic person cannot measure, analyze, or weigh the soul impulses of another; one can only compare and rightfully judge from that which he knows within himself. Thus, ESP cannot be completely weighed and judged on the level of the organic, energetic or factual sciences, as the higher power and expression of ESP is ever manifested in advancing and *progressive* stages.

Inasmuch as both higher and lower ESP exist in all men, there will be found with certainty similar or parallel evidences in all persons confirming the power of ESP. However, when science seeks to weigh and measure the intricate functions of the higher frequencies of ESP, this divine preceptor or lightning rod for God, when approached irreverently, will provide only mechanical analysis. The mystique of higher psychic power can be only partly gauged through physical instruments designed by man.

ESP can be utilized ethically and made to function on an enlarged scale for man only through spiritual ethic. Men in this age, accepting the evidence that ESP is a reality, will give a greater play and freedom to the power of ESP. The secular rigidities, religious taboos, and materialistic concepts which men have inherited concerning the psychic arts—particularly in the Western world—are now to be revised and eventually swept away.

THE ULTRA SENSE

When God placed man into the earth as a living soul, He activated in man five senses for his earthy mind to use. He gave to man a psychic energy body. This body is an exact duplicate of the physical body and is necessary for man's survival in a gravity world. This psychic energy body is an organized, deathless body with two natures: lower and higher. The lower energy body, or lesser etheric body, more oriented to earth substances, is used in combating and mastering the forces of Nature, the elements of fire, air, water, earth, and ether. God also gave to man a higher energy body, called the immortal or everlasting body. Though man would die in countless times throughout the aeons, reincarnating over and over, the essence of the lower and higher energy bodies would survive to be used again and again until a certain mastery of consciousness is attained.

To each of the five senses God gave an energy to be drawn upon and used. To the sense of sight He gave the energy of the light of the sun. To the sense of hearing He gave the energy of gravity and rays of the moon. To the sense of taste He gave the power to draw the energy from the chlorophyll of the plant-life world. To the sense of touch He gave the power to draw upon the mineral kinetic energies imbedded in form and in stone. To the sense of smell He gave the use of the ionic and pranic energies of earth's atmosphere to draw inward air through breath and respiration and to manufacture the blood or life force for the physical body. All of these powers — psychic, kinetic, planetary and gravity — man uses with his earthy or lower mind, that he may survive and master the earth, its resources and its power.

To the higher energy body made of cosmic-life frequencies, God gave a higher mind with an ultra or sixth sense as a door ajar through which to make union with Him. God instilled into man this ultra instrument of perception with the forewarning that man must use the ultra sense reverently, creatively. To do other than this would defeat the purpose of his life on earth. It was the plan of God that the five senses become obedient to the ultra sense or higher ESP, and thus make man into a son of God in action. Consequently, when man denies the ultra sense and enslaves himself solely to the lower aspect of his five senses through acts of sensuality and materiality, he short-circuits the pure and more accurately true attributes of foreseeing and foreknowing.

To depend upon the earthy mind and the five senses alone, is to use but a fragment of one's memory, imagination, and will. To use the ultra sense or higher sense perception as the shepherd over the five senses is to make the senses the servant rather than the master of one's mind and emotions.

From age to age, men depending solely upon the lower aspect of their five senses have fought a repetitive and losing battle in a mortal world. When higher ESP is nullified by the inflexible earthy mind, man is shut away from God.

Man cannot hear what God would say to him nor see what God would reveal to him. He cannot know the greater gifts that God would give to him. He cannot be enlarged by God's restoring life in him, nor can he speak as an authority for God. Having lost touch with the true Source of his life, he is aware only of himself, of his physical and mortal concerns.

The senses can be perfect recorders of the emotions and thoughts only when one unites the power of ESP with the higher ray of his own ego and the Will of God. To permit the ultra sense to function as the supreme ruler over the five senses is to unite with one's spiritual destiny, rather than with one's physical fate. Ultra sense or higher sense perception gives to man the way in which he may command his destiny. The great mystics, sages and masters of the earth have used ESP as a golden antenna for God. Under the Will of God, they have freed men with a vision beyond the senses.

To be lost materialistically in the labyrinth of the five senses — to be solely dependent upon them — is to live in part and to see through a glass darkly. To understand and to be aware of the ultra sense is to chart one's life upon the creative sea, a delightful ocean of supernal creation for God.

THE INHERENT PSYCHIC NATURE

To acquaint oneself with and become aware of the meaning in higher sense perception, one must accept the fact that he has used the various aspects of his psychic nature in many lives.

In the ages past, when this earth was mist-like, the five senses being hypersensitively active, a higher etheric inductive ESP had command over the senses. With the increase in density of the earth and the congealing effects of gravity over the ages, man — through experimentation in touching, tast-

ing, smelling, breathing, hearing and seeing — gradually began to neglect his higher sense relationships and to depend
less and less upon his ultra sense. Today in the world there are
some who yet retain the etheric techniques of the Lemurian
powers of ESP kinetic energies. And some function now
through post-Atlantean or Egyptian ritualistic memory in
the use of ESP.

In the course of man's evolvement on earth, all have retained, to some degree, banked fires of psychical power residing within the lunar abdominal brain, or solar plexus. And
there are some who have access to ESP powers drawn up
from the well of memory in the atavistic psychical brain, or
Quelle, seated at the base of the brain or the lower portion
of the skull. Such psychical impulses are stimulated in
dreams, in karmic trials, and in crisis initiatory events in
one's life. It is God's intent for man that he use the higher
psychical impulses to precede or go before his senses. It is
also the intent or plan of God that man use his psychical
potential as a holy antenna for creation, that he may develop
a whole consciousness.

Men of this age desire more than anything to understand
themselves. And men truly in love with life will desire to dare
to go *inward* to understand. Men will turn to the great
prophets, sages, and teachers of the past, and to the most
exalted One of all — the Christ — to understand this mysterious holy power given to men which may become a bridge of
light between death and life, darkness and light.

The timely recognition of the higher psychic faculties in
man is now preparing him for an astounding mental and
emotional expression. Should men fail to recognize this
subliminal power of the mind to be sacred, all will be lost
or in vain. Jesus, the Son of Man, came to give the ethic
for the use of spiritual powers; before Jesus, the ancient

Rishis of the East came to give man the way to develop these powers.

Before the coming of Jesus, the majority of men used ESP through group etheric instincts. Men in tribes and lesser family-genesis followed and obeyed the instinctual psychical ESP impulses to protect their crops, their herds, and their families. The psychical ESP impulses before Jesus were used to shape and expand the lesser emotions of men. After the Christ Spirit took command of the inward minds of men, the spiritual aspect of ESP moved into the Jesus-impulse directing initiation into the higher mind of the individual. However, traditional and secular early church fathers, discarding certain inherent and supportive wisdom carried over from ancient teachings, frowned upon the individual ESP, repressing both the higher and lesser aspects of the psychical nature. In the medieval Christian church, persons externalizing their psychic natures were persecuted. Thus, the mystic body of the church gradually atrophied, and men of the Western world as a whole have through misconception ostracized the individual having psychical powers.

In ancient Lemuria, men lived within a psychical ESP etheric matrix clairsentiently and clairaudiently under the direction of the Over-Lords or Hierarchy, the Father, and the angels. Lemurian ESP powers were etherically inductive. The Atlantean ESP powers were forcefully kinetic. The post-Atlantean or Egyptian ESP powers, before Christ, were ritualistically astral. The Christ mentality, since Jesus, is seeking to initiate all who are ready into the higher expansion of the ESP powers of the spirit.

Many students of occult knowledge compare the present age to the age of Atlantis when the dark scientists and occultists of that era, using the nefarious side of psychism, were responsible for the sinking and destruction of their continent. They look upon the calamitous events in the present atomic age with fearful eyes, fearing a disastrous ending to the humanities in the present time.

In the rising crest of Egyptian grandeur and accomplishment, the adept-priests of Ammon, using remembered Atlantean occult practices, achieved mighty and unique things, building vast empires directed by the priest-kings or initiates. Under priestly tutelage, pharaohs produced a glorified Egypt which is yet to be fully understood in the present age and time. As the pharaoh-initiates reached their ascension arc, through the use of a superior psychical knowledge they commanded vast lands, wealth and culture. These exalted egos inhabiting Egyptian bodies influenced the total Mediterranean orbit of cultures, including Greece and, later, Rome. However, in the latter Egyptian dynasties, ending with Ikhnaton, children born in the royal environments of Egypt were thereafter unable to activate the former pure Atlantean psychical powers.

After Atlantis, all royal Egyptian infants at birth had their skulls tightly bound so as to exert pressure upon their skulls and also upon the pituitary gland, thereby producing magnified psychical power. With the passing ages these spinal pressures were less effective, even with these superimposed stresses; the Ammon priest-kings and their priests fell into the lower or nefarious psychic practices. The Egyptian rulership receded into ritualistic decay.

There is a cardinal law ruling and governing all psychical powers: when stimulated by psychical pressure, by drugs, or by any other outer means, psychical power, using the destroying and the death aspect of the life force, degenerates into lower expression.

When a nation or a person is on the rising crest of creative evolvement, the psychical power inspiring and stimulating this rise produces pure spiritual manifestation. When nations abuse the accumulative soul-perception impulses or psychic stimuli embodied in the mass of people, the result is amorality and loss of ethic.

Psychic power, while unpredictable in the untrained individual, is predictable when used as a gift of God. Psychic perception, used devotedly and rightly, inevitably provides a unique, regenerative, vital and creative expression for God.

The center of the periscope of the subconscious or the obelisk-like column of psychical energy seated at the base of the brain may be compared to a fern frond. In the undeveloped psychical person, the frond is tightly curled in an inverted circular fashion. In the developed spiritual person, the frond uncurls and rises, pressing upon the higher mental and spiritual atoms governing the pituitary and pineal glands. The more highly evolved one is spiritually and the purer his motives, the more erect is the upward column or frond of the psychical powers.

When psychical energy is stimulated outwardly by a situation seeming too burdensome for the senses to comprehend — and the frond or column of psychical power is at its lowest point of placement — the will is subordinated to the lower aspects of the senses. Then the senses and the psychical power are uncoordinated, and one is subjected to the lower phases of karma. Persons depending upon the force aspect of their psychical natures rather than upon the peace aspect of their souls become involved in initiatory, subterranean, astral chimeras. Pure spiritual power is supported by the more wholesome contemplative aspects of the psychic nature.

The psychical periscope may also be compared to the stamen in a five-petaled flower — the five petals symbolizing the five senses. When the stamen is yet to be full blown, one must depend upon his five senses to receive the hidden fragrance or scent of the flower. This is true in psychical power and the senses; thus, when the inner periscope of psychical power is unopened and partially active in the fiery matrix of the subconscious, one is dependent upon the karmic aspect of his five senses to gauge, to judge, to weigh and to act.

When one uses the lower sense perception through materialistic mental concepts or seeks to further his materialistic ambitions and advancement, he weakens the volatile energies in his psychical power. The lower psychical powers become devitalizing agents producing listlessness and depletion in vitality and demotion to egotism.

The full flowering of the senses, and their accuracy as recorders of the life force in man, are at their best when men make equal the senses, the psychical, and the spiritual. All experiences in life press man to make this possible.

All suffering comes from imbalance of the psychical forces in the body, the emotions and the mind. Men are rejuvenated, regenerated, and resurrected through right channeling and ethical use of the psychical energies.

Psychical powers become spiritual powers when men love life, rather than self. As long as men are self-lovers, they will demote their spiritual gifts.

The nervous system, the glandular system, and the organs of the physical body, inclusive of the heart and the brain, are subjectively responsive to the psychical aspects of the soul; the organs seek to respond positively to the spiritual aspects of the soul. The subjective powers of the soul are spiritual. It is the work of every living conscious being in the earth to unite the subjective facets of the soul with the objective facets of the mind.

The psychical nature must be coordinated equally with the physical to be a reliable instrument in the emotional as well as in the mental expression. When the pure psychical power of the soul becomes a spiritual power for the use of the soul, men will produce perfect bodies expressing a pure heart and mind for God.

A person failing to use the higher value of his senses and depending solely upon primitive psychic sensing power, becomes a subverted mystic — over-idealistic — leaning toward unrealistic values and perceptions. Also, any person depending completely upon his senses without yielding to the higher psychical foreknowing is stoic-like, hardened and impenetrable.

There are two sides of the psychic force: (1) the crude, electrical, experimental, exploitative; (2) the diamond-like, intuitive, spiritually realistic. When one is exposed to or attacked by the cruder facets of ESP, he is magnetically drained of vital energy, and the defense levels of his lunar reflective brain situated at the base of his skull and the direct lunar brain situated in the solar plexus activate porcupine-like pricklings; he feels a needle-like piercing, and painful, uncomfortable awareness.

The higher and harmonious, harmless ESP flows into one's whole nature, stimulating peace and healing trust. In the crude phases of ESP, exchange of magnetism between persons is never equal. True communication between persons, to be lasting, occurs through the fusion of spiritual or holy magnetism given off by each person.

Electromagnetism is the stuff of psychical energy. The higher magnetism of the emotions produces a satisfactory and gratifying sense of love and charitable thoughts. The lower magnetism, filled with resisting gravity energies, induces devitalized nervousness, depressed thinking.

Brash or overbold egos exploiting the lower psychical powers through deliberation incite the lower electron energies, producing a combative fiery vibrational field of energy. The continued use of psychic force by an untrained will distorts the etheric body, causing the ego to be obliquely centered in the mentality.

Persons fearing forceful psychic power in others have reason to do so. However, when intrusive psychic power is understood, there are ethical measures and protective insulations which one may call upon spiritually. One calls upon these in remembering his protective angels, and God as the Protector over all.

To know oneself, one should define the power of ESP in his own nature, not as something fearful and to be avoided, but as a means by which he may gauge the barometer of his own unformed being.

One who emerges into true selfhood looks upon psychical power in himself and in others as a necessary attribute of the soul, even as he looks upon the breath of the physical body as necessary to the life of his body. He knows psychic power, trained or untrained, to be a vital facet of the spirit.

The breath of the body is continually renewing and recharging the higher psychical life vitality and life energy of the body. The higher psychical energy of the soul works to keep alive the versatile animation of the spirit. He who masters the higher psychical energies becomes a transubstantiator for God.

Man began his life in this world by being dependent upon psychical power. He will end his life on earth by having dominion over the psychical forces of his nature.

In all ages there have been advanced egos having knowledge and command of the psychical transmutation and transcendental powers. These are the teachers and the avatars sent of God to instruct and to point the way for the use of spiritual power, that man betray not his soul, himself, or God.

The soul history of man is the record of man's use of will and of his victory over the darkened portions of his will.

Man entered this earth to incorporate into his soul, into his mind, and into his will the energies, the substances, and the forces of his cosmic being.

The science of being is established when man knows himself to be a body of energies inhabited by a soul and a quickened spirit in the course of developing a magnificent mentality through creative processes.

In the history of every man can be seen the story of resistance to light. Paralleling this record may be seen the wounds and the scars, the griefs, the ills, and the disappointments of physical human futility. When one thinks himself to be a world unto himself dominated by physical self-will, he is fated to fail. When one thinks that his higher psychical powers make him unique or exceptional, this is a fallacy. Through repeated research into spiritual initiation, one learns that all persons have psychic perception. The angels working with the science of being, overdirected by the Will of God, during the hours of sleep seek to make man aware that the lightning rod of the spirit, or psychic power, is to be used purely, morally, and ethically. The angels are the major mediative presences enabling man to extend his psychic powers with harmlessness. The cherubim and the seraphim angels are especial initiators into psychic powers. The Masters, visible and invisible, are the initiators as to the ethic in the use of psychic powers.

II

PSYCHIC MASTERY

PSYCHIC FORCE AS THE LIFE FORCE

The will to live is a survival impulse charged with psychic fire. Love of self and the use of force, anger, and hostility will disarrange the psychic energies, overcharging one or more glandular centers of the body. The result is an erratic personality, a forceful will and disorganization of the body functions. The best in the spiritual life of each person is expressed when the psychical force is harnessed to the higher disciplines of the spirit. Rhythmic psychical channeling assures one of longevity years and of effervescent associations. Mystical equanimity based upon free creative psychic flow assures one of enduring love associations. The increased preciousness of life rolls out into the life of the present and into lives to come.

One cannot overestimate the sacredness of a contact with one who has commanded and used psychical life force in a healthy manner for many lives. Such persons are sacred persons; in their presence one is healed, revivified, renewed

32

in courage. When such blessed contacts are made, one should remember that he is close to things spiritual, for all persons having healthy, harmless, psychical presence are healers and anointers.

Psychical force, as the life force, assures man of repeated lives or of many existences in the earth. Psychical force has been given to man primarily that he may be ever in a state of moving, vibrating, and sounding while of the earth. In the sea of life force or cosmic psychical energy, man swims and moves. To resist the tide is to die. The emotions, the mind and the will of man, outpicturing his mentality and his soul, are in an incessant state of journeying toward a sublime goal, for deep within man is a desire to swim toward the supernal sea, that he may return to the original calm of his eternal spirit.

The volatile, versatile, selective quickening power of the psychical force surging through the organs and glandular system of man keeps him in a constant state of restlessness and exploring, giving to him a divine discontent, willing him to master gravity.

Some persons contain an erratic energy rate of psychic force, having abused or denied psychical power in former lives. Refusing to give psychic force a balanced free play diminishes vitality. Such persons become the soul laggards and must be supported by the more energetic and vital persons in the world.

There is nothing more repelling than a wilful use of the psychic force for greed and exploitation. Egotistical psychically charged persons — understanding not the dangers of the psychical fires in their own beings — are like stingrays, destroying to gain for the sake of their own egos.

True initiates are intuitively aware of and repelled by persons having overestimation of self. Egotistical beliefs generate an overextraverted personality. Psychic excitation extends one's own gravity karmic shadow, inviting upon oneself a breakup rather than a breakthrough into life.

Persons entering the world with certain psi powers developed during former existences, yet having been untrained in former lives in the ethical use of such powers, invite tribulation for themselves and disaster for those with whom they would share the results of such powers. Encased in an astral bubble of their own glamor, they think themselves to be in command of their own fate and of other persons. Sometimes they *are* karmic agents met in timing to a karmic discipline or lesson.

Overdependence upon the shadowed psychical powers inflicts pain upon the user and upon the one receiving the questionable benefits of psychical partial knowledge. A person deliberately using extrasensory perception out of timing is an unqualified channel for psychic power. To place one's complete trust in an untrained and unethical psychic is to violate one's own right to discover and experience. Repeated will-surrender to an untrained psychical source stultifies the seeker's need to search within his own heart for union with God.

One giving out psychical knowledge or information while yet a novice in these powers is in a state of karma. The ethic in the use of psychic powers is to remember that one's own karma colors all interpretations of the psychic state or event. Only from the initiated may one receive clear, unsullied, selfless representation of the psychic state.

If untrained, one limits the clear externalization of ESP powers and invokes karma upon the one with whom he shares or displays such powers. One using the psychical arts *for the sake of* psychical power is yet encased within his own egotistical shell, and is thus karmically unreliable.

There is a death wish working with the lower side of the psychic force. One cannot be healed if he lives on death thoughts. If one continues to think on death, the psychic force will oblige him. The destroying principle when out of balance uses the crude contesting destroying psychic energy to bring to one wishing to die death to his cells and organs; the fire of death comes to him who wills it.

To seek to escape one's duty or responsibility, and particularly to refuse to use the higher aspects of creation due to inertia or procastination, is to invite one's own physical annihilation through psychic force. The banked fires of the life force desire to be used progressively. If one fails to recognize these primordial preparatory fires as the altar flame of his spirit, he invokes upon himself stagnation, and sometimes obliteration and death.

Hate is the lowest aspect of psychical force. As love is a transfiguring and transforming force, hate is a resisting force. Hate acts as a psychic acid upon all living things, thwarting the impulse of life and growth.

Overflow of psychic energy acts as a force. When one uses it as force, he becomes a destroyer. To use it as a flowing stream of peace and harmony is to become a healer and to heal.

Persons having an abundance of pure psychic force are dynamically charged with life, eager for life, going forward. Their tensions are relaxed; they are enthusiastic and healthy, inviting manifestation and creation.

A pessimistic and depressed spirit distorts and negates the creative, inspiring light of the soul. A depressed person believing he has failed himself, and being unwilling to discipline the psychical fires within, exposes himself to the actual manifestation of his fears.

PREDICTION, PROPHECY AND REVELATION

All persons having the pure higher psychical powers inoffensive to others have earned them as holy-stigmata fresh springs of the soul. Such persons are placed by apportionment into the life or community of those having a need or being in a state of crisis in things physical and spiritual.

Foreknowing aspects of ESP powers relating to the progression of the self, used directly and indirectly, may be classified in three divisions: prediction, prophecy, revelation.

Prediction in the lower psychical levels may be classified as a *predictive possible*. An untrained psychic uses prediction powers rather than prophetic powers. Prediction works with the karmic fate of man, or that which he has made himself, or sown, and now must reap — and is therefore subjected to the reshifting, cycling tides of karmic law.

The gift of *prophecy* comes from the illuminative oil of the spirit and is stated as a *prophetic certainty*. True prophecy is the finger of destiny pointing toward an absolute pattern or blueprint as designed for man through the plan and Will of God.

Revelation is the work and gift of adepts foreordained under God to lift the cosmic veil and to give vision into God's handiwork for all mankind, for all peoples and for the blessed events concerning the humanities in the world.

To *predict* is to insert suggestibly into the play of the will and mind of him who receives the prediction. To *prophesy* is to give hope, stamina, poise, insight, foresight, inspiration and comfort. To *reveal* is to give faith in God, in His purpose, and to bring mankind as a whole closer to its divine destiny in the earth.

EXTRASENSORY RECEPTIVITY

There are functionings of mind and intelligence beyond comparison with anything one may know in or of the earth. These divine units of consciousness seek to communicate with him. As long as men seek to limit their classification of ESP, they will fail to unite with the intricate and complex aspects of the invisible intelligence supporting spiritual communion and communication; they will remain on the outer side of spiritual reality. To make a definite hookup with the vast system of communication between Spirit's declaration and the soul of man, one must move beyond lower psychical ESP; he must open the mighty wave lengths of ESR — extrasensory *reception.*

ESP is presently limited because the materialistic minds of men desire always to compare ESP with something they have experienced on the physical planes. Beyond the experiencing wave length of man's lower sense perception are divine and holy intelligences waiting to inform and teach him.

Investigation of lower ESP power concentrates one solely upon one's own experience of perceiving. One must seek to extend the frequencies of sight to *perceive* the real in things, objects or persons *beyond the register of the lower senses.* In lower perception one is only qualified to compare what he experiences through ESP with the familiar things of the physical world. Hence he more often colors all he experiences through ESP with what he would like them to be rather than what they are.

In extrasensory receptivity, the one receiving and experiencing must be united with the cardinal master spiritual codes to evaluate or gauge beyond the physical aspect of ESP. This perception and prompting is of a soul-awareness. Through the opening and use of the master codes or archetypal symbols, extrasensory receptivity by degrees becomes spiritual seership and cognizance.

Psychic Experience

There is more in the life of man than visions and revelations. In the higher psychical and spiritual life one reaches toward something beyond visions and revelations. Jesus, the Masters and the greater Rishi guru-teachers of the East all point to union with God as being the infinite and ultimate.

When wholly engrossed in the physical body and its pleasures and sorrows, man is incapable of experiencing the Absolute in his finite nature. Being a differentiated portion of God, one can experience God only as to what he consciously believes and knows of God.

The yeast of consciousness is stimulated and kept alive on the physical planes by psychical energy. Consciousness of the psychical expression of the ego would be non-existent, dead, nothing, without the etheric fiery-like animation of psychical energy. Thoughts on God are spiritual thoughts. The higher psychical energy upholding the yeast of consciousness, when turned to God, gives illumination of the mind.

Psychical energy, psychical force, psychical power, and psychical perception are four different aspects of the psyche or soul nature. These four aspects of the soul work in different manners in the life of each person.

Psychical energy is the cosmic life substance supporting all life — sentient, plant, animal, and man. Psychical energy is experienced in the life of man biologically, physiologically, psychologically, mentally, and spiritually.

Psychical force and forces are inductive and *intelligible* drives of the collective unconscious, stimulating the outer consciousness, occurring in energy tides and cycles. Psychical force is experienced under the controlling law of ebb and flow, or the dualistic and polarity laws of cause and effect of the greater alternates. Psychical force incites, stimulates, and activates the law of karma, sowing and reaping, action and reaction. The ego velocities or the drive and thrust of the mind and emotions in man are kept alive by psychical force. Psychical force also keeps alive the stimulus for rebirth, enabling man to reincarnate.

One must contain a tremendous or extra plus amount of psychical force to be harmful to himself and others. When this occurs he may be used as a double agent of psychical force, and thus be a karmic agent in the lives of others. A person receptive to the shadowed side of consciousness may project psychical force by deliberation, and thus wreak havoc in the lives of others for many lives to come, interfering with the ebb and flow of fate — and even to the extent of delaying the spiritual destiny of his victim.

Psychical perception — an instrument of consciousness — when unethical and untrained, can be used as a trickster to produce humiliation, to deflate an inflated ego. Psychical perception, when used ethically as an extension of the five senses, is experienced through the higher seership or inner sight, clairvoyance, vision and revelation, clairaudience or inner hearing, obedience and discipline, inspired speech or logos, charity, tolerance, spiritual love and healing.

The soul of Nature, as well as the soul of man, has its psychic impulses. Nature works with the planetary rhythms and cosmic energy cycles to keep alive the energy flow in the vital or etheric body, thus providing for man in sickness and in health. The kinetic effluvia overflow of Nature in the etheric body contains the answer to man's life, growth and experience of the earth. When man unites spiritually with the soul of Nature, psychic phenomenal powers through Nature-processes are demonstrable in their highest quality and are of utmost value to the spiritual life.

One is recharged with psychical energy in the etheric body through desert experience, mountain climbing or altitude height. Through fasting, Nature's kinetic psychical energy may be transmuted to spiritual energy. Through bathing in pure water, in oceans, in springs, one removes the psychical soil or karmic effluvia from the etheric body. Through prayer in Nature's environment, one draws to himself the power to command Nature's psychical energy and becomes a healer-conductor or distributor of spiritual reviving and resuscitating power.

PSYCHIC INTELLIGIBLE ENERGY INFLUENCING CONSCIOUSNESS

Psychic energy vitalizing the mental faculties is a knowing energy instrument for the development of consciousness. Since the discovery of electricity men have utilized electrical energy, little understanding its source and its essence. So have the majority of men unknowingly used their emotions and minds to channel psychic energy, psychic force and psychic power.

Electricity is a cosmic elemental energy used as a servant for man. Psychic energy generated by man is an instrument of consciousness and intelligence. As a being generating psychic energy, man is the servant of God energized by intelligible psychic power.

Some persons are born to the world with occult inclination due to having used occult power as a scientific expression in former lives. One of the most outstanding benefits given from the adepts of the higher occult is the understanding of the system of karma. Karma, the necessary law of cause and effect, makes reasonable the seeming imbalance in the apparent manifestation of evil and of good. Through the law of karma, the psychic-intelligible without variation brings home to each one the lesson to be learned, that he may experience a greater receptivity to all of the equalizing balances and just ways of life.

There is no dead psychic energy. Psychic energy intelligibly sustains karma. Psychic energy having a kinetic effluvia, or a pregnable vitality, keeps alive and outpictures all offenses requiring rectification. Minds heavily laden with fear of retribution attract heavier karmic emphasis into their lives. Suffering caused by an overgenerated psychic energy is a cauterizing fire upon the nervous system, the heart, the soul, and the mind. Anyone destined for greater spiritual fulfillment is subjected to accumulative karma so as to clear the soiled field of the psychic state, that greater evolvement may come and thus give peace to the state of serving.

Psychic energy in the higher frequencies of the higher mind sustains all pictures of good. The grace record of man is kept alive through refined, illuminating, exalted psychic energy.

The spiritual adept is trained to draw upon the higher currents or wave lengths of the higher psychic energy or prana when he wishes to send to the sick or the needy a resurgence or renewal of life. He turns his visualization and attention toward the Source of supreme vitality. Visualizing the White Light or highest aspect of prana, the healer unites his own cosmic substance with the creative cosmic substances. In selflessly directed healing, the healing vitality in the healer increases, and in the one to be healed a recharging is given in strength, vitality, and hope. One receives a complete healing from a cosmic initiate's sending when he has a total accepting and a believing desire to be healed. When the one sick is feeble in belief, psychic energy is low, and less receptive to healing. However, one may be given a relief or respite in suffering whether believing or unbelieving.

A karmically laden knowing-soul enters the earth to use his *knowing* and to dissolve his karma, and to simultaneously slough off weaknesses of the past. With a little gain in each life, he serves, creates, and manifests. All of this he can do for the grace of this world and for the life to come. Psychic power to the advanced soul is beyond karmic sentient fire. He knows that psychic power is a life force working through him in specified rhythms and cycles to be used with versatility and creation.

With groanings, travailings and with rewards, something is mastered and conquered in each life. All souls remembering and drawing upon the grace side of their akasic records use psychic power in the highest ranges. All advanced souls *are* conscious dynamos of spiritual power, and use spiritual ranges of psychic power, not in the sense that they think themselves to be God, but in the sense of knowing that psychic intelligible energy is the universal-thinking energy of all creative souls.

All things given of God are magnificent when seen with the ultra sense or the higher aspect of the psychic nature. To subject oneself to the lugubrious or melancholy side of the psychic nature is to be exposed to the subtle forces of the dark. The darkened strata of the negative mind are nourished by the shadowed minds of the fallen angels and of the unrisen earthbound dead. The initiate on seeking the open door to psychical power is sometimes exposed to shadowed entities residing in the lower subtle labyrinths of accumulative negative thought. Great is the blessing for the one who has passed over the shadowed portals of the mind.

There is a certain kind of insecurity and jealousy existing in an overcharged psychic mind. Untrained, unprepared, undisciplined, inflexible, and unethical envious, covetous and lustful persons are sometimes used nefariously by the little-understood subtle powers of the dark to challenge the true motivation of the higher states of evolvement. When separative and unrelenting, these inverted souls are unrestful, rigid obstructors to the pure or naive mind.

In infinite being, one is in a state of constant awareness within the presence of God. In infinite wisdom, one is in a state of constant union and communion with the Mind of God. In infinite love, one is in a constant state of blessing, anointing, healing, manifesting. All men, one by one, must enter the door to the Blessed Infinite. The eternal is in each life. Man is but half of himself until he is united with the whole of his emerging self. Each life contains something of the quest for the eternal. When one reaches the elevated side of the rise in evolvement, he knows that until then all else has been self-delusion.

One must take hold of all he has proven to be good; he must bend it in an unending chain, letting not one link of understanding go. The truly blessed person is a spiritual scientist observing and participating in the greater cosmic drama of life. All life is an animated and velocified school of experience, experiment, and exploring. Psychic nature keeps alive the inquiring side of the consciousness. Psychic power thrusts one onto the scene of the action required by the soul in each life.

THE DEVELOPING WORLD OF MAN

Men are as yet in the unknowing side of their purposeful energized, mechanized involvement with life. When inert and unresponsive, they little understand their own world of self as united with universal life.

The muscular system is the burden bearer for the physical-body struggle. The nervous system is the psychical supporting antenna network for expansion in the mind. The glandular system is an energizing, undulating ropelike, agitating bridge for the emotions and mind.

One believing himself to be just a body makes an idol of his body. All must sooner or later be made aware of their glandular and nervous systems. Psychical energy and psychical force use the nervous system and the glandular system to refine the body and to open wider and wider the facets of mentality.

Science begins now to cross over the inhibiting barriers and enter into the discovery of the universal continuity in all

life. The present unknowing in science is scaled to or measured by traditional approaches to the discovery aspect in the
mind of man. God gives so generously in all things; so will
He overabundantly give to the age of science a more flexible
mammoth searchlight to reveal the underlying causes directing man and his purpose in the earth.

The psychical life in man is now entering into a less gen-
eralized aspect of clarification. Upon this will rest the fate of
religion, of education, and of man's breakthrough into mental
reaches never before known in the developing world of man.

THE PSYCHIC SIDE OF INTELLIGENCE

All lower aspects of the psychic nature are caused by an
unregulated glandular sub-charged emotional tension. The
higher intuitive aspect of the mind or the ultra sense is unable to function completely or articulately through ordinary
brain-dependent processes of imagery.

In all psychic experiences, high or low, something of a
plus nature enters the consciousness mind; another form or
extension of intelligence or comprehension is experienced.
Psychic forms, codes and symbols are unfamiliar to the ordinary brain thinking process. The process of psychical thought
is conditioned by repetitive demands on the more refined
processes of the nervous system. One less sensitive to the
intelligible energy nuances of the mind is unable to understand the more sensitively creative psychic aspects of communication. A long process of training as to psychic codes
and evaluation of parabolic revelations must be undergone by
all persons seeking to clarify the psychic side of intelligence.

The higher side of psychic intelligence is an instant, accurate and informing instrument. One experiencing this is
more than a participant and an observer. He knows and
understands what he sees and hears. Every psychic experience
carries its own mystic identity; its message and its mission

can be perfect in clarity and veracity when persons using the higher aspects of the psychic nature experience illuminative grace during psychic experience.

Veiled or mixed shadowed vision is experienced only by one unripe or unready to activate what he sees or experiences in his psychic nature. The Divine mentors or higher mentors telepathically supervising man's spiritual rise oversee all psychic development. These Divine mentors working with the angels set up impenetrable psychically charged barriers for the unruly experimenter. There is a cardinal law protecting the psychic aspect of the mind: *He who is not loving cannot abide in the holy city of the higher mind.*

Psychic persons, or persons using the foreknowing aspect of mind, are considered eccentric because they are geared to vibrational ranges of thought response beyond the average person's capacity to think. Actually their brain currents are super-saturated with energies both in high and low frequencies. Over long periods of time psychic currents directing thought set up grooves of acceptance or rejection of ideas, symbols, patterns, attitudes, and reflections.

The higher psychic mind is prepared to accept a state of constant discipline. The perfect psychic mind eventually must become its own censor, accepting and rejecting, proving and weighing. The true or the false, the real and the unreal are sifted, adjusted.

The pure and higher psychic mind is a combination of attentiveness, concentration and reverence. The higher psychic mind is jewel-like, centered in a mentality of flawless, selfless love. Such a God-centered person prays to serve God as one of His holy forerunner-spirits in the earth.

Prescient souls having psychic purity lean forward into the unborn and unmanifest world. They are as the prow of a ship going before the body of the ship, touching the new, testing new and alien waters. Long before the clumsy and awkward can perceive, the seers of God see, know and hear what the destiny is, under the Will of God.

Lower psychic thinking can be opened prematurely in the less evolved and less prudent by stress, shock, or drugs. In the highly evolved, the higher psychic thinking or foreknowing is opened in a natural spiritual evolvement flow. In spiritual evolvement, one opens the seven planetary portals of the glandular system conjoined along the spinal canal. The upward psychic flow becomes spiritual and mentally inspirational.

Psychic mental force, when scattered due to outward pressures, produces erratic symptoms in attitude and action. When synchronized in harmony with ethic, discipline, service, and spirituality, one experiences the Divine inner aspect of the higher polarity within the mind.

Ethical persons having and using psychical powers do not use them *as psychic power*. The process of assimilation of the higher variables of the mind enables true seers to move beyond the limiting personal identification or concentration upon the source and cause of their divine compulsions directing and motivating their extended mental skills. Their power within the universal mind is a cohering and illuminating instrument. Their sole purpose is to extend the overflowing charismatic ideas into the time and tide of acceptance in the world.

All prophets until now have suffered in a world of non-acceptance. Seers know that to be at peace they must come to expect nothing from the present. Living in things yet unseen by other men, the first requirement of the prophet is that he must unite with the eternal sense of timing. Prophets geared to the archetypes of a nation are karmically tied into national progress or the national disasters of their nation.

Such seers suffer grief and sorrow for the soul of their nation. The mass ear is deaf to the national prophet in the present time, or in any age in which a vast dissolution process is enacted in the world. The voices of such prophets seem muted, being washed under by the unconcern of frantic and fearful men. The greater poets of a nation are often prophets in disguise, singing their songs to hardened hearts and ears. Prophets writing a foresighted history for men are feared by calloused short-sighted men who have faith only in the awful specter of a disastrous present.

Uncreative psychic impulses thrive in mushroom fashion when nurtured and expressed by an overfearful mind. This type of psychic power is mesmeric and is produced by those living in constant states of apprehension and fear. A death-wish individual — by constantly dwelling upon the aspect of decay, death, and violence — can produce hallucinatory visions accompanied by actual manifestation of dire calamity and often death.

Psychically inclined persons dwelling fearfully on their unfaced guilts, living close to their shadowed selves, and refusing to accept their karmic responsibility, often produce, while awake, a chimera-like reflective state of conscience. Such visions are clothed with the masks or visages of persons formerly harmed, neglected, or abused. This apparitional psychic state of mind is sometimes suffered by one who is being initiated to higher soul-powers.

Until one is consciously aware of the higher effects of a channeled life, he more often experiences psychic power in the dream state of sleep. The psychic vibrating symbols developed for untold ages through evolutionary and evolving life may be absorbed and eventually activated into the objective mind.

Man sleeps, spending one third of his life dependent upon the higher and lower aspects of his unconscious mind. This mind, while in the state of sleep, more than any other facet of his consciousness is an agent for lucid undistracted thought process. Only on awakening does man lose touch with this highly satisfactory freeing power of the unconscious.

Sleep is a vibration of high supersonic energy. While one is in a state of rest, he is being activated by cosmic energies, sounds and tones that he is unable to absorb and relate to in the daytime action. The acceleration of the soul-hum at night enables man to use sleep, the mystical third of his mind, that he may learn and remember the cosmic truths as related to God and man's omniscient being to come.

III

MODERN-DAY PSYCHIC ARTS

Guidance and Karma

All persons leaning upon or depending upon either the higher psychic arts or the lower psychic arts are seeking guidance. Man, so often confronted with the complex and conflicting issues of life, is pressured to look outward for his answers. Failing to find the answers within himself, he intuits that he must look to the mystic overflow of revelation existing in the world.

All men have within them parapsychological depths of remembrance. There are periods of deep nostalgia occurring in man whereby he longs to unite himself with a knowing, guiding and informing principle. Thus, some in the world turn to external forms of psychic expression. The universal law supporting coincidences will sometimes send to a person a way in which he is exposed to a source of psychic help, guidance or healing. When this occurs, he should be flexible, setting aside any form of hardened skepticism, but he should also be careful that he is not overcredulous, inasmuch as his own conscience, faith and will stand exposed to forces yet unknown. One should remain an observer, but also receptive to what is being revealed or manifested in a psychic art.

One cardinal rule protects and insulates a person who is the recipient of psychic manifestation: "Despise not prophesyings, prove all things; hold fast that which is good." (I Thessalonians 5:20, 21)

The informing and guiding principle is constantly working for all persons. One need only be aware of this great law to receive its blessing and strengthening.

Man is in a university. Tutors are everywhere. A small covey of quail will inform and teach man concerning communal laws of life, or a colony of ants will inform and teach him concerning the laws of industry.

When one reverently and expectantly asks for guidance in desperation, guidance comes. A call from the soul never goes unanswered. If the answer comes in the form of higher psychic counseling and guidance, one should apply it only if it is wholly affirmative when weighed against his reason, his conscience and his intelligence.

A psychic source of information coming from another person, personalized directly to one's needs, is subjected to the law of sowing and reaping, or the law of karma supporting the life of all human conduct.

Love is the only existing emotion free of karma. The *solar psychic,* or high mystic initiate, is a healer using the power of selfless love. Having mastered his emotions, he has the power to heal and to change the timing process in personal karma. Such initiates have certain knowledge of timelessness. They have the power to rearrange one's karma and move one beyond the time range of karma. However, they do not have the power to prevent a person from being involved in collective or world karma. Until all men have reached a higher state of love beyond self-love, vicarious supports from the initiated will continue to be needed that men may be raised into light.

Joan of Arc under Archangel Michael was a solar initiate. Her soul chose to be involved in world karma on a national scale. When her work had been fulfilled, she became a victim to the dweller action of her nation. Her betrayal, even as the betrayal of Jesus, was necessary that men of her time might be exposed to spiritual laws governing their actions. Only in looking back may the life of a prophet, saint, or martyr be understood. As Jesus said, it was necessary that the Son of Man die.

A highly evolved mystic while living in the human world—even though under the direction and guidance of the Archangels, the angels, the Masters and the saints—does not at all times have an open and available circuit continuously accessible to spiritual knowledge, information and protection. No one save Jesus has ever had this accessible and unceasing open circuit or flow of communion with the Father. Even Jesus in His last hours was denied communion with His Father in heaven, so that He might give something to the human life wave in the power of resurrection.

Anyone expecting a person having high ESP powers to be a perfect being is expecting the impossible. Joan of Arc was deserted by her "voices" in the hour of her capture, only to have them return for brief intervals before the time of her burning.

It is by necessity that one while living in the world of flesh must pay, to some extent, the toll to the flesh. It is true that highly evolved persons have less worldliness or fleshly instincts and are therefore excluded from much of their human karma.

To be in the world, to live in the world, is to be confronted by world issues and world situations.

Men of scientific, probing natures in the scientific age look on the mystic side of life with cynicism. It is vital in these times of exploration into the powers of ESP that men retain a reverent respect for the versatilities of the mind, particularly for the little-known side of man's volatile psychic power.

CABALA AS A PSYCHIC ART

Many persons, having no mathematical sense, satisfy their needs for union with an ordered universe through their study of and application to the cabalistic sciences. A true cabalistic scientist is a rarity in this modern age. Occasionally one becomes exposed to a person who lives by cabalistic formulas. The art of cabala as used before and after the life of Jesus came into the world to support the scientific age of the present time.

The tarot and playing cards are left-hand projections of cabala. These have been stepped down from the abstract world of myth symbol mathematics into a source of entertainment. Cabala is a science of symbols and myths represented by procedures objective, subjective, inductive and scientific. Thus, of all the psychic arts, cabala is the only system retaining its purity. Cabala, an ancient art, was formulated as a system of ritualistic concentration to overcome manipulative psychic magical forces. The system of cabala when rightfully and ethically practiced will unlock doors to the past, and give penetrating and accurate insight into the future.

All symbols and formulas of cabalistic origin are the offspring of the archetypal master symbols. To use them in proper sequence is to produce an exceptional mind force capable of channeling psychic energy with ethic.

Cabalistic formulas unite man with universal cause, opening him to the flow of universal ideas, and thus organize his practical and outer existence.

The tarot science unites man to Quelle or the subconscious, emphasizing the power of foreseeing and prognosticating. Tarot leans the emotions of man far outward toward things yet to come, overstimulating his inductive imaginary expectancy. The use of tarot to probe the future denies one of the practical unison with the past, the present, and the future.

Prophecy gained through the tarot sciences does not strengthen man for the practical, intermediate stages for fulfilling his prophecy. The tarot science invariably carries with it a fearful aspect of prophecy, fatalistically suggestive to those who are dependent upon the psychic arts. Thus, many persons submitting their suggestible wills to tarot foretelling very often open doors to negative conditions in their lives which could by the use of cabalistic knowledge be overcome.

Cabalistic science is a long art, that is, complicated, requiring concentration and contemplation. True cabala touches the higher mind, enabling one to master the forces of the lower mind, assuring a calm spirit and wisdom in crisis. Of all the external arts of the psychic life, cabala is the most reasonable, logical and rewarding.

The science of cabala has contributed to basic art forms over the centuries, inclusive of music, painting, poetry, and drama. In all forms of allegorical expression may be found the supporting ideation of cabala.

Anatomy, when approached through the system of cabala, opens the door to man's understanding of the super-charged intricately developed processes of the human body.

Cabala is the slide-rule for chemistry and for the physics of inorganic and organic life, and when applied in the realm of consciousness existence makes death and life acceptable.

The cabalistic system of the West can be compared to the yantra system of the East. Both systems have been used by man to regulate and to transpose the formidable forces of the unknown facets of the mind into creative aspects of the spirit.

Yantric formulas stem from man's inductive cosmological sense of universal order. Cabala stems from union with cosmic and universal law upholding and supporting destiny. Both sciences have a spiritual kinship and have been used by the leader-initiates to direct, to guide and to inspire men in times of tumult, chaos and distress.

The face of cabala appears again and again on the surface in human affairs. Sometimes, a fragment of cabala is used and called numerology. Numerology, however, is more psychologically effective in the individualistic action of men. When expanded upon the blueprint of the Pythagorean system, one unites with the cosmic flow of sound operating as vibration in the life of personality.

Numbers when applied as a psychic art prove out beyond theory that man is indeed a precise instrument operating within precisional law. To understand the science of numerology one must be a seeker after harmony.

The energy vibrational forces within numbers pertaining to the vowels in the name of a person represent his akasic strength as earned in former lives. The consonant power as related to vibration in the numbers in a name, indicates how one will use and channel the vibrational power of his vowel numbers.

Cabala, however, is an art attuning one to the infinite positives. Numerology is a science attuning one to the acceptance of the finite alternates. Numerology works with the law of coinciding principle, that is, one finds himself living in a house having a number exactly correlating to the vowel numbers in his own name, or he purchases a seat on a plane having his own number, and at last he dies in a hospital room having his own number.

The perfect law of proportion controlling the destiny of man may be found in the science of numbers. Wherever numbers are used as the platform to psychic research, one cannot be lost or go astray. The science of numbers will uphold and support one's search and research into the many labyrinth-twistings of the psychic world.

It has been often seen by teachers of the spiritual arts that persons overmystical and in need of organizing their psychic natures are karmically led, more often against their wishes, to earn their bread through jobs such as bookkeeping or computing. This is a touch of grace, and a divine testimony to an intelligible force directing the life of a person.

One learns in the system of cabala and in its sister science, numerology, there are no accidents. The cosmic system of balance for all aspects of life is mathematical. Men have only now entered into a mathematics beyond man mathematics, a cosmic physics preparing him to accept the interrelated processes of life as a reality.

HABITUAL CARD PLAYING AND PSYCHIC FORCES

In the world there is a long history of the use of physical objects to channel and to extend psychic energy. Desire to use such objects stems from the memory of the use of magical powers in other centuries and eras. In each era man moves a little closer to the knowledge that the physical world is made up of atoms, energy, vibration, ether and light.

Wizards, witches, so-called wise women or wise men, understood intuitively the kinetic laws of energy. Dependence upon the teraphim magical powers was known in the time of Abraham. The Bible mentions the use of teraphim in Judges, chapters 17 and 18. The teraphim powers were a fragment of memory stemming from the time of Atlantis when levitation powers of mammoth proportions were used by certain leaders of that age and period. Today, anyone using psychic kinetic powers contains in the astral core of his being an overabundance of electrically charged psychic energy.

The adrenal glands are in command of a certain will aspect connecting man to the forces of Nature. Using the power of suggestible will, inverting it into the molecular masses of energy, one can with practice control or fix an object that it be not moved, or one can move objects according to his willing and desiring. This kind of willing is used unconsciously in all sorts of competitive sports in the present time, especially in games of chance where gambling is involved, or in the playing of cards for gain or money.

The psycho-suggestible will is intensely overcharged in games of bridge or where all forms of repetitive card playing are practiced.

The cards of the tarot are kinetic divining agents attuned to vibrational laws of energy. One using the tarot cards to reveal the future is assisted by the psychic cognition forces existing in the lower astral planes.

Regular playing cards are remnants of the kinetic cognition powers and etheric ritualistic powers out of Atlantis, China, Persia, Arabia and Egypt. Regular playing cards, when used with psycho-suggestible will, develop powers of foreseeing and prognosticating.

Persons habitually playing card games for pleasure come under control of psychic forces and become highly charged with psychic overflow in their thought processes, often having hysterical, highly nervous dispositions. To such persons, however, playing cards has a soothing and quieting influence on their excitable temperaments; returning to the card table channels these overcharged psychic powers. Such persons may develop a high degree of psychic experience with the dead. In their dreams may also be seen much of the symbolic myths portraying the original magical source of their interest and attachment to playing cards. In dreams, they unite with the Quelle myth symbols and draw from them a certain energy.

It is difficult for a person with an intense psychic nature to break the syndrome of card playing. Only a deep desire to enter into a higher creative aspect of one's nature can free a person from habitual card playing.

To be caught into a psychic fascination snare due to any form of card game is to overdevelop the competitive forces in one's nature. Certain persons playing cards, having over-belligerent natures, instinctively turn to card playing for therapeutic reasons. However, with time, it will be seen that dependency upon card playing as an outlet for their psychic natures develops psychic reflexes, rather than spiritual reflexes, to the values of life.

Rivalries, tensions and jealousies develop between card players because men come to know each other at a card table in a subtle manner that they cannot learn in any other way.

The spiritual scientist does not condemn card playing. He sees it to be an allegoric outpouring and freeing of the hidden myths residing in one's own subconscious mind. However, he also knows that to every person caught into a hypnotic suggestible way of life, there comes the time when one must say "Enough," and move onward to a more fluidic and expanding process of his soul.

Any repetitious overconcentrated and exaggerated attentiveness upon a singular facet of one's nature steals from or robs the versatility of the life force. To over-use any one talent is to short-circuit the source of inspiration and make sterile one's creation. The very aspect of being born in many existences reveals to man that the scheme of Nature and the plan of God is a versatile way. He who finds this law lives harmoniously.

ASTROLOGY

There are high and low psychic arts. A psychic art when used for personal gain and manipulation of the will of another may be considered a low psychic art.

Astrology has been considered to be a low psychic art by astronomers. However, in the present time astronomy and astrology are beginning to converge. The astrologer is to be recognized as a scientist operating and functioning adjacent to the science of astronomy. The open portal door to recognition of astrology as a true science is at hand.

Astrology, the study and science of the stars, is related to the temperament and energy life of man. The insight gained in astrology, when esoteric and spiritual, may open the door to one's akasic records and to the mystic mold charting his destiny.

Mundane astrology has been accused of being a psychic art when stemming from charlatans and impostors, thus diverting many from its beneficial and directing influence in their lives. Mundane astrology, purporting to direct and control human fate, is considered by progressive astrologers to be a limited science.

Astrology has intrigued and challenged the minds of all thinking men because it is a true science when linked to eternal intuition; but, if used through psychic extension and personal opinionated reflexes of the mind, it can produce disillusionment. Men have inherited this science from the sages or scientists of old who charted their lives upon the zodiacal force ruled over by the great galaxy Over-Lords or Hierarchy.

Astrology is now beginning to be reassessed and applied by authorized scientists. Astrology is on the threshold of being proved to be not only a workable system as related to man's energy life, but will also be accepted by all forward-living persons as a way and means of mastery of life forces in the emotions, in the mind, both subconscious and conscious.

Men will soon come to use their ephemeris of the personal life alongside of the graphs and blueprints of astronomy. Science is now beginning to see the imprudence of isolating this ancient wisdom. Even as in the field of medicine much research is being done to recover the ancient herbal arts, so will astronomy acknowledge that man is influenced by the planetary energies, by the lunar energies, by the solar energies, by the galaxy-system energies.

The theme of life in the present time is explosive. Man is exploding out of the boundaries of specialization and separation. The interflow of the life theme of the future is scientific, and ultimately spiritual. There are too many coinciding truths in the science of astrology to deny its evidence in the physical, emotional and mental life of man.

When one is a *natural* astrologer, that is, born to understand astrology automatically, and uses it as an interpreting agent for the processes of life, he is a dedicated astrologer and free from the psychic downpull of the lower mind which would interpret and emphasize the negative and frightful aspects speaking on the zodiacal wheel or chart.

To come under the influence of a person who overemphasizes the negative aspects in a zodiacal chart is a karmic circumstance. When one seeks out an astrologer for counsel, help, reinforcement and support—if he is unfortunate in selecting an astrologer who has overdeveloped his psychic interpretation of a chart—he endangers and exposes himself to the will aspect of the one reading his chart.

The circular wheel of a zodiacal chart is a matrix of concentration. In reading many charts over a period of time, an astrologer develops supersensory powers in looking into the circular astrological charts of others.

David, composing the 23rd Psalm, looked into the circular sphere of the heavens; starting with the eastern portion of the sky, he charted the 23rd Psalm, taking the sign of Aries as "The Lord is my shepherd," and Taurus as "I shall not want"—and continuing through the other zodiacal positions, gave to man a great mantramic formula for life. So also should each astrologer unite himself with the greater cosmic wheel of life on looking into the chart of another.

It is dependent upon the intuitive and spiritual evolvement of an astrologer as to how a wheel or chart is interpreted. However, in the present time science through instruments will gauge and measure the energy fields of the zodiacal human chart, national chart, and world chart with a total detachment, wherein personal psychic forces will be laid aside. Men will move forward through the scientific thrust into astrology by accepting that man is etherically responsive to the masterbuilding forces of the universe.

The fields of psychology, psychiatry, medicine, education and religion will include in their service to man a mechanized system of astrology approved by science. However, the first-hand personalized interpretation of astrological charts will not die, as individual doctors, teachers, and other professions will by necessity color the interpretation of a chart with human and psychical reflexes of the human mind.

Much of superstition will die in this age and much of old folk and psychic remedial arts will be extended and revived. The ancient gods of the Greeks in this age of modern science will come to be known as hierarchy forces of zodiacal origin.

Every god worshipped in the past is a coinciding agent to some phase of the psychic nature of man. Man in each age relies upon inner illuminating powers and psychic forces accompanying the milieu of the age.

The minds of men have been bound into a steel prison cage. Desiring to be thought open in their minds, they have closed the circuits of their minds to the vast interflow of wisdom and knowledge accumulated over the ages.

Astrology has survived because its basic structure is true. However, as in all of the arts of learning, psychic and scientific, man can only learn and apply what he is. And man can only bring to life what he knows in his own consciousness.

To be the recipient of an honest interpretation of astrology, one should seek out a person with a humane and impartial heart and also having a mind willing to acknowledge that he is an ego always in a process of learning. One should be cautious in placing his life in the hands of someone who thinks himself to have come to the end of knowledge, believing himself to have all of the answers. Until mankind reaches *pro-genesis,* knowing will be formed and shaped by trial and error.

In each life something is gained; in each era something is maintained. This is how God desired it and willed it for man. Astrology and astronomy as partners of the future will produce a zodiacal wheel giving play to forces and energies yet uncharted and understood by man. The present ephemeris used by mundane and esoteric astrologers will be simplified and enlarged, yet seeming complicated to the present scientist of the stars. A breakthrough in space exploring will recondition and reproportion man's interconnecting links with the planetary and starry bodies of the universe. Energies undefined will be understood and mastered, giving man an open awareness as to his whole body, his whole nature functioning in the life of his mind and soul.

Men must go forward and accept what is offered in this new, great era before them. Their minds cosmically organized must now concentrate upon interterrestrial influences, interterrestrial life other than the life on earth, and interterrestrial life similar to the life of man on earth. To do this one must be thoroughly indoctrinated into the nature of his own being.

To maintain the equilibrium of his past gains in this eternity system, he must draw upon charitable depths in his own soul-willingness to accept what is, rather than what he wants it to be; and above all, he must know that his course is universally charted, and that he can no longer blindly exist in the world.

To refuse to go forward would mean death and obliteration. The very angels and God are presently shaking and sifting this eternity system in which man dwells. The key word written upon the archstone is *unison*. Unison, however, without charity and mercy, is destruction.

It is written in the great book of the holy archives that all men must go forward and that, when men have learned this to be so, great avatars are sent to show them the way. The avatars of this era for man are not the scientists. The avatars are teachers, lesser saviours, and spiritual leaders.

It was written in the Star of Bethlehem that mankind should have one Saviour to lead them, but it is also written that mankind should have lesser saviours to do on earth what He in heaven desires to have done for Him. The coming of Jesus as a cosmos soul changed the axis rhythm and vibrational hum of the earth. Thereafter, the planets in their orbs around the earth and the sun accelerated and intensified their energies, penetrating more specifically the energy fields in the body and mind of man.

As men now move toward a new epoch rise in world consciousness, they are becoming the recipients of magnified cosmic light. The processes of their physical, emotional, mental and etheric bodies are becoming sensitized, that their expanding ego-powers may have supporting vehicles in their world of exploring, learning and creating within a Christ emphasis upon consciousness.

Galaxy forces and energies formerly sealed away from man are now saturating the axis core and the magnetic points in the earth and the astral core of man, playing upon his spirit, will and nervous system. With the coming of the Christ-Spirit elevation in the earth, man began a period of initiation assisted by planetary forces and energies. The display of unique expression in consciousness in this age is only the beginning of a realistic rather than mystic approach to the life of the mind and eventually to the life of the soul.

In this period, man will develop mind processes and an enlargement of thinking in a way formerly obscured to him. Until 2000 years have been fulfilled after the birth of Christ, the majority of men will think through the subconscious influences of the race and of the family.

To serve the unknowing and to raise them into the light, God sent certain initiates to the earth in the 1800's. He will continue to send them until the year 2058. The specific work of these initiates is to give illuminative enlightenment to the less evolved. Such initiates are knowers and doers of the right law, the just law, and will use ethically the scientific techniques linking the mind and the soul. It will be their labor, devotion and aspiration to make union with cosmic law, teaching man self realization and universal realization. Such initiates come protected with an armor of light, using the processes of light. They will be protected by insulating spiritual forces sustaining their spiritual powers. All initiates in previous lives have been abused, bruised and outcast. In a materialistic and uncaring world, they have borne the brunt of the ignorance of sensual and unknowing men.

The soul's passage into the earth is not a treadmill. Men do not come to the earth meaninglessly. The only abnormalities in the progressive states of life are when someone has offended the great laws of being and of life.

Among the planets especially initiating the avatar souls in the future are the planets Uranus, Neptune and Pluto. Looking into the charts of such men, an astrologer united with the cosmic graph of souls may read an avatar's chart and foresee the impact of these three planets upon the life of the masses.

Until the eighteenth century the planets Mars, Mercury, Venus, Jupiter and Saturn were the main actors in the drama of initiation. In the eighteenth century, coinciding with man's awareness of Uranus as an actor upon the planetary stage, he became receptive to a mighty overflow of galaxy energy moving into the solar system of the earth. This galaxy energy working through the planets Uranus, Neptune and Pluto began its stimulating work upon the adrenal glands of mankind. Also, with his inductive awareness of Neptune and its energy flow upon the pineal gland, man began to awaken and to recover powers in his higher mind that he had used in the elevated Lemurian and Atlantean times. In the eighteenth century this tremendous galaxy flow began to press upward the pineal crown of man that he might better unite with the Christ Light seeking to come into the mind.

Pluto, identified by all initiates as being one of the main actors on the scene of new-era initiation, began its work of destiny by transposing the great galaxy power upon Quelle or the subsconscious matrix of the mind of man. Henceforth mankind would be concerned with the unconscious, the hitherto unknown aspect of consciousness. Thus, today, men in the world, though not as yet aware of this, have mechanized themselves subconsciously to the energy reflexes of Mars, Mercury, Venus, Jupiter and Saturn. They must now assimilate the radical and overenergizing power of Uranus, the psychedelic, exaggerated, imaginative and inference effects of Neptune, and must also incorporate into their natures the Pluto suggestible interflow absorbing the magnification of things of the past long-hidden and buried in the dormant side of their natures. These three planetary initiators and galaxy mediators now concentrate upon men in energy tides and flows, working through the Christ Light that man may know himself.

In the zodiacal chart of each person may be found strengthening points and penetrable points of weakness. Man may look to the sextiles in his chart to see the angel doors whereby he may overcome and survive the tribulation aspect of his fate. Each person should look to his trines to see protective fortresses of mediation, such as the saints, the Masters. Wherever one has a trine, he has a higher point of telepathic reinforcement from greater souls, making him a receiver of protection, insulating him from the dark. Wherever there are squares in his chart, there is the key to his initiation and to the way of his resurrection, whereby he may alchemize and transform the condensed karmic squares containing the evidence of his past wrongdoing into transcendental strengths and power of the spirit.

IV

PSYCHIC COMMUNICATION AND THE

QUELLE MONITOR

Quelle, the lower subconscious and higher unconscious aspects of the mind, is a karmic monitor of man's psychological processes in the earth. It acts as an intervening, limiting lever, preventing man from psychic overexperimentation upon his fellow man. Quelle determines that each individual be free to live through his own willing and doing regardless of inner or outer mesmeric, psychic or hypnotic influence. Quelle sees to it that man goes only so far in tampering with the soul, mind, and will forces of himself and of other men.

The individual karma of each man must be balanced, permitting the soul to aerate his spiritual life. Psychic life cannot be the predominating principle within the revivifying vitality of the spiritual surges received from the soul. Until man learns to understand all sides of his psychic nature, he is a recipient of intermittent surges of psychic power and also of intermittent resurgences of the spirit.

In the latter part of the last century, coinciding with the ending of the Civil War, the collective unconscious of man in the Western world began to be opened in a very special way. Widespread interest was focused upon the phenomena aspects, stemming from communication with the dead. Until this day there are thousands of persons who find solace and relief in communicating with the dead. Parallel to the establishment of spiritualism and spiritism, two phases of psychic power were activated: automatic writing and the use of the planchette or ouija board.

Alongside of the development of spiritism and spiritualism, occult schools were formulated and established. Communication with the Masters was accepted by many intuitive souls who had through the ages of reincarnation encountered these Elect as their tutors and instructors. All interested in spiritism, spiritualism and the occult sciences had one thing in common: they were disillusioned with church or religious interpretation of life after death, the meaning of the eternality of the soul, and the church's failure to give ethical formulas for one's individual spiritual development.

Automatic Writing

The psychic art of automatic writing is a form of mediumship; it has been used by many persons on the halfway path between mystic and initiate. Three things are required for a clear manifestation of automatic writing: a desire to communicate with some source a little more advanced and less restrained in mentality than one's own; a subconscious desire to look in or tune in to guiding or directing forces; a compelling mediumistic aspect in one's own nature used in past lives.

In all of the external arts of psychic communication, one must be prepared to accept that any external instrument or object used as a bridge of transporting one over the barriers between the physical and the psychical is but a temporary support and unlasting phase of the psychic nature. Thus, automatic writing is but a relay station into the communicating aspects of superior or advanced knowledge.

All persons practicing the psychic art of automatic writing are in the beginning excited and stimulated by some of the accurate proofs and statements given through automatic writing.

The Censor aspect in Quelle, preventing intrusion, guards and protects all persons using the psychic arts. If a person has heavily-laden karma shadowing his subconscious, Quelle sees to it that automatic writing will mislead, deceive and delude him. If he has grace from a past life, automatic writing will cease to function and flow with any coherence after a period of three years. To replace this and to answer his yearning to know, a spiritual attribute of his soul will appear on his loss of contact.

Surplus psychic energy in the lesser etheric body supplies the energy for all of the psychic arts. When this phase of communication ends, the energy flow supporting this communication will no longer cooperate, disconnecting itself from the brain and from the lower aspect of Quelle. In automatic writing one feels in his hands a weakness and tingling, and in his wrists will come a loss of vital energy; and over a long period the ether energy wrist portals will become devitalized from the overuse of this psychic art.

In the continued use of external psychic arts, such as card reading, ouija-board communication, automatic-writing communication, psychic power reaches a crest or peak and then reverses its progress by a gradual decline until it phases itself out.

In the natural order of progression, if a person has prayed for spiritual evolvement, he will find on the conclusion of his dependence upon a psychic art that a higher door will open to a better and more sensitive stage of evolvement. If one should seek to return to a favorite psychic art, he will find great distress set up in the psychic energy fields of his etheric body. He should be grateful, for he is being protected.

All advanced teachers on encountering persons excessively using the psychic arts seek to tactfully redirect their course; and if one has the grace and insight to respond, his teacher will assist him in freeing spiritual powers rather than psychic powers. One should recognize in himself, on being exposed to the psychic arts, that there is no substitute for the real, and that all side avenues will delay him and keep him from the most direct aim and desire of his soul.

All psychic-art techniques depending upon physical agencies or objects are dangerous in that they expose one to unknown forces with which he is unfamiliar. These forces are intelligible. If one uses the psychic arts with total dependency, making himself a vehicle for lower astral gurus or the unrisen dead, the result is harmful, as he has opened himself to an invasion from the subtle worlds against which he is incompetent and helpless.

All spiritual persons come to see that it is best to avoid psychic experimentation through the use of external objects. Having a certain fastidiousness or selectivity virtue-grace extending from their souls, the spiritual person comes to know that he should not subject his mind to the degraded or unholy thoughts of discarnate spirits.

An enlarged curiosity, a desire to gain knowledge without effort, a desire to have certain superior power, these stem from egotism in one's nature. Degraded entity presences can mislead a vain and egotistical person into loss of honor, fortune, and even of life.

Regardless of how pure or right one feels himself to be, he can be made a victim of the shadowed world when he feels that he has superior authorization from being supplemented by entity forces. All too often such persons find themselves being the manipulated rather than the manipulator.

There have been rare instances in which certain naive, totally trusting persons have been used as instruments of the psychic art of automatic writing to write a book or a poem, to compose music, or to paint a picture. Such persons knowing no other way and being undeveloped as to the full range of spiritual powers are protected by their own naivete grace. However, the psychic art of automatic writing is not a spiritual art. It is more often a chimera veil giving off in part.

The only true, lasting and satisfactory method of spiritual communication is through the processes of meditation and alignment between the mind, the soul and the higher self. From such alignment come veracity, clarity, purity.

Many persons, having retained the memory of dependency upon the use of the psychic arts in former lives, on returning to earth turn to them, seeking to use them once more in the present life. However, there must be progress in each life, as even in the psychic arts there is a flow of progression. A psychic art used in a former life is never reproduced in the present life in exact fashion.

When man is born to the world, the rhythmic law of forwardness seeks to improve and advance him in each life. And unless one comes into the world still intoxicated by, and clinging to, the excitation gained from the use of the psychic arts, if there is grace he retains the upward side of the essence of these powers in his psychic nature; his soul leads him to crave something more than the outer covering for his gifts of the psyche or soul. All of the mediums and psychics of the present age were well versed in the psychic arts of the past, as in the creative arts a child prodigy, such as Chopin, may come to the world with his former-life soul gifts compacted in the early years of his life. This is true also with those who have used successfully the psychic arts in a former life.

The compelling psychic force flowing first from the astral core alongside of the spine into the etheric body of a psychic may be best gauged in its earliest manifestation, and, therefore, its fullest flow. This is especially true when the psychic art is dealing with the psychological nature of man, that is, man-to-man feeling and thought process.

Primal, psychic healers enter the world with memory of union with kinetic life force used in former ancient lives. This flow of psychic energy and expression is unusual and more likely to be lasting.

Ouija Board

The most etherically devitalizing psychic art is the use of the ouija board. Any psychic art drawing upon the heavy ether or ectoplasm in the etheric body is a draining process. Long before the ouija board or the yes-and-no planchette system was used, men had used the lottery system, the scrying system, the reading of tea leaves, gazing into bright objects, into water, into the clouds of the sky, the sand, the fire, and into inscribed circular objects, and phallic symbolic artifacts.

It is a primal instinct to look and to divine through one-pointedness or concentrated intensity and to try to see visions, omens and signs. When man discovered the power of concentration, he experienced his first union with the psychical power in his nature. This power was the power of inner sight or using a third aspect of seeing through the inner eye. In the primal action of this power, man knew that the life force was supported by an automatic etheric Over-intelligence; and he knew that he could shape and form ether through thinking and feeling, and that energy was obedient to his will. He also knew in his primal nature that others could shape and form ether through feeling and thought.

The hunger to return to the trusting and pure side of the primal nature is innate in all persons. The innate knowing that man has within himself the power to extend his psychic exploring is in each person. In some, this power has been retained more than in others. Persons with mystical minds having a certain obstinate willing have more often these psychic will-shaping powers.

Present-day aggressive persons are more likely to have mental-will psychic powers. The mental-will psychic powers are the property of the lower mind. Subjective passive persons have more emotional and instinctive psychic powers.

In the use of the ouija board, when two persons seek to operate and to unite their psychic forces to communicate with some contacting entity, the reliability of this contact is made possible when one of the persons using the ouija board is a subjective psychic or intuitive and the other is a mental-will psychic. In this, they use the alternating currents necessary for clear contact with entity forces.

Ouija-board experimentation and research cannot reach beyond the wave lengths of the entity dead; thus, if one is seeking to receive authentic communication through the limited instrumentation of a ouija board or planchette, he reaches into the thought wave lengths of those who have died. And only the dead who are aimlessly engaged in the astral world are communicable and available through the psychic art as expressed in a ouija board.

One cannot expect to get sustained authentic revelation from a ouija-board source of contact. Entities communicating through a ouija board are still influenced by their earth-limitation karma, and are thus no more reliable to inform or to advise than they had previously been while living in the physical world.

PALMISTRY

Man has been in command of the life flow of energy for aeons. In each life he reproduces a new physical shape and form, never identical with the form or body of the past, but bearing always without variation some resemblance to the body of the past life. One of the most acute and sensitive resemblances registering upon the body of man stemming from past life is to be seen in the palms of his hands and in the shape of his hands.

The hands of man are antennas of healing, of touching, of ministering, of labor, of creation. The fingers indicate sensitivity, virtue, philosophy, beauty, harmony, love. As much and even more than the tongue can say, the hands can reveal what a person is in the life of the past, in the life of the present and in the life to come.

Dexterity of the hands speaks of skills flexibly learned in former lives. Beauty of the hands speaks of esthetic life in former lives. Coarse turned-back thumbs speak of harsh, forceful wills. Long forefingers speak of hypnotic power in former lives. Upright midfingers indicate a well-balanced mind. A distorted and sensitive marriage finger indicates lack of harmony in partnership in former lives. The smallest finger, when separated and wide apart from the hand, indicates a desire for spiritual retreat in a former life.

Thousands of tiny brains occupy the hands, seeking to complement and even excel the greater brain encased in the skull.

The ancient Rishis understood the great mudra laws of hand posture and the freeing of the pranic fiery mind flow through the hands. The science of the hands is so ancient that man has no way of tracing this history.

In the left hand of man may be seen things of the spirit and of his past life. In the right hand of man may be seen the life of the now and of his effort and his struggle.

Commercial, professional palmistry as a psychic art is limited to character analysis through charts and maps, to the shape of the hands and of the fingers and of the lines in the hands. Such blueprints are no more than a graph to record impressions of struggle and development.

Hand scrying is a psychic art when a person having psychic power concentrates upon the lines of the hand. While touching the hand of the one he reads, he sees beneath the lines into the effluvia recordings of the soul speaking through the hand.

The eye of man and the hand of man contain more concentrated revealing ether than any other portion of the human body. A psychic scryer of the hands unites himself with the revealing ether in the hand, and thus can see literally things existing in the past, in the present and in the future.

Few persons have the gift of refined hand scrying in the present days because palmistry has fallen into a lower psychic art. In the view of most persons, it is a source of entertainment, of amusing character analysis.

No one psychic art can contain all of the facets of other psychic arts. The gypsies, so known for their reading of the palms, are old Egyptian souls fallen away from the Ammon occult powers. Gypsies use the psychic art of palmistry to penetrate neighborhoods and communities. Their divination powers, however, far exceed those of the Westernized ego who still looks with condescension upon the processes of psychic manifestation and demonstration.

The Western ego on the self-genesis level feels himself to be superior to any helps from the wave lengths of interior knowledge. Now that science is beginning to prove that man has an energized, intelligible consciousness, the Westernized ego will accept the psychic arts as being a process of energy forces in the nature of man. However, the more materialistic Westernized ego will ignore the higher aspect of ESP — intuition; and will thus deny himself the free play of the understanding of his own nature and being. In time, one by one the touching points interconnecting the psychic forces in one's nature will become an accepted part of self-understanding.

The Westernized world is presently being exposed to depths and breadths of understanding and self-awareness. This will eventually bear the fruit of spiritual understanding.

Should one have the gift of hand scrying, he should use this gift with reverence, knowing it to be sacred. One will best contribute to this age of birth to the high psychic potential in one's nature by being unashamed of his gifts of the soul.

By looking upon himself as a spiritual scientist and a researcher into the wave lengths of the interior consciousness, he will obtain for himself an extension of spiritual power and thereby command the psychic forces of his nature.

HANDWRITING

The science and study of graphology very often leads to clairsentient seeing into the ego life-stream of another person. Psychic sight can be opened through making contact with effluvia energy in handwriting using ink. The etheric content in the blood of one writing with ink unites with the fluid chemical content in the ink. This acts as a point of informing energy to the one having the gift of penetrating effluvia energy. Effluvia energy is a combination of intelligible ether plus magnetism.

WATER SCRYING

Water scrying acts upon the same principle as handwriting. One having a heavily charged lunar psychic nature responds to the informing principle concealed in all things liquid.

There is a certain mystic, moodlike penetration into all liquid life. Some clairsentient persons receive their best visions or inspirations while bathing or taking a shower; others, by contemplating a small stream or brook, a lake or a river. Any moving pure water can open primal etheric gazing powers.

A solar initiate can use moisture scrying, fire scrying, earth scrying, air scrying and universal scrying. A lunar initiate as a rule rarely uses more than one technique of clairsentient scrying.

SKY SCRYING

In certain seasons, such as the autumnal equinox, the winter solstice, the vernal equinox, and the summer solstice, there may be seen in the clouds of the sky, by those having etheric capacity to see, molded sculptures, scenes and faces in the clouds. Such cloud formations are a part of the world unconscious shaped in mirage fashion by the angels that he who has the sight to see may be made aware of the myriad moods of mankind.

The earth is a sphere of congealed pranic or etheric light. In certain periods solar light and lunar light unite, forming a screen to activate soul memory against the reflected screen of moisture and atmosphere onto man.

Men take for granted these sky sculptured forms as being coincidental shapings, or often think them to be chimeras of their own imagination. However, one still retaining something of the mystic in his nature knows these mirrored images to be a promise of his own expanded consciousness uniting him with the Mind and Will of God.

UNIDENTIFIED FLYING OBJECTS

Some of the U.F.O. phenomena are mirages astrally seen and are a part of collective, subjective wishful projection.

Some are tangible terrestrial orbs produced by the cosmic energy forces.

Some are physical secret research aviation projects of this nation and other nations.

Some are spiritual globular spheres etherically envisioned and formed for the seer by intelligible spiritual presences. When this occurs, one is being initiated into light, ether, and energy. Spiritually, these spheres may be seen when one has opened the sixth layer of ether in the eye.

One should, on seeing an externalized spherical object, ask for revealment. If it is the Will of the Father, he will receive the spiritual answer in the inner planes and thereby gain in progress and in rationality.

Bible Scrying

In the intuitive side of man working with the psychic forces, there are certain religious manifestations of ESP and psychic power. One never-failing, reverent source of guidance is Bible scrying. In early American history, this psychic art was used intensively by certain pioneer mystically-inclined persons, among these some of the signers of the Declaration of Independence.

Before men had access to the Bible they depended upon a certain tone echo in the ears to remembered passages of the Scriptures pertinent to their need and instruction. Memory of phrases and passages in the Bible seeming to contain the whole solution to one's need in a particular time comes from a certain churning effect caused by a union between mind and soul. To this day many have the gift of remembering a particular phrase or passage in the Bible which comes to one's rescue in time of need for comfort.

In the psychic art of Bible scrying, one holds the Bible in his hands and asks God to let his hand open the Bible to the needed page and a particular passage giving the answer to his need. One who uses this art with reverence invariably is given a correction, a strength, a guidance, and very often a prophecy.

The Bible, the sacred book given to man in its Old Testament aspects for the family-genesis phase of life, and New Testament for a self-genesis expression, is watched over by great Recording Angels who see to it that this sacred book may be, chameleon-like, suitable to any situation in the life of man. Until men have reached the completion of self-genesis, this book will remain sacred to men, supporting all things pertaining to their spiritual progress and their physical moral conduct.

GLOSSOLALIA

Glossolalia or the speaking with tongues is a part of the outpouring of Holy Spirit; not all have this edification. It is one of the gift aspects of the soul, and primarily gives release to the logos center in the throat, which in turn sets up action in the will, memory, and imagination processes of the mind. Unfortunately, many do not understand its "run away" nature in the psychic portals. Through glossolalia one can open himself to satanic as well as spiritual forces, which can be observed in a three-year period after its appearance. However, if this gift of the soul is not the whole dependency source of communion with God, and is kept on the leash of reason, much can come in its complementing aspects of the spirit.

Everyone enters the world with one gift of the spirit. When developed it is the *mystic key to the lock* and opens the treasure gifts of all of the other gifts of the spirit.

CRYSTAL SCRYING

All superior psychic arts depend upon the power of a certain attentiveness. Without concentration, the intelligible flow of psychic power cannot speak into the mind of man.

Concentration is a *willing* exercise. To concentrate upon things of the past one must tap either world memory, soul memory or ego memory. To concentrate and to receive accurate and helpful information, to be informed, to learn, to see and to foresee is only given to those who have in former lives ethically used the psychic arts under the tutelage and instruction of sages, gurus, or avatars.

Persons having the power to penetrate the reflective informing ether have lived in a state of alerted foreknowing and foreseeking for many ages. Many in the world use the gift of attentiveness and one-pointed concentration in the ordinary processes of life. Should one seek, however, to come eye to eye with the ESP gifts of his soul, he must be prepared with a resiliency and a fortitude to meet equally his earth anxieties and responsibilities with spiritual awareness, faith and understanding. Only in this way may he remain useful to his age and period of time, for a psi gift without usefulness or being of some service to someone is a waste against the flow of creation.

Psi powers are creative powers. When not used for the service of others to create and to make new and to give hope, they fall back upon the one having such powers. In analogy it is similar to a man having a fire on his hearth whereby he warms his neighbor with hospitality.

The higher psychic powers and gifts of the spirit when not used in the service of the Holy Spirit become a consuming fire to burn and to destroy one's own body, emotions and mind. Some psychics in the world, looking upon their psychic gifts as sacred, seek to carry this flame and fire from place to place. As metaphysical troubadours they must wander into other environments so as to leave a little warmth. It is unfortunate that in the present time of egotism even though all are fermenting in the juices of their own unused psychic powers, a metaphysical troubadour finds in each new place only a few responding to his powers. Only those who have encountered a cold reception to their spiritual powers can estimate the suffering caused by non-seeing eyes, non-hearing ears, to that which is being said through them.

However, there is presently in the Western world the beginning of a response beyond curiosity to the psychic interplay in the mind and affairs of men. Certain seers are receiving prominence and acceptance. Popularity of a seer carries its dangers to the seer. Psychic power stemming from spiritual sources moves in a flow. When overused due to outward pressure from unknowing minds and selfish wills, the result is devitalization and degeneration of the psychic flow. Too often one can see how psychic flow is degenerated by overuse. Thus, in the present time of a factual look at the psychic sciences there will come a reverence, a respect, accompanied by an ethic in the use of psychic and spiritual gifts.

Science presently engaged in the mechanical development of exploring psychic gifts is beginning to see that protective measures must be given to those who are uniquely organized psychically.

In the time of the early Christian period in Ephesus, in Chaldea and in other ancient places along the Mediterranean, acquisitive men searched the slave market to find gifted oracle psychically-inclined persons. On buying them, they placed around their necks a velvet collar with a chain and led them from place to place, selling their services. Unfortunately, this state of existence for a psychic person still exists in this time. While slavery of psychics no longer exists, rarely does one find a psychic person who has not been at some time or another the victim of exploitation.

Publicized psychics must bear the brunt of ignorance and exploitation. Thus many persons having psychic gifts conceal them, intuiting the necessity for maintaining the purity of the psychic art functioning through them.

One of the ancient psychic arts preserved and still used today is the art of crystal scrying. All seers having access to the kinetic layer of energy in the eye have psychic penetration powers into jewels and stones of the earth. Each jewel left in the earth by the mighty convulsions during the earth's creation contains the mirrored light of creation. And of all of the objects used for psychic seership and revelations there is no better instrument than a jewel or a stone for revealing and discovering the things of the past, the present and the future, for in the condensed vitality energy of a stone can be found a cosmic key to the meaning of life, especially a stone in a rounded or oval form.

In the jewel and in the stone, congealed light can picture and portray what has been, what is and what will be. Ancient peoples have made jewels and stones sacred from time to time—the American Indians with their turquois, the Incas with their gold and silver, the Egyptians with their lapis, the Hebrews with their ephod jewels, the Chinese with their jade.

In all continents may be found a reverence for the sacredness of jewels and stones. The wearing of amulets, the zodiacal jewels assigned to each person — all of these are part of divination resources and strengths.

Crystal, the mysterious, has attracted seers for ages. The crystal mass has been more than any other life mass filled with psychic energy. Cold to the hand, demagnetized to outer electrical influences, each mass of crystal contains in its centered core a shining, reflecting, etheric energy point of akasic fire.

A mass of crystal when used reverently by a spiritual psychic becomes an extension of his own etheric body. Highly magnetized by the effluvia of the psychic it becomes a third eye. As a concentration orbit for his psychic powers it can be used to reflect as a reflecting mirror upon which salient dramas are pictured.

When used with right attentiveness, a crystal acts as a drawing, pulling influence. If used unethically, a crystal can be a hypnotic instrument, drawing persons to an unethical psychic. The crystal can become a will hypnotic forcing point of energy.

Persons using a crystal mass usually become unexplainably attached to this orb of reflected light. A seer using a crystal ball for the means of intercommunication comes to look upon it as more important than any other article in his possession. Complete dependency upon such externalized objects prevents one from fulfilling the need of the contemplative side of his spiritual nature, as to overextend any psychic gift and to use it in total dependence is a form of idolatry. When the contemplation aspect of seership is absent as it is more often in crystal gazing, one fails to make union with the universal Source or the One Spirit directing the affairs, minds and hearts of men.

Overconcentration powers of a psychic nature are a form of fire. One using the crystal gazing art should devote two-thirds of his spiritual life to selfless service, prayer, devotion and contemplation, giving but one-third to this most pointed and selective gazing power of the eye.

The scenes, the dramas, the pictures, the perils, the tumults reflected into a crystal ball are the reflections of the lives of others in the world and not the reflections of the life of the seer. It is a rare seer of a crystal ball who can see things for himself or concerning himself in gazing into a crystal ball.

Thus, to be but a reflector of the affairs of others in the world and not a participant is to lose step with the life flow and interplay necessary to spiritual and psychical progression and growth.

To professionally use or to earn a livelihood through the use of a crystal ball is to push aside the solar and lunar influences of moment by moment self-experience. To live always sensationally oriented in psychic excitement through the vicarious reflected portrayals of the lives of others is to offend the law of timing. A true and high psychic power carries with it protecting and insulating influences which determine that one become not a victim to overlong psychic drainage from others.

Overuse of any psychic instrument, be it the use of tarot cards, playing cards, planchette or crystall ball attracts the fakir, elemental, magical influences. Intense, heated psychic power occurs in the brain of one overusing the instruments of the psychic arts, causing pituitary gland irritation.

The crystal art of seership is a psychic art and should only be used as an intermediary researching and exploring instrument. Indeed all of the superior psychic arts can be used safely when used in proportion to common sense.

One should never use a psychic art through instruments as a fun instrument. The unseen forces protecting the psychic arts will induce unpleasant results when the psychic arts are used in any manner other than sacred.

PSYCHOMETRY

The psychic art of psychometry or reading the reflected light in handwriting, in objects and in environments is a familiar psychic art to spiritists and to those seeking to understand and to make viable the psychic manifestation.

In psychometry one draws upon the kinetic energy reflected light contained in environments and objects. To clairsentiently touch and to communicate with the reflective effluvia in environments, one can psychometrize, that is, center his psychic power into an environment or upon an object, and thus draw into his active psychic portal the knowledge he seeks to gain concerning persons who have previously lived in or visited the environment.

A psychometrist, by holding an object in his hand, can bend the time barrier, or energy flow, and see with etheric hindsight the time or period in which the object was meaningful to the consciousness of the owner. He can tell the origin of the place of the object; and if the information desired is personal, he can identify the owner and outstanding incidents in the life of the owner. He can also describe the appearance of the owner, the emotions of the owner, and the mental state of the owner of the object.

Psychometry comes under the heading of the psychic art of clairsentience. The psychic art of clairsentience extends the sense of smelling, touching, tasting and seeing, and sometimes hearing. The clairsentient psychic first feels what he seeks. The clairsentient often becomes that which he seeks. The true clairsentient has the power to become the stone. Through teleport powers he can transform his consciousness to a state of organic life relating himself sentiently to the meaning and intelligence in organic and inorganic life.

Many persons having clairsentience have the experience of becoming another person, thereby entering into the most inner processes of a person. A clairsentient can also use this power as related to objects, houses and environments.

Psychics renowned for their investigation powers regarding criminal acts use clairsentient powers to track down a criminal. This is a form of psychometry.

One of the mediumship side-attributes of psychometry is the blindfolding of a psychometrist. A tightened bandage around the head pressing upon the base of the brain produces the same effect used in old Egypt to bind the skulls of the young, whereby an overcharge of psychic flow is pressed up into the pituitary and pineal glands, thereby increasing the psychic state of seership.

Psychometrists overusing this brain-binding psychic process endanger their minds and mental wills. Often brain damage is the result of such extreme concentrated pressure. The etheric sheaths protecting the brain from excessive psychic energy and force are violated and destroyed when any form of external pressure is used to gain excessive psychic power.

Dowsing

Men have built-in psychic geiger counters and water dowsing wands which can lead them, if they will, to all of the food they need and all of the water they can drink or use. The divining, water-dowser psychic uses the primal etheric memory to find water. This memory exists more often in men without glamor or clamor in their psychic natures. To recover one's union with the providing essences in Nature, one must retain a certain clairsentient union with the hidden resources of Nature.

Successful mining prospectors also know the law of clamor subduing, that they may develop their inner kinetic geiger counters leading them to the discovery of precious ores and metals.

Pranic Finding

In a finding of lost articles or persons, the psychic perceiver projects his searchlight of intelligible perceiving. Thrusting aside the fixed time or place assumption, he sets into motion the recovery of the object or person. Through this process the article or person comes back into the time range of the one seeking to recover or find.

The perceiver, in seeking to find an article or thing, must first know that if the article or thing truly belongs to the possessor no other person can have or claim it. Understanding the law of composite association, he knows that the article is saturated with the effluvia or pranic magnetism of the one owning the article. The perceiver pierces the barriers or walls of time and space and of distance and placement, setting into motion the law of finding and recovering. He builds a psychic energy cord of retrieving, using the magnetism of the one absent from the article to draw and bring back to the possessor that which seemed lost.

Should a person have an article lost and not recoverable, this indicates that the one claiming ownership has in some manner failed to earn the stewardship of the article. All initiates having divine recovery attributes are assisted by the angels. However, there is a sensitive *ingathering* psychical process one must set into motion so as to receive the direct angelic helps and assistances in recovering so-called inanimate articles.

In seeking to find a lost article one must know that he is united with the life functioning of the article, and he must assure himself of the necessity for the article's return, realizing that all objects and persons have a psychic interrelation and a communicable point of vitality. From this sense of knowing, the psychic searcher unites with the animating life force sustaining all objects in the universe. Every true seer has the power to draw to him or to his mind that which he can see or behold in magnified sight.

When one finds a lost article, he is using kinetic psychic powers. When one diagnoses illness through psychic power, he is using etheric psychic powers. When one is receiving warnings of dangers or trials of death, he is being reinforced by angelic psychic suggestible helps.

In psychically finding or locating a person living or dead, one enters etherically into the magnetic energy auric field and unites himself with the feeling and thinking processes of the person lost or displaced. Starting in the last known environment, one opens himself to the identity tone pitch of the one absent; fusing himself with the missing person's animating life force, he penetrates the communicating fiat of the person. He familiarizes himself as being in the mind and feeling processes of the one absent. He calls upon the divining power of persons in the environment near the absent person to come forth and to disclose or to make public the whereabouts of the missing person. This procedure can be used also in finding and recovering articles. Should one fail to find the person, this will prove to be out of timing to the individual karma of the one seeking to find and of the one lost or missing. However, the process of recovery will have been set into motion, and recovery or knowledge of the person or object sought will occur in some manner. In event of failure to find, the angels will rationalize the loss and the one seeking will make adjustment to the loss. The one lost, being known of God, will be watched over, wherever he may be, by the law of timing and finding.

The art of pranic finding is a clairsentient, telepathic art. The finder must use the techniques of the spider building his webs; plunging into a seeming void, he must scale time and distance to reach the object or person lost.

Prana is the highest form of energized ether. When used by the power of will projection, it becomes a uniting, tangible field upon which all things become at one to one another.

To use pranic finding one must know there is no separation in life. The pranic high-ether is the supporting life substance of the One life.

PSYCHIC POWERS OF A THIEF

There is a psychic wave length operating between a thief and a thing valued by a person. Any person having a valuable object such as jewelry or any form of object animated by a sense of possessiveness may during certain negative planetary aspects draw to himself covetous, possessive, or thieving minds, hands, and hearts. One invites a thief to steal from him when he has in his own nature a fear of loss and an over-protective possessive feeling for an object or a thing. When one takes stewardship carelessly, failing to fulfill the right care of possessions, he offends the law of stewardship and also attracts covetous minds and thieving hands.

Psychic force is intelligent, especially when concerning geting or having. Psychic force used by a cunning mind can ferret out the the very object one wishes protected. There is a radar-sending existing between a thief and the object he desires to obtain. Thus, all thieves use a subtle, lower form of extrasensory perception which leads them to take that which should not be taken.

When one is the unwitting victim of a thief, he should search himself as to his stewardship reverence. One should gratefully thank the Father for his possessions, keeping always close to the blessings of divine substance. Such persons know they cannot be separated from that requiring their stewardship. Also, such persons are givers rather than takers. Their hands are not grasping hands. If things are taken from them, it may be seen that always the Father provides them with more than that which has been taken.

One of the more sordid aspects of covetousness is that which exists during or just before one having possessions has died or immediately after the death of one having possessions. There are certain persons having vulture-like psychic antennas in their nature who value more the possessions of the dead than the possessions to be gained in worthy works of their own living natures. This unholy psychic atmosphere produces in some instances violent, angry and unreasonable separateness between relatives and friends during the time of death; sometimes a hidden side of one's nature rises up to surprise oneself as to his resentment and his acquisitive attitudes toward the possessions of the dead.

Inasmuch as the one who is dead still remains for three and one half days close to the environments of his possessions, these thoughtless and covetous dissensions disturb the one who has died and interfere with his after-death repose and retrospection.

To spiritually add to the peace of one who has died, one should release the one who has died and his possessions to the Lord of Life who equates and gives all life. In God's equation there are no accidents. All possessions are earned either in this life or in a former life. To seek to have what does not rightfully belong to oneself through the virtue of one's own earning will open the Quelle discipline in karma and invite poverty, lack, and suffering.

Psychic Healers

There has been a special interest in psychic diagnosis of ailments and illness in the human body in this age of psychic research. To the mystic-minded this is a wonder gift. To the occultist it is a natural offshoot of the psychic nature to explore the unseen or the etheric processes of man.

Psychic healers have been active in the earth since the memory of man. Ancient man discovered through Nature's etheric processes the psychic attunement between certain herbs and certain illnesses. At this time man's etheric nature was totally under the direction of the etheric Over-lords establishing mankind in the earth; men knew astrally what herb correlated to the inner astral counterpart of an outward disease in the physical body.

In the earlier stages of man on the earth, men had the power to heal the wounds of their bodies through drawing etheric-life substances into their bodies. Even as certain creatures can reproduce a portion of their bodies by drawing upon the etheric causative controls of life, so did men in the beginning of the earth use these laws.

Man has submerged his etheric healing-power memory into Quelle. Sometimes into the world there enters a soul who has this ancient and primal etheric healing power still active in a certain portion of Quelle. With this power is also the power to analyze, feel, diagnose and heal.

Such healers, when free to express this primal etheric power, do remarkable things. Their gifts to mankind are often looked upon as freak circumstance or as supernatural. However, such souls, when their akasic records are read, may be seen to have followed the mystic heart-path for many lives. Through some form of soul alchemy they have failed to develop the skeptical and denying side of their mentality. Not fatalistic, but more in accepting a universal life of love, these healers drawing upon etheric memory are sparsely placed into the life stream of man.

The akasic records of certain psychic healers reveal them to have used the healing arts by being in accord with the plant, animal and angelic kingdoms. In today's world they still recharge their healing powers by drawing upon the etheric energies in the plant life, the kinetic energies in the stone, and the sentient life of the animal; and they are always accompanied by the angelic suggestible influences.

Persons not having free flow in their psychic natures turn to such healers with their weaknesses and their hopes, knowing they have been in the presence of exceptional insight. However, not understanding that a person having one psychic gift does not have all psychic gifts, they are often disillusioned and disappointed when the primal etheric healer fails to have an accompanying modern practicality. It cannot be expected of a person having one perfected psychic gift that he should have all of the spiritual gifts.

Many healers with primal etheric healing gifts do wondrous things regarding the human body, but in their own evolvement are incapable of extending the powers of seership or of opening the veils of the future. Persons expecting them to do so, very often are the agents who blemish or cast doubt upon the spiritual veracity of the healer.

Scientific research will see that each person has his own measurement and capacity of individualistic psychic power. While some of the psychic arts are accompanied by adjacent attributes in certain persons, only in one who has become an initiate can be found the composite of all of the spiritual gifts, and rarely are these manifested in coordinating action. This by necessity must be, because even the one called initiate must have his specific point of expression in each life.

Jesus of Nazareth is a perfect example of cosmic centeredness. He was a teacher, a prophet, a healer, a kinetic scientist. He had the power of astral or etheric projection. He had the power of levitation and transubstantiation. Man eventually will be and do all of these things, but he will be them only after he has experienced everything possible to be experienced physically, emotionally, mentally. He will then use the etheric laws for healing, not as a primal etheric man, but he will use the powers of healing as a cosmic, spiritual man.

Just as there are creatures found living in the earth and swimming in the sea, having survived the great glacial and catastrophic ages in the earth, so are there souls retaining the primal etheric powers. They are retained as grace remnant egos out of the wisdom of God's equation, so that men may perceive in them a reflected primal purity residing deep within their own souls.

When modern man who has been asleep to, or has forgotten, his primal etheric memories draws upon the primal etheric healing resources dwelling deep, deep within Quelle, these memories will come forth into his consciousness in a different manner from that which is produced by a primal healer still having this power as the functioning atmosphere of his nature. Thus, primal etheric power tapped in Quelle by spiritual aspirants produces karmic upheavals necessary to be cleared away before healing may be manifested. This must be expected by one who would heal others. In the present and modern time, one's nature is not oriented to primal impulses. Healing in the modern age will thus draw upon the remedial powers from many sources.

In the average man, the primal healing arts are submerged or buried. They may be drawn upon and touched during sleep while dreaming. They may also be quickened into action through the opening of the akasic records. However, the primal healing arts touch and heal only the basic malfunctions of the body.

In man's coming to birth in his mind, the hidden inner physician will lean toward the direction of healing through the forces of the mind.

Quelle, or subconscious mind, is presently preparing man to die to the primitive myths dwelling within his lower unconscious, so as to open to man a non-irritating conscience aspect of his soul and to unite him more sensitively and justly with the higher conscience aspect of his soul.

The progressive new era or age of man will no longer overemphasize primitive challenges of life. Life of the future relates to soul to soul, mind to mind, rather than to the brawn to brawn of the past. The unique variableness presented to the mind of man will require all of the psychic resources dwelling in the wealth of Quelle and in the mind.

Very special angels now work with the mind of man. The Christ Light is seeking to penetrate the right hemisphere of the brain of man. The Quelle pressures and overflow in the subconscious of mankind are purging or throwing overboard accumulative primitive aggressions of the ages. Thus men are presently inclined to more calculated violence toward one another than has ever been known in their existence.

Men are not as yet in an era of perfectedness. In the beginning of the new era, competitions of the mind force will be far more dangerous and deadly than men have ever known in aggressions of the body. The fearful dangers of telepathically induced illnesses into the pathological side of the mind through mesmeric and hypnotic suggestion will be mastered and understood. There will be advanced ethics regarding the preservation of man's thoughts established by explorers and researchers of the psychic and mental life.

As men inherited the Ten Commandments, so will they be given through angelic and inner-plane guidance a reclassification of the ethic as taught by Jesus in the use of the powers of the mind. It is stated in the ancient schools that man should think with his heart and feel with his mind. This will be the basic support for all thinking in the age of mind.

Flexibility and the Psychic Powers

The higher aspects of ESP are creative and spiritual. Spiritual powers come forward into the life of man, proving all things. Spiritual powers need not appeal to the credulity of man. Spiritual ESP proves itself through "the demonstration and power of the spirit."

Psychic powers are forces. One must sift the psychic force and its message and its meaning, even as one would in mining the ores of the earth separate the lead from the gold. One should never permit himself to accept psychic force as being the whole. To be overemotionally involved in psychical expectations is to invite forces of the dark.

Sixty percent of lower psychical ESP is inaccurate because of faulty concepts regarding psychical laws and ignorance concerning the origin of psychic information. The best advice to follow concerning psychic events is to remember that the true spiritual scientist operates with detachment and impartiality. A sense of detachment is necessary and a reliance upon a higher directing and guiding principle which will correctly gauge or assess any form of psychic phenomena. This guiding principle is *God in man.* "Wait on the Lord" is an admonition which may be used in such matters with rewarding and gratifying results.

Psychic clairvoyant powers do not make a person holy. To properly gauge and measure psychic powers, one would need to have access to the past-life records of one having psychic powers. Mediumship powers appearing suddenly in the life of a person may be set off by some former-life overflow of the subconscious mind.

Psychic power when used by an untrained mind with immature emotions is similar to a horse taut to the bridle, yet retaining certain unpredictable wild phases in its nature. It is not by accident that a black horse symbolizes dark, magical psychic powers, or that a red roan symbolizes unruly psychic powers. The white stallion so often seen in preparatory instruction represents the last phase of discipline in taming and transposing the psychic force into the spiritual.

It is unfortunate that persons having manifestation of certain psychic powers often shut themselves away from instruction, and thus refuse to avail themselves of spiritual instruction and powers. The majority of persons having one or more manifested aspects of psychic powers are satisfied to remain psychic rather than become spiritual.

Refusal to accept that one can err in certain aspects of his psychic powers, refusal to take responsibility for his mistakes in the use of his psychic powers, refusal to admit that he is operating on hit-and-miss accuracy will build serious karma upon the soul's record.

Spiritual power needs no defense. It *is,* proving itself clearly, perfectly.

A higher lunar psychic may by grace attract a Master or teacher on the inner and sometimes the outer planes. If he will consent to follow the spiritual instruction and disciplines given by the Master, his psychic powers will be expanded into spiritual powers; he will become an initiate on the inner planes of instruction and will thereby render a valuable contribution to the world.

V

THE ROOT RACES AND THEIR

PSYCHIC POWERS

African primal psychics are earth scryers. Polynesian primal psychics are water scryers. American Indian primal psychics are fire scryers. Caucasian primal psychics are air scryers or etheric telepathic scryers gathering their powers from mind-to-mind processes rather than from Nature. Western-ego primal psychics are humanity and energy scryers. The East Indian primal psychics are higher astral akasic scryers.

Mother Shipton of England, so exact in her predictions regarding the scientific age, was an old Druid cultist. She used the Lemurian lunar-moisture scrying powers, drawing from the psychic foggy blanket covering her native England.

The island of England is a tremendously charged moisture psychic portion of the earth. Previous to the time of the Romans, the inhabitants of this fog-blanketed island were reincarnated primal psychics. The resilient courageous power of the Englishman is due to the fact that he still retains a close rapport with his primal psychic etheric supports.

The country of Ireland where so many persons are considered to be fey, using naturally and openly the psi powers, is encased in an envelope of green, misty lunar fire.

The people of Ireland, originally the blue-eyed and golden haired Aryans of the Himalayan mountains of India, chose this land that they might extend their initiatory knowing into the Western culture.

All ritual in the early Christian church was established out of the heart remembrance of Persian souls who had taken bodies in Spain and Italy. The ritual which formulated the cementing factor in the church can be traced to Persia and Zoroaster. Egos who had lived in Persia using Zoroaster's magical rituals reincarnated into Spain and Italy; they established the ritual of the medieval Christian church.

The ritual in the medieval church contained a strong conjuring power supported by elemental spirits. The use of the bells, the incense and the various steps in rituals for the mass were drawn from remembered magical powers used formerly in Persia. Today, the magical processes of ritualistic power are to be changed, so that man may be no longer dependent upon the magical procedures supporting worship.

Ritual forms a psychic envelope or matrix for worship. In new-era psychical impulses, new rituals are born. Science will play an important part in producing new approaches to God, thereby calling up other ritualistic formulas.

Egos formerly incarnated in Greece established the Aristotelian philosophy in the medieval church. Souls reincarnating into the new era of interterrestrial knowledge will replace the Aristotelian philosophy with a new-era logos. The evidence of the beginning of this new logos may be found in the works of Teilhard de Chardin.

The Hebrew race, a pure extraction from the Atlanteans, has the most inverted psyche of any peoples of the earth. The Hindus have the most inductive psyche of any peoples of the world. The Africans have the most parapsychological psyche in the world. And the Westernized mass egos have the most extroverted psyche, and are therefore more materialistically inclined.

All oriental people have accumulative psychic dynamism. Western persons express individualistic and scattered psychic dynamism.

The great avatars choose to embody in masses of people where psychic power is homogenized. Thus, the West must turn to the avatars of the past who have centered themselves in the equalized psychic processes of the soul. An avatar requires a mass psychic body to work through to give his message to the world.

When souls incarnated in the West have incorporated the parapsychological heritage received from the dark races, the inductive heritage received from the yellow races, and the intense inverted psychic dynamism incorporated in the Hebrew race, the West will receive its avatar. This will occur 2,500 years after the birth of Jesus.

The soul struggles in the present era are occurring that man may accomplish this, and thus recognize the great teacher who will come to give balance in the Aquarian Age. This teacher will not be the Christ, but will be a lesser saviour who will reveal the Christ as He *is* to mankind.

Primal psychic powers are possessed and used by the four root races. The black race, the red race, the yellow race and the white race — each root race has its own distinct psychic processes and a way of uniting with the unseen forces governing the psychic nature.

The black race primal psychic has access to a greater depth of parapsychology than any other people of the earth. Their origin myths are still foremost in the imaginative processes of their thinking. Their thinking is united with the primal ether powers. The black primitive healers using psychical arts can manifest phenomenal happenings in the physical world due to their being wholly cognizant of the subjective influences in man's inherent earthy nature.

All people encased in tribal patterns retain the primal etheric powers. Being unrestricted by civilization restraints, their thinking and feeling are supported in a manner submerged by men living under civilization's repressive laws.

The more civilized a person is, the less he has direct access to the primal inherent psychic powers. However, these primal powers are dormant in the Quelle portal seated at the base of the brain of all men. In certain times, under stress and pressure, these primal etheric powers move forward into the mind of man. He meets these powers according to his degree of evolvement.

Any person becoming ultracivilized, accepting total repression of his psychic nature, cuts himself away from his primal myth powers. He loses contact with the myth memory flow of consciousness supporting his reincarnation strengths.

It is important that each person, on opening the psychic portals of his nature, be fortified with ethical instruction, so that he may use the beneficial aspects of the primal flow rather than the hostile and aggressive side of his primal nature.

The experimental psychic arts when manifesting primal etheric powers become abnormal to one who has progressed with the upward flow of evolvement. Disastrous consequences result when one without preparation or understanding yields to the primal etheric side of psychic powers. To be overstimulated by a primal thrust of energy stemming from decaying habits and ideas exposes one to archaic laws of retribution out of timing to the laws of cause and effect in the present.

Certain persons having access to primal psychic memory desire to keep before the gaze of others the old techniques and practices used in dead cult formulas of the past. To do this produces a form of witchcraft and sorcery.

The Masters, teachers and presences of the spiritual worlds seek to keep alive the free flow and progressive side of the psychic nature. To lean upon the archaic psychic arts and to use them in the present offends the law of progression.

The primal psychic arts still exist. Men still use them and suffer from their use. Among the Tahitian peoples the voodoo powers and doll magic are still practiced. The use of blood to call up visions or to conjure and call up the dead exists today. The modern psychic arts will gradually replace the archaic primal psychic arts.

Many persons puzzle over the difference between the supernatural spiritual and the archaic psychical arts. One will lose his way if he supposes or concludes them to be one and the same. The archaic psychic arts draw their power from the fears of men. The spiritual arts are supported by faith, hope, vision into the pure, the good and the true.

Some of the primal psychic arts existing in the world are of a high order, expressing the divine primal side of scrying, healing, and of energy or kinetic control of phenomena.

The American Indian still manifests the power of fire scrying, the changing of weather, the reading of the reflecting etheric patterns in sand. As a race, the American Indians are old Atlanteans who have retained the higher Atlantean clairsentient powers of foreknowing and foreseeing.

The history of the Western continent red race can be understood through certain linkings to the initiatory schools existing both in the Western and the Eastern continents. The initiatory schools were common in the Atlantean civilization.

Their polarity points of instruction still remain in the earth. Persons clairsentiently attuned to Atlantean memory can travel etherically at night to these initiatory points and schools and can recapitulate or recover in their etheric processes the edicts used in those former times. Such persons having the power of cognition and night-flight return to these old initiatory schools. They travel by night, thereby recharging their psychic vitalities. With proven formulas, they gather protective strengths based upon natural psychical laws which are beneficial to man and his life on earth.

The psychic nature of nations and their resulting progressions may be traced to their reincarnation origins.

In the present time one understanding or having inner research powers learns that the majority of highly evolved egos living in France were formerly embodied in latter-day Egypt. And in England the majority of egos retain more closely within their memory their attitudinal reflexes of the karmic inheritance out of Rome and Spartan Greece.

Reincarnating egos move as a nucleus into nations so as to reinforce a particular aspect of conjoined national as well as individual evolvement. The psychical energy of nations is powerfully regenerated by souls having a common pursuit in gathering and gaining knowledge available only through indoctrination into a particular race or nation.

Four continents on earth beginning with the letter *A* are presently experiencing the most intense psychic pressures. In these four continents there is now occurring a higher genesis-rise in all phases of expression. From this rise the world evolutionary map will change for the better over a period of ten thousand years.

Chanting

A constructive and pure relic of memory in the primal healing arts is chanting and use of certain sacred tones and sounds to cure and heal diseases. In the Rishi line of instruction in India, man has retained the audible sound memory-power in the use of the OM. The constant sounding and speaking of this uniting Word vibration effectively changes the aura, rearranges patterns of karma, producing wonderful healing and spiritual effects. To use the power of audible sound, one should have the grace of instruction, or else he can upset the total health of the etheric body. The sound OM used indiscriminately can produce a dissolution process in the energy fields of the etheric body.

Sound plays upon the subjective receptivity of the psychic portals in the etheric body. Drums used by primitive races are inductive telepathic suggestible devices to penetrate and influence separated communities. Chanting used to change weather is a form of mantra suggestibility falling upon the vibratory receptivity of the subconscious mind.

If one has not yet united with his own key tone in his ego, he can be penetrated by magical sound tones used by persons having knowledge of the nefarious side of chanting. Psychical hypnotic chanting can be sent on telepathic sound waves by one having knowledge of the inferior magic. If the aura is insulated, one is protected from harmful nuances of destroying sound. An insulated aura protects one from the overpowering influences of cosmic sounds as well as from intrusive persons who have knowledge of the use of sound-wave sending.

One need only reflect upon a time when he has had an experience in failing to erase from his mind the subtle inference voice tones of a person implanting some idea contrary to his own ideals. These words of negative suggestion linger in the aura, churning over and over until one finally detaches himself clairsentiently from such inference offending one's own principle.

One of the strong powers of Satan is suggestible subtle speaking into the aura of the initiate. Jesus gave man the Comforter on His leaving the world. The Comforter is the Holy Ghost. It is He who speaks through the audible sound as the Spirit of Truth. When one relies upon the Comforter, his aura cannot be penetrated by the voice of Satan.

When one has been subjected to nefarious sound telepathy, he is in a continued state of astral argument with the suggestible sound phrases implanted into his aura. With spiritual conviction he can obliterate and erase the alien sound waves disorienting the placidity and harmony within his aura.

To set aside one's will and to be totally passive to hypnotic external sound of chanting produces a mesmeric eroticism, exciting the erotic side of one's nature. This invites spirit obsession and possession. To be spiritually receptive to the true mantramic suggestibility spoken by oneself will provide miracles in healing.

Chanting formulas when designed to destroy the will of another are evil. Spiritual mantramic formulas are molecular energy tone sounds to erase karma, to cleanse, to heal and to unite.

Each person has an ego tone. When time is ripe, his angel will send to him the one who will attune him to his own tone sound. He can open the door to this grace by first uniting himself with the harmony tones supporting universal order. He can also through love speaking slow down the over-aggressive aspects of his own nature and temperament.

The primal art of chanting used by a dedicated medicine man produces healing. From a deliberate sound arrangement of tone chanting a medicine man can redirect the malignant energy processes of a diseased condition, translating sickness into health of the body, the emotions and the mind.

One can through meditation and the use of mantramic speaking penetrate his own sacred tone existing in his spinal canal. He can through intense devotion, prayer, and meditation change the vibratory wave lengths of his ego into the resplendent self-music to be found in illumination.

Repeated and regular meditation produces union with the audible sound centered between the eyebrows. This is the perfect way for the modern initiate and mystic to know himself and to know life for what it is.

When the audible sound is free, the psychic processes of all bodies are in a state of balance, harmony, peace and bliss. One can then be said to have entered into fulfillment of the spiritual life.

MUSIC AND TELEPATHY

Of all the languages universal and cosmic, there is no greater blender and unifier than music.

Music begins as tone in the great Hum or in the WORD sounding through the greater archetypes, from whence it is sent down due to the gravity pulls of the physical earth where it falls upon the astral nadis centered in the astral core around the spinal canal. Here, as vibration, it flows into the aura and then into the oral etheric vortices surrounding the ears. Vibrational flow transmitting music as sound, harmony, and melody is heard by the hearer as to what *he is* in his evolvement. No two persons hear in the same manner. The nuances of sound cannot become more than *one is*.

The clairaudient and clairsentient person hears and feels the source of music and, if highly evolved, he can also unite with the celestial underflow in music. He can in his feeling and sensing transpose music etherically and thus heal and rearrange crystallized patterns in karma. Masses of persons hearing etherically overcome mass karma.

Persons with telepathic receptivity and sensitivity are strongly attached to the musical astral cuneiforms floating in the etheric and psychic atmosphere of persons. They are telepathic receptors or receivers of thought sent on wave lengths of music. Thus, their telepathic intuitions are received as certain songs sounding over and over into the aura and onto the ears. These sounds also fall into the cuneiform points of the body such as wrists, ankles, etc. One should alert himself to fixity musical sounds and musical phrases repeating themselves over and over into the ears. Such sounds are a form of telepathy seeking to tell him something vital transpiring in his inner world or in the inner world of those around him.

Hearing and experiencing in telepathic wave lengths of sound long-forgotten themes of music can be a code sound of one sending from the world of the dead.

Hearing music of childhood repeatedly sounding in the ear can be Quelle's way of flowing out of the subconscious long forgotten debris intruding upon and affecting the attitude of the present.

Hearing subtle music over and over having sharp irritation and intrusion of the mind's peace shows that one has astral vulnerability to a mischievous astral psychic mind. One should erase these subtle tones by prayer and meditation, or should set up a counter sound with singing or chanting.

The angels with their power of suggestibility are the greater senders of telepathic sound into the emotions of man. Much of their healing and lifting for man is accomplished by penetrating the master-tone in the ego of the person they would lift, console, or heal.

In the spiritual art of contemplation, sound as music is a master accompaniment to contemplation. All initiates work to achieve at-onement with the Master Hum of the universe or the Word. To be a receiver of heavenly telepathies through sound is grace.

VI

THE LUNAR PSYCHIC AND SOLAR PSYCHIC

All psychics come under three categories: the lower lunar psychic, the higher lunar psychic, and the solar psychic.

The lymph system of the lunar psychic is highly charged with moon vitality. The kundalini powers in the spine, working with the glandular system, press upon the lymph chain of the physical body and upon the corresponding currents in the etheric body, giving a mystical, magnified enlargement of things seen and heard. To see things through lunar light produces in the psychic a powerfully charged emotional reaction to the world unseen by others.

The lunar psychic lives in a mood consciousness. The exterior world of consciousness is experienced dramatically in the higher lunar psychic; sensationally, in the lower lunar psychic. The lower lunar psychic sees the inward world through the mirror of his own emotions. The higher lunar psychic experiences his visions and dreams through a certain kind of self-induced suggestibility whereby he sees, but does not understand always what he sees. The higher lunar psychic intuits in depth what he sees, but he is not always able to put into words what he sees or why he sees it. He is unable to convey to others what he sees. He knows, but does not always know why he knows.

Certain higher lunar psychics, giving information about life after death, see men after death through the reflected lunar light; they often believe the shining radiance of the etheric bodies of the dead to be angelic. A solar initiate seeing men after death recognizes men to be not angels. Having the androgynous sight, the solar psychic would see into life after death and know man to still be man after death, an angel always an angel.

The solar initiate can see all the lunar psychic sees. However, he sees beyond the lunar psychic into dimensions of light. On extended wave lengths of light and sound, he sees, hears, knows and is informed as to what he should do with his information.

Intuitive sensitive persons having aversion to the lower psychic arts are justified in that all psychic untrained immature emotional persons are uninitiated. Their untrained psychic powers are pressure-produced by some derangement of the glandular system due to karmic unethical offences in the use of the life forces or of the psychic arts in some other life. Persons excessively displaying psychic powers are astrally oriented to the subtle worlds. Their psychic energies are charged with inverted magnetism; as dividing agents they play upon the fears of unknowing persons to upset and to agitate.

Fortunately, the uninitiated psychic has a limited period of thirty-six lunar month cycles to produce powers of phenomena by drawing upon his glandular system. After this period, he becomes dependent upon another order of intelligence commanding the kinetic forces in the astral planes.

A higher lunar psychic is an astral psychic having access to the reflective light of the lower astral world and to the higher aspects of the First Heaven. Lunar psychics, both high and low, use their power of ESP to see all things clairvoyantly in *reflected* light. They are profound night dreamers of the weird, the fantastic, and the magnified. Lunar psychics use the power of psychometry, of character analysis, of physical-body diagnosis. The lunar psychic is responsive to hypnotism by persons in the physical as well as in the interior subtle worlds. Lunar psychics use their powers to unite with the moon changes working through families, the animal kingdom and Nature.

When untrained, the lunar psychic unconsciously uses mesmeric powers. When trained and assisted by the angels and the Presences of heaven, they draw upon the *reflected* Scrolls of Light. Their psi cognition powers, when assisted by the angels, are remarkable. When dependent on their own memory energy coils and their psychical instinctual responses, their prophecy is predictive, not always coming to pass.

A lunar psychic, being astrally oriented, can shift from the low octave of psychic power, producing fearful phenomena, or can progress to the higher aspect of spiritual seeming miracles. More often, however, such phenomena produce wonder-psychism. If the emotions of the lunar psychic are immature, he has not the ability to comprehend or to interpret intellectually what he is seeing, hearing, feeling and expressing. Such psychics are dependent solely upon the pituitary gland. Overdependence upon the pituitary gland produces an irritation to the brain and to the etheric body. This in time drains off psychic intelligibility. The etheric-body drainage due to psychic excess causes mental and emotional imbalance. All lower lunar psychics are exposed to such dangers. If there is heavy karma, tragedy is the result.

When there is an irritated psychic action in the etheric body, the lower astral psychic creates havoc wherever he is placed. He is forced to rebuild his psychic vitality from the effluvia-magnetism within the spinal canals of persons in his environment. As a psychic drainer, he draws upon the lunar magnetic fire in the solar plexus of persons with whom he has daily contact. He may be said to live upon the magnetism of others. Such persons are overpossessive and separative, causing irritating situations to occur, and depleting the vitality of persons close by.

If the psychic drainer is a reader, he draws upon the magnetic effluvia of those he contacts, that he may add to his own magnetism, and thus astrally read in the magnetic-blood effluvia the ego memory of the person he reads for, concerning the ambitions, the fears; something of the ancestral memory is also read through the magnetic effluvia moving out of the blood energy vitality of the persons for whom he reads. Such psychics become highly stimulated and recharged when reading for a subject receptive to their mesmeric influence. In spite of this, such psychics have a place in the life of man, sometimes rendering a service to the knowing researcher. In the presence of a lower astral psychic, if the one being *read* is spiritually protected and insulated, he may see himself and his affairs mirrored in the phenomena as expressed by the psychic.

As long as one does not consent to come under the influencing and willing of a lower astral psychic person, he may gather knowledge from such persons to his advantage and enlightenment. It is sometimes the case that a highly evolved person, while experiencing drastic initiation, is led to a mesmeric lunar psychic, that he may learn certain things about himself that he refuses to admit as existing in his own nature, and thus speed up the resolving process of his karma.

Mediums who have yet to earn angelic protection, working with spirit life, are to some degree mesmeric psychics, being subjective to the unrisen and risen dead; and, not being fully conscious while entranced, can be used by the unrisen dead to exploit the psychic forces. They thus are unreliable instruments for pure or true psychic revelation.

Unethical mediums having exploitation facets in their own nature accumulate, over a period of time, astral soil and dangerous cursing ability. However, if a medium contains a pure heart — and more often this has been developed in a former life of innate goodness — such mediums are sacrificing persons. Setting aside their own will-ego power they consent to mirror or to become an instrument of psychic reflection.

Mediums having the gift of clairaudience can reproduce and materialize on the physical plane sounds from the little-known wave lengths of the interior worlds. Mediums having the open astral eye in the lower subconscious of the Quelle matrix, using a heavier vibration of ether and ectoplasm have the power to reproduce to the sight of others fearful and also familiar apparitions.

Psychic powers are extended, increased and transcended in a medium when purity is expressed in the heart. However, mediumship of a totally subjective and passive nature prevents the medium from progressing into self-initiation. Therefore, a medium does not evolve as an initiate evolves. An initiate of the spiritual life commands, understands, and has access to both the astral and spiritual worlds. An initiate is in command of his own ego, fully aware and conscious, inwardly and outwardly, of all encounters astrally and spiritually.

A lunar astral psychic penetrates the kinetic mind cluster energy fields of the ego he *reads*. All lower astral psychics

have an unwholesome curiosity or desire to penetrate the
energy field of others. Thus, they attach themselves to psychic
development groups, or they single out certain persons that
they may recharge their own psychic energy fields. They do
not understand how to draw upon the higher spiritual cosmic
energy to rejuvenate themselves, as the initiate knows and
uses.

To supplement his energy, the psychical medium must
depend upon certain exchange of energy between spirits,
elementals and persons. The spiritual initiate is recharged and
revitalized through meditation, contemplation of Nature,
cosmic energy, and mediation with holy, purified life-renew-
ing wave lengths directed by the soul-light as sent from
heaven.

Aimless happenstance psychics with untrained psychic
powers produce fear and glamours, living upon the decaying
emotions of others. Their outer lives reproduce personal
chaos, soiled environments, and untidy personal appearances.
They draw upon the excrement-like atmospheres of human
depravity, often being attracted to bars and chaotic noise.
Such psychics are by nature slanderers and dividers, living
upon the destroying principle under the guidance of the dark
angels and the shadowed brothers.

The aimless psychic floats aimlessly in the sea of life, expecting others to be responsible for him. Such persons having
obnoxious psychic powers inflict pain upon others. These
persons, as a rule, lack intelligence to intellectualize their
turgid emotions. Living upon unreality mental stimuli, their
irritation-reach more often extends only to karmically associated persons who are drawn into the disastrous area of
their influence.

A solar initiate cannot be penetrated by a lower astral
psychic. No matter how a lower astral psychic may try, he

cannot penetrate the ego energy field of a higher lunar initiate or a higher solar initiate. His penetration is limited to
those who fear the lower psychic energies and forces.

Persons born spiritually evolved are insulated in their solar
plexus or lunar-brain center, and are immune to soiled penetration by a lower astral psychic. The only time the higher
lunar and higher solar initiate is exposed to the lower astral
psychic is when the higher lunar or solar initiate must add to
his healing knowledge to learn something concerning the
soiling human aspect of the psychical nature.

All higher initiates are at some time in their lives exposed
to the lower psychic forces as expressed by subtle beings and
human beings, that they may better understand the psychically charged atmosphere produced within the lower astral
planes, and also that they may have command and mastery
over any reflected soil of the psychical nature within their
own natures as retained in their shadowed bodies from former
lives.

The cosmic psychic nature is open to the higher initiate. It
is his work to become a cosmic universal initiate. To do this,
he must familiarize himself through a certain inductive sensitivity supporting the emotional and mental human life of
man on earth. To accomplish this, he does not become a
medium; he becomes a spiritual unifier and a mediator.

Through increased and accelerated initiation, the cosmic
initiate or solar psychic is made aware of dimensions beyond
the subjective and passive states of the emotions and the
mind. Cognizant of all he sees and learns on the inner and
outer planes, it is his work to make others aware of the unseen
dimensions existing in the universe supporting the life of man.
Not only is it asked of him to demonstrate the universal
phenomena he sees, it is also asked of the higher initiate that
he manifest and give outer form to what he sees. Through

some form of creation he must give tongue, voice and sight to what he knows and understands.

The lower astral psychic, failing to respond to the creative aspects of spiritual initiation, excessively depletes his energy in the lesser etheric body, and eventually falls into a state of inertia and fatigue. Without defense, he becomes an agent for the shadowed brotherhood. One of the ways that one recognizes a higher lunar psychic is that he has a greater degree of energy after sunset; the lunar brain retaining the solar life fire energizes and stimulates his psychic forces after the sun goes down.

The lower lunar psychic, however, is dependent upon unrisen-dead ectoplasm and upon the sub-magnetic resources of the physical world. When active and aware of the use of his psychic powers, he draws his energy from the sub-human levels rather than from Nature or spiritual levels.

The lower lunar psychic engrossed in the excitation of psychic powers, failing to understand the ethic in the use of these powers, has not the capacity to deliver himself from the accumulation of the astral soil or karma he draws to himself. A subjective lower lunar psychic must await many lives to free and extricate himself from such decaying atmospheres.

The spiritual initiate, in contact with others through healing helps, understands the necessity for the elimination of karmic soil. When he is called upon to instruct and heal others, he uses certain cosmic initiatory understanding to impersonalize or to dissolve any karmic retention through association with one who comes to him heavily laden or burdened with karma.

The lower lunar psychic is vulnerable. Therefore, his time as to the use of psychic powers is limited, when he becomes overweighted from the burden and saturated by the karma of others. Invariably he invokes upon himself heavy karma from those under his influence and from his own karmic past, and thus he is distracted from any further personalized use of his own psychic powers.

The sealed-in protective guardianship of the higher worlds permits psychic intrusion only so far. Great angel guardians overseeing and preserving the laws of soul-penetration set up impenetrable and protective etheric walls. It is a blessing when this occurs to a novice of the psychic life.

Failing to understand the blessing in this phase of correction, one sometimes turns against all things psychic, thinking them to be a dimly remembered foolishness in his own nature. However, if he responds to the upward flow of his divine gifts, he will begin to spiritually hunger for a true enlightenment; and a right and ethical channeling for his psychic powers will come forth. His soul will send forth the call, and his teacher will appear.

The protective aspect in all psychic awareness in the low or higher degrees of the psychic nature is the desire to render a service. In the untrained psychic, power is precocious. In the initiate psychic, power is illuminative.

A higher lunar psychic works to become a solar psychic. When the desire becomes intense enough, the divine companions of the higher worlds will provide him with greater insight into the limitations of his own nature. He will be given the good dharmas or supports to assist him over the formidable abyss standing between him and the solar initiatory powers.

The lower lunar psychic is inflexible and unteachable, thinking he needs nothing beyond the hookup of the source from which he receives. He is unable to explain what this source is. Many times he calls it "a voice" or he calls it "God," or he may believe it to be some prominent oracle from the past. Whatever he calls his source is usually of his own invention.

The higher lunar initiate having moved into adjustable receptivity intuits the source. Through right methods of prayer and meditation, he prepares himself to eventually recognize the wave lengths of communication.

The three steps of psychic power are initiatory steps. One is in the primary grades as a lower lunar psychic; in the secondary grades as a higher lunar psychic; and as a solar initiate one has moved out of the algebra of mystical metaphysics into the higher physics of archetypal dimensions.

PSYCHIC EXPLORATION

One should determine before he enters into psychic exploration whether or not he has any facets in his own nature of the exploitative. If he has a natural, honest, and reverent research approach to the psychical world, he first recognizes there are no magical answers, no magical corridors, and no magical instantaneous approaches to the psychic world. He must factually see that psychic energy is an existing force supporting the various nuances as experienced in the emotional and mental nature of man. There are no instantaneous magical formulas to a true ethical spiritual life. One who seeks to gain instantaneous psychical power to enable him to conquer all the unhappier and less easy aspects of his environment and world, his person — and especially to produce some sort of panacea which would give him mastery over his own human karma in this life and other lives — is doomed to failure, to grief, and to sorrow.

Wherever one sees today a promise of an ESP power enlargement through advertisements in books, through various aspects of personalized psychical classes, or wherever a person enters into, in any manner, a desire to magnify his own psychic powers and to attain their mastery through some easy access, he is inviting upon himself acceleration of karma and also a too hasty development of certain energy-charged psychic portals in his own nature.

The glandular system of man, as yet so little understood, is the key and the clue to the maintaining and recharging of man's psychic nature. If one happens to be born with an overemphasis upon one glandular portion of his body, he expresses his psychical nature through one particular gland starry center.

The most important aspect in initiation of the ego is will. All initiates to be used of God must come under the Will of God. When any person intrudes upon the will of another —through uninvited hypnosis, through subjective astral mesmeric influence, or in any degree seeks to divert the will of another person and to exploit it, to gain or to in any manner attain a certain power over the mind, emotions, and will of another—this is of the dark. All initiates understand that the true life of willing is also the life of being. When one on the path of the spiritual life surrenders his soul-life will to any human person, or subjects himself to the will of another, he invites the shadowed and lower psychic world; and, in the processes of initiation, he will invite the forces of the dark who will challenge him and entice him into diverting chimera-like situations issuing out of the astral world.

The lower astral world is a world of tumultuous forces. One exposes himself to the lower astral world tumults when he has within himself any forceful desire to attain psychic powers and to thereby gain influence over the lives, minds, and affairs of others. To truly experience the finer side of the play of the psychic forces, and discrimination concerning psychic energies, psychic forces, and psychic powers one must be willing to serve God and to earn these powers. One can recognize a true initiate by seeing that he seeks not to personally influence the will of another. The initiate knows that to do this is to offend the Will of God seeking to be made manifest in the minds of all persons. It is God's plan that man achieve through his own identity. Even though man is supported by all forms of mediative association, it is a necessity that one must be confronted by the shaping of his own destiny. Man must be an identity centered in his own true desiring. He must know his desiring and utilize it, so that he may render the creative aspects of his desires in a perfectly manifested form.

Man and his universe and the order of his universe are dependent solely upon his use of willing and the understanding of his own desiring. To overzealously attach oneself to any form of action, is to use will as an overpositive influence in one's own life and one's own being, and also in the life of others. To be overpositive is as harmful as to be underpassive. One must find the golden middle way or the beautiful spirit of moderation. He should live always centered within the Will of God which contains neither a hard thrusting nor forceful action. The golden middle way is the balanced and peaceful way.

Lower psychic power when used as force is harmful, defeating one's right, not only to experience, but to discover and to add to his own versatility of the spirit. All spiritual initiates refrain from association with overforceful persons, knowing them to be as yet disoriented to the flexibilities of the spiritual life. The true spiritual person reaches not into the life of others with force-willing. He knows the first law to observe is that of a relaxed atmosphere which is conducive to spiritual communion between the higher aspects of the mind and the soul. He understands that the greatest attribute of all sealed into himself is a portion of the Will of God. When the initiate finally reaches forth and makes union with the ray of his self-desiring, he makes a simultaneous union with God. In self-knowing as a part of God, or as one of the particles of God, he discovers that the very first part of his being is *willing*. All psychic action is a will action, and this action must be totally in ethical hands. The initiate on the spiritual path knows that psychic power can be wrongly used or abused, but he also knows that it can be used in the Will of God as a mighty and creative aspect of his nature, producing in the nature of others a spirituality, a healing. Hence, psychic power when used to channel love is the greatest power man can know on earth.

VII

ZODIACAL POWERS AND THE GLANDS

The lunar and solar psychics are initiated through the planetary energies playing upon the astral fire in the astral core along their spinal systems. The glands of the body are planetary receptive generators. It is the work of the astral core to send the charged planetary energies into the etheric body.

Karma, soul and ego evolvement determine whether one is a lower lunar psychic, a higher lunar psychic or a solar psychic. The planetary emphasis playing upon the glandular system determines what kind of energy a lunar psychic uses in his psychic powers, and how he differentiates it is determined by planetary pressure playing upon his emotions and his mind.

A lower lunar psychic may be a Uranian psychic and thus have levitation powers. A higher lunar psychic using kinetic psychic power also uses levitation power to raise the emotions and mind of man. This, a solar psychic using Uranian kinetic powers can also do.

The astral body or emotional body is a complete ovoid sphere centered along the nervous system of the spinal canal. The astral currents influence directly the emotions of man. To be primitively overcharged astrally, one draws excessively upon one or more glands of the body. The true initiate has a balanced working harmony within his glandular system.

One may find his glandular nature and his astral nature clearly revealed and defined in his own astrological or zodiacal natal chart. If he happens to have a pronounced Venus grace in his zodiacal chart, he has a balanced nature of psychical harmony as related to the spiritual life.

A Venus negative psychic is very often a self-indulgent, indolent person. Through a mystic clairsentience, he wills the love of others. One who does not understand the lower Venus indolence or fatalistic attitude thinks such a person to be one who is totally dependent upon love. A Venus negative psychic is always in a position where his abundance of self-love gives off the emanation of love effluvia, making victims of those who love him.

The high initiate of Venus' psychic power is an initiate of cosmic love, universal love, divine love. And his spiritual life is supported by love. When the heart is pure, such initiates are truly the John-the-Beloved disciple. In the Rishi teachings the high Venus psychic is known as the bhakti or heart yogi in which the divine nature of his love is essential to his life, and all who are associated with him are blessed in the peace of his love.

If one happens to have overemphasis upon the Mars aspect of his nature in his zodiacal chart, his astral and emotional inclination and his psychical powers are kept alive by the energy of the planet Mars which plays upon the pancreas, liver, and the spleen. He will find that he is more inclined to use the psychic faculty of clairsentience, that is, he senses rather than knows. His sense of smell is magnified. A Mars magnified sense of smell provides psychic clairsentience. This gives an acute power of diagnosis of diseases to highly evolved doctors or physicians.

If Mars is well aspected in one's zodiacal chart, he has the power through the solar plexus to give off to others a feeling of super strength, and to generate well-being to others. Healers having an elevated Mars position in their zodiacal charts are coordinators and strengtheners to environments. Especially if they have the grace of a highly evolved mind, and a keen one-pointed or God-oriented spiritual intellect, such persons are able not only to sense through things and to describe and tell of a vision in other dimensions of life, but they are also able to penetrate the truth aspect in the minds of others and to represent truth in its highest nature.

Persons of higher Neptune psychic natures are dependent upon the cosmic pressures of the pineal gland. Such persons are highly sensitive, delicate, refined. Their psychic powers are sensitively spiritual. All high initiates have Neptune favorably aspected in their own charts. Such initiates having the gift of a delicate and intricate disclosure, their powers of revelation probe depths and reaches little touched by others in the world. Joan of Arc had such perception.

Persons especially influenced by the planet Uranus are kinetic psychics; having extended powers of the adrenal-gland action in the psychic nature, they are electrically charged persons, and are often disorienters of others or become karmic agents to others. Persons having strong Uranian aspects use their psychic energy as concentrated ESP, drawing upon the adrenal gland's forceful action. If the Uranian psychic is negative, he becomes a disorganizing agent in the lives and affairs of others. The Uranian psychic is sometimes feared by others; yet having many aspects to be admired, he very often comes to the world with versatile transforming powers of creation. It is not until one is exposed to the negative Uranian psychic in intimate or personal nature that he is aware of a subtle destroying power. The forceful Uranian psychic, enforced by an overly astral, charged adrenal gland, during certain negative planetary aspects will be a most painful associate to those who love him. As an initiate on the path, he is gifted, having inclinations toward the new era and leaning toward the higher genesis levels more often than lesser genesis. If he is unevolved and has an inventive mind, he is inclined to use other persons as experimental pawns. One should be alert to the materialistic Uranian psychic, as he is an experimenter, experimenting upon persons, experimenting upon life, looking not back when losses occur, but moving forward always at the expense of others and even of himself. He is an isolated person; satisfied with living alone, he is content only when he is himself engrossed completely in what he is doing. The lower Uranian psychic person indirectly seeks recognition; he subconsciously desires to be known and accepted without question for what he is; but once receiving it, he has no value for it and moves on to other worlds to conquer. The Uranian psychic of scientific inclination is a kinetic psychic; he is an offshoot of old Atlantean times now preparing in the self-genesis age for the time when he shall add to himself both mercy and heart. His chief lack is heart and mercy. One should understand when he is overly attached to a Uranian psychic that he will live in a state of continued excitation and that he must be wholly consenting or subjected to the will of a Uranian kinetic psychic.

The illuminated Uranian psychic sees the world as a cosmic whole. He is united to universal cause. He is dynamically charged with energies and forces beyond the wave lengths of ordinary man. He is not a visionary. He is united to the vision of the future. Jesus used the Uranian powers to kinetically reorganize and to sensitize the energies of this earth. The high Uranian psychic is an illumined seer; as a healer of the fears of man, he is daring and courageous. To be under the leadership of a Uranian initiate is to chart interterrestrial life. The black magic of Atlantis is to be healed by the Uranian higher psychic.

The planet Neptune is a galaxy mediator, taking from the great galaxy system supporting the solar system of the earth. Neptune is an initiatory planet. One being initiated under Neptune is exposed to the fanciful chimeras of the wish level of the astral world. If one is untrained, the central nervous system is affected, producing hallucinatory states of consciousness. A mature person undergoing Neptunian initiation frees the vagus fire in the nervous system. The pineal crown produces the power of revelation. The highest aspect of clairvoyance is produced through Neptune's osorius or highest pranic atmosphere, that is, wave lengths of revelation superior to mortal sense.

The lunar psychic using Neptunian power is a vague mystical psychic. The solar psychic using Neptunian power is an initiate using spiritual power in the highest degree.

The Neptunian energy rays play upon the pineal gland and the imaginative processes of the mind. The lunar initiate failing to understand the power of imaging through the process of imagination is a receiver of images rather than a sender of images. A solar psychic initiate using Neptunian planetary power receives his images from the greater archetypes and sends them through the power of his own imaging, knowing and creating. All great mystics having sending and receiving telepathic powers have access to the Neptunian fiery crown in the gleaming brain.

The Saturn lower lunar psychic receives his mystical psychical knowing by uniting with the traditional psychic reflexes of memory. The lunar psychic under Saturn's influence appeals to the fears, to the guilts and to the conscience of those for whom he psychically sees or hears. He unites with the punishing and retributive aspect of psychic powers. The higher lunar psychic using Saturn psychic powers attunes himself to the griefs of man, to the homesickness of man. The higher lunar psychic using Saturn psychic powers has déjà vu powers or the power to recognize former environments in which he or others have lived on earth.

The higher lunar psychic under Saturn has the power to read the akasic records regarding ancestral streams. The higher lunar psychic with an elevated Saturn can provide certain instruction regarding the higher astral and psychic planes. The higher lunar psychic can also invoke healing mental processes for those whom he would help or serve.

The solar psychic initiate using Saturn powers is a teacher of high order, a healer and rearranger of karma in the lives of persons heavily laden with debts from past lives. A solar psychic initiate with Saturn well aspected is insulated and protected in his own life regarding intrusion from the dark. He is also believed on as being an infallible representative of the light. He attracts to himself persons to whom he is the teacher—persons who are faithful, devoted, loyal. This initiate has an unending rapport with memory of the soul and of the world.

A lower lunar psychic when strongly charged by Jupiter's fire is an extravagant, wasteful psychic. He is unable to organize his psychic forces or powers. He is a devitalizer of his own etheric energies and of the energies of others. He is a diviner of the psychic fire in the astral core of other persons. And he is used as a pawn in karmic situations to upset the spiritual progress in the life of others. He is especially known to speak out of timing, saying awkward things. In the time or need of praise and reassurance he dowses the inspired fires of those needing comforts, helps and supports.

The lower lunar Jupiter psychic is especially a misleader of persons regarding advice in investments in money or changing situations. Their advice and psychic clairvoyant seeing for others is used by the brotherhood of the dark to treacherously divert naive persons into pitfalls of delaying actions.

The higher lunar psychic using the Jupiter psychic expansive hopeful enthusiasms gives encouragement. He stimulates the environment with his emanation of cheer. He is a healer of environments, of business, of professions.

The lower lunar Jupiter psychic is one who rejoices in the downfall of others; who delights in pointing out weakened situations. He adds an unholy glee to sorrowful conditions.

The higher solar psychic initiate using Jupiter powers is seated in an overlook over the affairs of men. Cosmic powers and universal laws work directly with such initiates, producing noble and generous directives so that the many may prosper rather than the one. The solar psychic initiate reinforced by Jupiter's elevation in his chart will be especially prominent in the mind-to-mind and soul-to-soul age now opening to mankind.

A solar psychic choosing a zodiacal chart for rebirth with Jupiter placed prominently in his destined way will be among the leaders of mankind in the space or interterrestrial age of mankind. Such initiates will have at their command interconnected psychic communication with the tones of the greater archetypes governing this eternity system. The solar initiate using Jupiter powers is a spiritual mediator for the multitude.

The lower lunar psychic having Mercury planetary powers uses certain aspects of his mind and of his speaking, when under psychic pressure, to tell the unusual. With an unpredictable, unknowing perception, he puts his finger upon certain things not seen by others. Yet he is unaware of how he does this. This is a quicksilver sort of action containing elements of truth. When asked to explain and to extend what he sees or says, he is unable to do so. He is very often overproud of this aspect of his psychic nature, thinking himself to have something more special than others. By this he places an obstacle between himself and his own upward rise in evolvement. He may be said to be psychically prideful.

A higher lunar psychic using Mercury planetary supports has a scintillating penetration into the thought processes of other persons. When exposed to the thoughts of another person, he understands the person's thinking, but he is unable to help anyone to change his thinking process.

The higher lunar Mercury psychic is personalized psychically to the thought processes of others. He cannot see the soul-motivation of thought, neither can he unite himself with the memory processes of thought. He can only unite with the thoughts as they are read at that moment in the psychic light. The higher lunar Mercury psychic is usually admired and thought proficient by a person who is satisfied with having his mind and character read. Should one depend on such psychics to help him to go deeper into the why of his thinking he will be disappointed, and thus judge all psychic powers to be valueless, trivial.

The solar psychic initiate with Mercury elevated in his chart is attuned to the mental processes of anyone he desires to contact through the mind. He is a mental telepathic artisan. The Mercury solar psychic initiate can open the mind wave lengths of the informing principle and receive the answer to what he wants to know concerning the thought processes of the mind of the past, the mind of the present

and the mind of the future. The Mercury solar psychic initiate has the power to introduce into the mental wave lengths
of mankind new and original ideas never before contemplated
by man.

Pluto, when placed in a water sign such as Cancer, produces a person emotionally self-engrossed, living and depending upon the Quelle subconscious flow of feeling in his nature.
Pluto in an air sign produces collective instinctual knowing
in the mind; in the unevolved, causes snap judgments; in the
evolved, produces predictive insight and foresight. Pluto in
a fire sign inhibits the subconscious, causing the person to
inflict upon others a subtle atmosphere of disapproval. Pluto
in a fire sign causes an inner sense of inferiority, unworthiness;
when mastered, produces humility. Pluto in an earth sign
produces a slave-driver seeking to use the energies of others;
self-preservation protecting one's own physical self interest;
a long-range shrewdness.

Pluto is the planet of the unconscious or subconscious.
In world initiation Pluto works to keep alive man's primal
memory. In family initiations Pluto keeps the dweller action
and conscience aspect of the family alive. Pluto working on
the person seeks to keep him aware of the greater collective
unconscious, uniting him with the interflow between all souls.
Pluto holds the key to the unconscious memory of mankind.
When Pluto is well aspected to Saturn, man has an initiate's
memory as to the creation of the world.

The lower lunar psychic having Pluto emphasis in his
chart uses the subconscious-mind telepathies, drawing upon
the Quelle fire supporting hostility, hate, separateness and
fear. He will see and hear the negative rather than the
positive in the lives of those he contacts. When called upon
to pursue his psychic powers for the sake of others, he will
fortify and keep alive these decaying hates in the minds of
those he touches. Clairsentiently he will play upon the fears of

others, using them to his advantage. As a separator he carries with him telepathic inference powers. He stresses the unpleasant and the obnoxious. As a homing pigeon he goes directly to that which is most feared in the minds of others. If his victims are superstitious or covetous, he encourages them to sustain and to act upon these lower attributes of their natures.

A Pluto lower lunar psychic is a destroyer of hope. Eventually, such psychics fall into the snare of their own despicable inductive practices, and become a part of the league of fallen souls.

The higher lunar Pluto-reinforced psychic is a quiet, inoffensive, non-intrusive healer. He works behind the scenes to soothe and to calm a person overcharged with anxiety and fear. Not always aware of his own mysterious power to penetrate the subconscious minds of men, he uses his healing powers in the night as a night healing minister working in the suggestible realms of sleep.

All persons having highly charged Pluto psychic powers have a certain color and texture to the skin. Being exposed intensively to the Plutonian lunar fire in the night hours, their skin takes on a slightly greenish hue in the daytime hours. Rarely does one find a Plutonian psychic with rosy-colored skin.

By the skin tones one may recognize the more powerful planetary charges in the psychic nature. The psychic under Venus has a milk-like skin with rosy tones. A Saturn-influenced psychic has a skin colored by violet tinges beneath the skin. A Jupiter skin tone in a psychic person gives off blue undertones with greenish inner tints. A Mars-influenced psychic gives off orange and red undertones to the skin. A Mercury psychic gives off yellow undertones, especially to the eyeballs, to the tips of the ears. The yellow undertones of the skin may be seen in the Mercury psychic. The skin tones of a Neptunian psychic's lips, cheek bones and forehead are alabaster-like, clear, with peachy violet ether flowing toward the outer tones of the skin. This is a transcendent undertone to the skin given off especially when the Neptunian psychic is in a high state of exalted spiritual power. The Uranus psychic coloring of the skin alternates between violet and tinges of grey-blue. When the spiritual power is supreme in a Uranus psychic, the color is a rosy violet beneath the skin. When the psychic power is of a low degree, the skin color is a slatelike blue-grey with seeming circulatory congestion beneath the skin. In the low psychic this color penetrates, and the slatelike color is reflected as a cold, calculating light in the eye.

All solar initiate psychics have fine texture of the skin, translucent in appearance and at times seeming transparent, giving off opalescent coloring and shadings.

VIII

IDENTIFYING CHARACTERISTICS
OF PSYCHIC EXPRESSION

THE EYE

The most prominently revealing aspect of psychic power is sent from the eye. The shape of the eye, the color of the eye, the etheric shining ether centered in the iris of the eye — all give off psychic power. The eye being the center of self-consciousness is the number-one instrument of willing and sending.

The cowled lid or the cobra-lidded eye invariably reveals psychic power. Rarely does one find an advanced initiate not having a cowled lid. Such persons have been initiated in many lives in focusing their self-conscious sight inward into the higher consciousness of seeing and knowing.

Many persons having the cowled lid or cobra lid are not aware of their psychic nature, nor are they aware of their psychically suggestible influence on the lives of others. However, it may be seen that they do influence and very often control the lives of others through their use of psychic or inner perception.

A cowled lid or hooded lid of the eye reveals that one has used the third eye in an ethical manner in some former life. One having cowled eyelids is an overseer of things unseen. Such egos are linked to the inner processes of human nature; they carry a certain wisdom foresight into all human affairs, not always knowing themselves to be psychic and not always understanding their psychic flow. Yet their soul-powers see to it that they keenly intuit the basic issues of life and that they are usually found in environments where their spark of God-inwardness lights up the environments of trouble. Helping and resolving, they are catalysts of hope. *The freeing of their spiritual power is service.*

The hypnotic eye may be discerned in the iris of the eye. Persons having the power to will others to do their will, through overflow of Quelle force acted upon by the astral fire, literally project rays of willing from the iris etheric center of their eyes.

Sensitive persons are repelled by eye-hypnotic-willing persons, often fearing to look them in the eye. The Western Indians in their knowledge of the will sciences used opaque concealing powers in their eyes, so as to avoid forcible hypnosis from the eyes of others. The Asian and Oriental souls still retain this power to make inscrutable and impenetrable their thoughts as revealed within the iris etheric point in the eye.

Hypnotic persons use this power of opaqueness, intuiting it to be their protection in the use of their hypnotic powers. Hypnotic persons are rarely willing receivers of telepathy from others. Directing all of their will through the eye and through the suggestible tones of their voices, they overuse the effluvia etheric contents of their psychic energy so as to gain the one power — hypnosis.

Suggestible receptivity plus the power of eye scrying is a balanced spiritual aptitude. When one has these two powers equally adjusted to helping others with a sense of selfless service, he is a high initiate.

All persons have been the victims of eye anger at some time or other in their lives. Lightning bolts of hatred coming forth from a hate-filled brain work with the destroying principle. Long periods of sending eye hatred destroy brain tissue.

Persons exposed to eye hatred subconsciously build opaque reflexes or reactions to hatred stemming from the eye of a person near by. Unexpected eye-hatred voltage can cause psychic trauma in the emotions, leaving literal scars upon the etheric body, particularly upon the heart center where all receptivity or receiving is experienced. All initiates know the power of love eye sending, of love eye glance upon one needing assurance, warmth and healing.

The psychic portal of the eye is inductive to the subconscious Quelle station at the base of the skull. The love eye sending draws one's emotions from the heart center and from the astral-core portal seated over the etheric matrix of the heart. All true eye sendings are accompanied by a smiling or a near-to-smiling countenance.

The Bodhisattva smile, as seen on so many sculptured forms of these perfected Saints of the East, is a symbol of love eye sending. The shape of the eye of a love sender and healer is semi-oval in perfect balance, both eyes being equal in serenity. To see eyes unbalanced as to intensity is to know that psychic polarity is yet to be completely obtained.

To see a photograph of an initiate yet to reach total polarity is to see a noted difference in eye balance and protrusion.

In a woman initiate the right eye is extremely prominent due to the need for the balance between Quelle flow and the left hemisphere of the brain. As a woman initiate advances and becomes polarized in clairvoyant sight, the eyes become more harmoniously balanced; pressure of psychic flow becomes equalized.

In a male initiate the left eye is at first more prominent. As the male initiate is seeking to balance the feminine principle in his nature, he must release the lower Quelle flow into the higher consciousness aspect of Quelle, into the larynx and into the left ventricle of the heart.

The male initiate, when his psychic flow is polarized, after reaching the forty-fifth year usually begins to bring balance to the eyes, that is, each eye has a similar outward pressure as to self-consciousness flow from within.

Madame Blavatsky's portraits may be seen to show an extremely strong right eye will-scrying gaze. Her initiatory powers were dependent upon the higher energy flow of the astral planes where she received the reflected archetypal light, and thus gave her written message to the world.

Eye scrying is an invaluable measuring, assessing process as to individualized psychic force or power. The more highly evolved one is the more peaceful and less intrusive his gaze.

A glance from an adept can totally rearrange the karma pictured upon the auric light of a person. All adepts having had constant discipline in the powers of concentration through the eye have the power to image and to manifest the Word into flesh.

Sacred is the gaze of the high initiate. All true dedicated disciples recognize their teachers by their teachers' eyes. Having looked into their eyes in former lives, they recognize them in the life of the present. Through that inner exalted ego-gaze, they are made to feel at home from life to life with that which shines from the inward light of their guru, teacher or master.

CHARISMATIC VOICE

A *charismatic voice* is a psychic heritage produced from many lives of emotion and feeling. A voice having charismatic and magnetic undertones to be spiritually effective must be supported by a selfless love generated by freedom of the love atoms.

A harsh, nasal, piercing voice is the voice of the hysterical pressure charges of psychic energy stemming from untrained emotions and self-will, and can only be freed through love mantramic speaking.

Love selflessness produces the pure non-intrusive voice tones. Rounded voice tones are united with the circular feeling flow of the emotions. To free the audible sound through the voice, one must channel the emotion flow toward the love of God.

The "voices" of Joan of Arc coming from the Archangel Michael and of her directing angels fell into her love atoms and her great desire to serve her nation. Joan heard and obeyed.

Spiritual voices heard and unheeded shut away guidance. When one refuses to follow guidance, guidance is withdrawn and one is left desolate in a harsh, unknowing world.

The voice of Satan pierced the ear of Jesus in the quiet of His desert retreat. He knew the subtle penetration of Satan to be the voice of evil. Wise is the student of the inner sciences to know clairsentiently what a voice contains. When the aura surrounding the physical and etheric body has been damaged, or if there is even a minute opening in the aura, a subtle voice can penetrate and remain there for long periods of time. Penetrating the mind, ears and nervous system, subtle voices are destroying vehicles.

On looking into his own mental conflicts, one can observe that he has throughout his life been a victim of subtle sustained undertones charged with inferences flowing into his lower mind.

Collective negative voice tones in the aura are sometimes telepathic, one not always having a direct vocal contact with the voice upsetting the peace and containment of the mind. A disapproving voice instilled in the aura can remain in the aura from childhood onward into maturity.

Every disciple of the spiritual life knows and remembers the beloved voice of his master or teacher. And if he has the grace, he can also hear the voice of his angels.

Telepathy is a powerful instrument of the mind and of the will. One can by speaking love-affirming sentences and love sending change, heal and rearrange the karmic patterns in the aura, and also mend the leakage in the aura through the power of the voice sent along the love wave lengths of healing telepathies.

All speakers influencing groups or the masses have charismatic power in the voice. Savonarola, martyred in Florence for his evangelistical John-the-Baptist power, had a mighty charisma. His martyrdom changed the flow of papal tyranny. His voice tones in the environment of Florence and of Italy cleansed the cesspools of corruption. From his period and era, man began another look into the Inquisition tyrannies of his time.

Oily, manipulative voices disturb one's self-containment. To shut away manipulative, psychic undertones within the aura or auric field, one should contest this hypnotic power with a direct challenge. Usurper voices can be erased with mantramic speaking and with spiritual exercises designed to open the audible current centered between the eyebrows. Through speaking the name "Jesus" or the word "Christ" one can heal, divert, erase and mend a mesmeric receptivity in the aura.

One should always analyze and weigh from whence a negative voice tone comes. He should determine in himself that any voice lingering continually in his mind is definitely not of his own mind or his own thinking.

All subtle, psychical powers are bullying powers building upon cowardice and fear. The first words the initiate learns to say in his expanding consciousness into the inner planes are "I am not afraid." In dreams, in all psychic experience, one must learn to say on reaching the boundary line between physical mastery and spiritual revelation, "I am not afraid," or he may use the name of the Christ. This one name — the name of all names—will take him over the abyss dividing the dark from the light.

The power of the Holy Ghost uses the audible sound power in the evangelist to influence the multitudes or masses in a religion. The roaring of John the Baptist as a lion was the evangelistical power of the Holy Ghost. The voice tones when free in the power of the Holy Ghost are a converting power. Miracles of healing can occur through the voice of the evangelist.

Words can be words of fire for the impure. Words can sound like the wind to overthrow hardened conditions. Words of water can be cleansing, baptizing words. Words of earth can break open substances of the earth, feeding the hungry. Each evangelist has his own element of the Holy Ghost, be it earth, air, fire, or water. When the Holy Ghost is present in the spoken word, mighty works are done in the Will of God.

THE LARYNX

Overcollection of psychic energy *upon the larynx* produces a harsh intrusive sound upon the hearer, reacting upon the speaker's nerve energy flow in the etheric body as grating sand upon silk. To change the intensive psychic accumulation in the larynx, one should speak love mantrams. Forceful psychic energy masses collect on the bones due to the lack of astral-core union flow. This produces inhibition to the blood cell and marrow in the bones, causing chronic and fatal diseases to the blood and cells. All psychic energy is supported by cosmic vibration and sound. When overenmassed upon any part of the skeletal system, this pressure upsets the total organization system of the etheric energy body, resulting in outward deformities and sicknesses of the physical body.

To organize and regulate the astral-core flow playing upon the etheric body, one should meditate and contemplate upon union with all life, upon God as life and love.

The flow of the life-energy currents begins in the astral core. The first aspect of energy flow is produced by the flow of the planets. Man receives this energy flow into the astral core acting along the spinal and nervous systems of the body. The life-current energy flow is transmitted into the etheric body. When free, this energy moves into the etheric energy body process as a finer energy, and when united with the soul produces radiation in the aura. If this life flow of energy is intercepted by resistance to life in any degree, the result is an overaccumulation of liquids in the physical and etheric bodies.

THE HANDS

The hand, next to the brain, is the most sensitively organized vehicle expressing the psychic flow between the senses, the mind and the soul. Psychic flow from the solar plexus governs the appearance of the hand, its shape, dexterity, movement, flexibility, grace or ungracefulness, and health.

The hands of man are directly charged and recharged by the psychic currents and wave lengths of the abdominal lunar brain centered in the solar plexus.

Persons having arthritis in the hands show an overcharge of lunar fire and psychic force playing upon the solar plexus, needing to be expressed outwardly in creation. Such persons are frustrated as to personal will and creation. When psychic creative flow is free, the hands become flexible instruments for the higher mental processes of the mind and for the soul.

The flow of psychic pressure in the solar plexus seeks to rise up the spinal column to the shoulders and then to flow downward into the hands. When this is repressed, the result is psychic blockage pressure falling upon the heart's sacred atoms.

Physical heart stricture is caused when the creative psychic flow playing upon the solar plexus is shut away by inertia, by laziness, by procrastination. One frees the psychic flow and the heart by desiring to serve, to heal or to minister to others through the use of the hands.

The hands are antennas for the solar psychic-charged force centered in the solar plexus. The healing art of laying on of the hands is a primal healing art. One can literally transfer his life force from his solar plexus to the body of another when he has primal etheric powers of healing through the solar plexus.

One can emanate healing power at a distance through teleportation powers or visitation powers by visiting the sick etherically and laying his etheric hands upon the sick.

In all instances of laying on of the hands, the one sick is recharged in his own solar-plexus lunar abdominal brain.

When a magnetic psychic healer uses the primal etheric powers of the solar plexus to heal, he awakens the primal instinctual life force in the etheric body of the one who is sick. And the one who is sick being once more united with his primal life force returns to the hookup with his own healing forces in his body.

The automatic brain of the body is centered in the solar plexus. It has all of the instinctual powers of rejuvenation and health. The hands are the outlet for this automatic brain. The automatic brain process centered in the solar plexus has developed throughout the ages. Its accumulative instinctual memory has a perfect recollection of how to restore and rejuvenate the body and to preserve it.

When one shakes hands with a person having primal etheric reviving powers, he feels the voltage of this supercharged intelligence. A handshake given with indifference or apathetic interest or from a person disliking another, or from a person not liking to shake hands short-circuits the charge of the life force seeking to communicate between persons.

Hands lifted in prayer contain in their touching palms kinetic psychic energy. The hands lifted as a gothic arch are pyramid-like. Cosmic energy is centered within any pyramid-shaped form. Accumulative kinetic psychic energy in praying hands can be used immediately after praying for the power of laying on the hands to heal. Also, the one praying can himself receive a free flow of energy stemming from the automatic mind of the body, or lunar brain. Thus prayer is more than a petition; it is an actual process or formula for self-revitalization, physical, mental, and spiritual.

Hands continually cold are due to a short-circuiting of the psychic flow in the lower mind and the lower mind's refusal to obey and respond to the demanding processes of life. The lack of circulation of psychic flow produces the cold hand. Psychic flow is controlled by soul flow. The unbelieving, resisting, negative power of the mind affects the psychic circulatory processes which in turn affect the physical circulation processes of the body.

To stimulate psychic flow, one should seek to develop cheerfulness, enthusiasm, responsiveness to life.

Cold hands are indicators that one is himself timid in his outgoing towards others. It has been proved in the Far East that one can master the temperature within his body. Through mastery of psychic laws, certain gurus of the East are unaffected by cold or heat, thus proving that the circulatory processes are in reality under the power of man's own willing and believing.

Moist hands in a person, proving embarrassing to many, are caused by a blockage between the sound currents playing upon the astral core or spinal nervous system and the etheric body. Such blockage short-circuits the emotional nature. When there is a perfect interflow between the astral core and the etheric body, the liquid content of the emotions is normally released through perspiration, the tear ducts of the eyes, and the kidney processes of the body. When this flow is restrained, heavy droplets are formed upon the etheric body similar to enlarged tears from the eye. This detoured moisture moves into the palms of the hands as a form of emotional repressed weeping. Only a powerful repressed emotion can cause this moisture of the hand. To search out and find the karmic cause concealed within the emotion will heal the moisture in the hands.

Listening to music, creation of mandala designs in painting — will assist in freeing the astral-core accumulative liquid of the emotions.

INJURY TO HANDS

Under the law of God's equation there are no accidents. Accidents are caused due to man's stepping out of timing as related to the rhythms and cycles of his own being. When one exposes himself to or attracts an accident or injury to any portion of his body, if he is an initiate of the interior sciences he should ask himself why this injury has come to this particular place in his body.

In the case of injury to hands or fingers, one can look into history of past lives as to how he used his hands—whether for good or for ill.

In some rare instances it has been seen in the akasic records that if one has had his hands amputated for theft in a past life, the etheric mold of his hands fails to be life animated with out-going vitality and flexibility. However, this does not occur except in rare intances when cupidity has been an obsessing passion. The next life's use of hands is in some manner less dexterous and less likely to follow one's instinctual bidding.

It has been seen in reading the present-life karmic record of a person having an injury to the forefinger of the right hand that the person had failed to defend a fellow initiate when slandered. The right forefinger is the accusing or pointing finger. When one receives an injury to this finger, he should ask himself whether or not he has defended someone who is libelously condemned.

To be injured on the thumb is to be warned that one is being overforceful; to be injured on the midfinger, that one is being mentally proud; on the marriage finger, that one should look to his ethic in partnership; on the little finger, that he is failing in the reverence aspect of his nature.

The automatic brain processes of the lunar brain in the solar plexus are intelligent, containing a rewarding as well as a punishing aspect to the physical and the etheric bodies. When the subconscious Quelle aspect of the psychic nature overflows with self-condemnation and guilt, the automatic brain reflexes in the solar plexus move to the portion of the

body where guilt lies. The result is injury, sickness or malformation to that part of the body.

The hand has a face, a countenance as important as the
face familiar to oneself in the mirror. Not only is it a servant
for the body, but it can also render a service for God. Next
to the face, the hand can speak and tell what one is, what one
desires to be, and what one can be.

The positive and negative principle works in all life, universal, natural, and personal. Man cannot escape from this
great law of cause and effect and from the positive and negative polarities upholding the functional aspect of life.

The palm of each hand contains a miniature sphere reflecting the spherical action of the solar plexus. The abdominal
lunar brain containing the lunar and solar fire may be visual-
ized as working clockwise and counterclockwise. The inner
portion of the solar plexus, or lunar-brain center, works in
counterclockwise fashion. The outer rim of the lunar abdominal brain, containing the solar fire as received from the
sun, works in clockwise fashion.

The palm of the left hand receives the counterclockwise
rotational action of the lunar fire. The palm of the right
hand receives the clockwise solar energy. Thus the two hands
of man work with the alternating currents in willing and
doing. The left hand is the receptive hand. The right hand is
the hand of aggression. The alternating flows of lunar and
solar fires in the solar plexus enable man to master gravity
in the daytime.

Quelle, the atavistic brain or subconscious mind of
man centered at the base of the skull, works in an opposite
manner to the automatic brain in the solar plexus. The center
of Quelle flow works in a clockwise fashion with the solar
fire of the sun. The outer rim of Quelle is surrounded by a
ring of counterclockwise lunar energy fire. These two great

portals of man's primal nature centered in the solar plexus and the base of the brain control man's primal instinctual nature. When unbalanced or out of alignment with one another, man becomes separated from his instinctual protection which he has acquired over the aeons.

All psychic processes in human life are dependent upon the balance between these two great instinctual portals of life preservation. In the daytime man is sustained by the lunar fire accumulation which he has gathered from the moon's fire during the night's sleep. In the nighttime man is sustained in his sleep by the solar fire he has accumulated in these portals during the day.

The moon-gathered experience in the center of the solar plexus makes man a reflector, obeying inductive and suggestible influences of the subconscious. When man consciously masters these portal energies, he becomes a will-initiate and creator. Until this time, he is dependent upon his lower mind and all its psychical instinctual processes. Man is influenced more in the daytime by the lunar fire stemming from these two portals of the primal life. He is a reflector in his actions. However, as man polarizes these two great rotating primal energy portals, he steps beyond reflected action and becomes a willing, knowing agent in command of the lunar and solar alternates in his body and mind.

When in command of these alternating psychic currents in his nature, man is a willing being. The hands are will instruments. The two hands, when coordinated to create, function as will antennas of the mind.

THOUGHT HABIT PATTERNS

There must be an even flow between the two great primal portals in man's etheric body before he can control the psychic processes through which he creates and lives on earth.

Habits from the past, crowding the lower mind, generate a psychic heat, causing mental explosion, neurosis, and erratic thinking.

Until one has developed an awareness of his dependency upon repetitious thought patterns and of his subjective tendency to think through the groovelike flow of the thought currents, he will continue to be the victim to past-life habits and present-life habits.

Such groovelike repetitious thinking defeats the intent of spirit. Spirit functions as a free flow of spontaneity. Thoughts used repeatedly supported by inflexible attitudes become hissing particles of resisting energy. When one reaches a time of upward rise in his evolvement, these thought habit patterns of energy resist the spiritual flow of originality and creation. Thoughts built up over a long period of time become actually entitized.

All spiritual scientists must move out of the contaminated reaches of decaying thinking, entering into wave lengths of thought yet to be established.

PSYCHIC CORPULENCE OR OBESITY

In some instances, when one is preparing for spiritual initiation, he develops a temporary aversion to the intimate processes in the physical body, having been inducted in religious ideas regarding the unworthiness of the physical body and the physical world. The spiritual scientist must weigh and reassess the why of his physical existence and the necessity to accept the physical body for what it is — a beautiful and miraculous mechanized instrument as a vessel for God.

A person having a preponderance of psychical power, when opening the door to the spiritual life, must literally clean the house of his body, his emotions, his mind, and his soul.

In many instances a person having used psychic powers on the lower lunar wave lengths of energy finds himself with a corpulent or obese body. While from every obvious aspect overweight or obesity would seem to be caused by overeating or by glandular imbalance, one of the major causes of obesity is psychic. The abdominal cavity of the corpulent psychic has received over long periods of time an overabundance of psychic-charged energy from the lunar counterclockwise action in the solar plexus. Non-assimilation of food, unbalanced protein assimilation have been the result. The lunar fire overpressure upon the glandular system is a cause of overweight or obesity.

The unbalanced lunar fire used in mediumship powers, the imbalance between ectoplasm and ether, the counterclockwise function of the etheric energy field produce a heavy body.

Many women preparing to take a male body in the next life become obese in the latter part of their lives. The lunar and solar fires being unbalanced and the emphasis being upon the lunar fire energy, the mind being overpositive, the karma of a woman moving her toward masculinity in the next life places pressure upon the etheric matrix. Thus it may be seen in a woman with an overpositive mind that if she increases in weight in later years, she is preparing to inhabit a male body in the next life.

The 42nd to the 49th year in the life of a man reveal what sex he will be in the next life. This is not experienced as physical corpulence, but if a man is preparing to be a woman in the next life, he will experience an excessive loss of weight in the buttocks and a non-aggressive thrust in his walk.

When preparing to be a male in the next life, the buttocks of a man will appear to more substantially support the upper torso. Such men in the latter part of their lives use more of the solar fire in their thinking and feeling. Their contact with the psychic nature through the primal portals relates to masculine willing, patriarch ideas, responsibility as to work and occupation. All of these are experienced by a man after the age of forty-two when his karma determines that his next life polarity experience will be masculine.

Psychic corpulence is caused by overuse of psychic power through thinking and feeling. It has been seen in the akasic records of some persons who draw upon the fallen Egyptian occult powers that they have a powerful lunar-functioning in the solar plexus. This produces psychic corpulence. Such persons cannot reduce the weight of their bodies through diet or exercise. Only through the slowing down of the sub-charged lunar fire can they maintain the loss of weight and become less heavy in their bodies. In right timing their souls will bring them a deep desire to use the Rishis' technique of becoming as a mustard seed. The suggestible technique or practice of visualizing oneself as minute or small reduces the lunar fire, equalizes the solar and lunar fire, and therefore produces a symmetrical body obedient to the will of the spirit.

When one approaches overweight from the viewpoint of food as being the total cause of surplus weight, he will fail to maintain loss of weight because the psychic hissing energy habit coils sustaining unresolved desires will still remain charged with their habit demands. One must find the clue to the psychically charged emotional desire and face it through some form of channeling, either by admitting some unresolved emotional or mental habit pattern exists or determining to dispel the habit through some form of creativity. If a person is spiritually evolved, he will face up to the negatives in his nature. He will admit to himself that he has a dormant irritability inducing outer hungers in craving for food or stimulants. To lose weight one must dissipate the psychic energies causing the weight.

Former-life habits remain imprinted upon the etheric body. The etheric body is a chameleon-like servant obeying and reproducing habit patterns from former-life indulgence.

To be overly flesh-conscious is disturbing to the spiritual life. Every person rising to a spiritual life who has unknowingly drawn upon the ectoplasmic powers through lunar fire must come to a halt and cease thinking through flesh-laden heaviness. In this time he will be given helps and guidance from the inner planes, sometimes manifesting through outward helps from persons, such as diet regimes and yoga practices. None of these practices would have availed previously had he not reached the right timing for shedding useless weight.

The inner Masters watching over the progress of an advanced initiate can see to it that one who has reached the end of psychic tumult experience through the flesh shall be led gently into relaxed and peaceful processes of rejuvenation, thereby assuring the initiate of mastery of the energy forces selfishly controlling the body.

Such initiates come to realize that these forces are using the negative habit patterns of former lives to sustain the expansion of flesh.

In initiatory rise one truly desiring to serve the light shall be given inward scientific approaches of visualization and suggestion. In the inner planes this is considered to be a death to the body and its demands. It is necessary that this occur before one can truly give freedom to the causal or higher etheric body.

CRUCIAL TRANSITORY PERIOD IN INITIATION

Many women on approaching the 42nd to the 49th year, if overcharged with lunar fire and overpositive in the mentality, release their children and divorce their husbands. Such a woman looks upon life with masculinity, often seeking employment to supplement income. She loses respect for her husband, thinking him too weak. In the self-genesis age in which reincarnation and karmic pressures are more highly volatile, divorce is becoming more and more a common thing.

If a man is karmically polarized to be a woman in the next life, he begins to be interested in things of the domestic life, such as cooking. He becomes highly critical of disorder in the household, hypersensitive as to the overdomination of his mate. Such men, when divorcing their wives, rarely find any person with whom to be congenial.

Looking into the history of the great male and female geniuses appearing in the world, it will be found that the majority of them suffered a domestic and personal climax between the years of 42 and 49. The life of Gauguin, the great artist, is an example of one who in his late forties deserted his safe banking profession to become an artist, leaving his family destitute.

Rebellion at 49 on the surface appears to be due to glandular change. However, on interiorly looking into the akasic records one can see that all persons who are vitally concerned with spiritual exploration and overcoming of their psychically-charged moods and temperaments, when spiritually inclined, should approach the 42nd to 49th years with fear and trembling. In these years of hypersensitivity, a mass weight of karma waits to confront the initiate. If there is a special calling for a spiritual work, this karma is four-fold, pertaining to race, religion, family, and to self.

THE SEXUAL IMPULSE AND THE PSYCHIC NATURE

The most powerfully sensitive psychical impulse is the sexual impulse. In the lower psychic nature the sexual impulse is gross, sensual, and unrefined. The sexual impulse heavily charged with sensuality takes rather than gives. In the highly evolved person, when chastity is overemphasized, this very often endangers one seeking a spiritual life to false prudery, coldness, frigidity.

Enforced celibacy in a person sentimentally evolved rather than spiritually evolved produces lust in the mind, lasciviousness, lechery. Born celibates have worked out their karma as to biological fulfillment in the earth. Made or enforced celibacy produces sadism, gluttony, envy, covetousness, hatred, perversion, rebellion.

Sexual power when absent from vulgarity is a pure natural attribute of the physical, the emotional, mental, and soul natures.

Women in marriage relationship, when naturally oriented to the purpose of motherhood, are intensely charged with pure psychic knowing as to when the sexual impulse of their mates is in harmony with their own giving. Such women work with a time-clock of their sexual fire, responding to the male without resistance or friction.

In ancient times mankind fulfilled the laws of propagation by responding to the psychic time-clock of the angels. In the present state of man's evolvement, an immature person seeking to be individualized — and very often feeling burdened and having faulty expectations regarding the sexual life and the wrong anticipation as to what the sexual life offers—fails in the sexual side of marriage relationships.

Persons coming heavily laden with immature ideas regarding sex have had in their childhood parents who are also immature in their sexual relationships. The highly evolved ego, when married, accepts the mutual interflow in the sex life.

Women being closely connected with the angels directing motherhood have special Guardian Angel protective helps. If they will turn to them, they will receive a divine intuition in their relationship in the sexual life.

Psychic telepathy between man and woman begins with sexual attraction. This is why certain men look on each woman as a potential wife or bed mate and why certain unmated women look upon all men as a potential father for their children. This is a biological psychic function abused only by persons having little understanding of the sacredness of the sexual force and its function.

Men and women are far from perfect. In the self-genesis age new discoveries in the genetic laws will produce many emotional hazards and casualties. However, eventually science will be an instrument to give men a clue to the sexual time-clock or seasonal flow of their sexual desires. The hormone system supporting the sexual life will be better understood. While natural biological selection of a mate will continue, through scientific discoveries man will be able to measure the degree of hormone function in his body. He will not mate under the direction of a computer, but he will be educated as to his own desires and to his needs in the fulfilling of the reproductive processes in his life.

Faulty Austerity and its Danger in the Spiritual Life

Self-discipline is a requirement in the spiritual life. No two persons look upon discipline in the same manner. It is common for those who are yet immature to look on discipline as stemming from some human person, such as parent to child, husband to wife, teacher to disciple. In the progressive spiritual life one comes to understand that the only discipline is within.

When one enters the path, seeking a gateway toward illumination, he places himself in the Will of God. The laws of God begin to function on a sensitive level directly into the initiate's life. Thus one must confront each weakness in his nature and temperament — and master them one by one. He does this by being telepathically attuned to a pure source of mediation. The angels make him aware of his faulty think-ing, acting, and doing. By a process of instantaneous reproving, his Guardian Angel accelerates the action of his conscience. Each day the accumulative negation is reflected in the auric encirclement around his body. On this circular receiving set, he is reminded of the wrong saying, wrong doing, wrong thinking of the past day. Every initiate is taught to look directly into the events of the day past and to resolve to do better on the coming day.

Many persons having lived in monastery-thinking and feeling in former lives seek to outpicture austere habits in the present life. Some having known poverty have exaggerated traits of frugality. Biased austerity is fatefully alien to a spiritual life. Any form of zealous intensity is a burning fire standing between one and the free flow of the spiritual life. One should search out his exaggerated tendencies, such as the belief that a vegetarian life is the only way to a spiritual life, or that beautiful clothing is an expression of vanity, or the refraining from certain environments, feeling himself to be superior to ordinary people. Jesus gave more than one example regarding the lesson of excessive austerity and overzealousness and the danger of fixity of purpose upon any one singular idea.

The spiritual life is a versatile life, a flexible life, yet it is not a giddy life. By seeking to be overversatile, one may become a zealot of versatility. The admonition in discipline to all initiates is: Tread lightly, hold loosely, keeping the gaze fixed steadily upon the light and only the light. Keep the heart warm with unpossessive love. Keep the mind tranquil by turning it always to the sunlight of union with the Mind of God.

Many persons are led toward the spiritual life through nutritional channels, as it is natural for a person in living a disciplined life regarding the intake of food to desire more realistically the true things of life, and therefore ultimately God. However, one should be alert that he does not make nutrition the whole way of life. In the spiritual life, one should seek to unite himself with the original, pure dietary laws given by the angels. The angels are still in command of these great laws. When one unites himself with the Agrarian Angels and the Dietary-law Angels, he develops a selective palate. By uniting telepathically with these great angel powers he translates his former appetite cravings into the true hungers of the body which provide him with a palate for the food suitable to his own chemistry.

It is very difficult to find any person seeking to be more spiritual who does not live in a constant state of desire for purity in all levels of life—the body, the emotions, and the mind. However, to produce the most effective balance in command of the psychical flow in the etheric body, one cannot safely be overconcentrated on food as a way of life. It can be seen that such persons very often fail to understand their own emotions. Being more mystically inclined, they are also unable to factually look into the processes of their own minds.

It should always be remembered that each plane of consciousness must be served, that discipline in the spiritual life pertains to a cherished care of the body, of the emotions and of the mind. All mystical persons desire to be good persons. This desire eventually and inevitably leads them to clarification of the emotions and mind.

The process of psychic stimulation binding man to sensuality is the easier way of life, invariably leading to pain and suffering. The passage way to peace is sometimes lonely and invariably long. Equal to discipline is the need of patience, of faith, and of a winged belief assuring one of a rise above the myth happenings and fallacies so prevalent in human folly.

Extreme vegetarianism keeps the etheric body in a constant loosened state which is not a natural process of the etheric body. A loosened etheric body intensifies the astral-core fire falling into the etheric body. When the etheric body is overloose due to overaustere practices in diet, one should be in a state of retreat, as any form of semi-fasting opens one to the lower psychic or astral planes. It was not by accident that Jesus was exposed to Satan when He fasted on the desert. This is a natural occurrence when one deliberately undernourishes his body.

A continued vegetarian diet with an intent to open doors to the spiritual life produces hypersensitivity, impracticality when one does not obtain the proper protein balance in the vegetarian diet.

Many persons are born with a very low reserve of survival ether in their etheric bodies due to some form of abstaining from the free flow of the life force in a former life. The true ethic in the vegetarian life is to avoid exaggeration. In the spiritual life one seeks to avoid the taking of life. Thus some persons turn to a vegetarian diet, very often being unprepared for this extreme change in the body. The result is an abnormal manner of thinking and feeling.

Every person has his own approach and his right to make a choice as to what he gives up to obtain spiritual power. However, when one has the grace to be under a true teacher or guru, he enters the gates of austerity carefully, moderately. Ethical teachers instruct their students to move slowly to gain best results and to maintain the momentum of spiritual and physical vitality. They teach their students to avoid plunging indiscriminately into extremities on all planes.

FASTING

Fasting has been practiced by all seeking to open the portals or gate doors to the soul. The prophets of old adjured their proteges to fast. Fasting is a spiritual act. When used rhythmically according to planetary rhythms, and within the cyclic laws of the spiritual tides, one can truly erase his karma, and thereby travel light or become a free agent to serve God. However, fanatical fasting can open the doors to the darkened inferior levels of telepathy.

New and full-moon fasts are effective for a busy person engrossed in materialistic processes of earning a living. The new-moon fast of one day, concluding with light nourishment, is especially effective for the male initiate. Women using this method of fasting are especially fortified in searching their own mental aspect of positiveness. The full-moon fast provides an insight into the feminine principle, into memory and into the akasic records, and enables the advanced initiate to research the pyramid ritualistic laws of old Egypt, as a full-moon fast loosens the etheric body in a specific way so that one may engage in more depth in night-flight during sleep. To fast on the day of the full moon and on the day of the new moon enables one to be cleansed in the physical body and in the etheric body.

A prophet's fast lasting seven days should not be undertaken under one's own self-direction, as a prophet's fast should be begun only in a propitious time of readiness which can be confirmed as to its right timing by one with understanding and authority concerning the spiritual art of fasting. A teacher familiar with the conducive spiritual tides can best chart the time according to beneficent planetary aspects regarding a lengthy or extended fast.

The taking of the Eucharist sacrament should be preceded by fasting at least one or more meals, so that one may truly absorb the sacred atoms of Jesus into his own atom body, thereby giving life to the full symbolic significance as received in taking of the Eucharist sacrament.

A therapeutic fast taken for the sake of health should be under the supervision and care of a physician. One should alert himself, however, to the spiritual nuances accompanying the art of fasting, as the etheric body in a fast invariably drains off psychic poisons. During a fast the astral core plays more intensely upon the etheric body, causing magnification and acceleration of astral sight or seeing. One can then expect to have some form of inner experience due to fasting, even though he has not anticipated this additional aspect would occur.

Some persons are born hungering to fast. To them fasting comes naturally, as such persons have fasted in former lives so as to purify their sensual natures.

Some persons are addicted to extremity in fasting. This produces the fanatical, psychically overcharged mystic. A psychically overcharged extremist sees in mirage or chimera fashion; their visions have little relationship to reality.

A sacrificial fast, that is, a fast entered into that one may achieve a vicarious purification for the healing of another person produces exceptional examples of strengths, endurance for the one fasting and also for the one for whom he prays while fasting. Sacrificial fasting should never extend longer than five days. In this sort of fasting, one should remain in seclusion, reading meditatively and praying often. Very special helps from the angelic kingdoms are given to such persons. The angels minister to the one fasting, giving to him vitalities.

No hunger is present throughout the period of sacrificial fasting. Mahatma Gandhi of India is an example of sacrificial fasting. His prolonged fasting was sustained by heavenly forces working with the archetype of his nation. In the case of larger concerns for a nation or for a world condition, only a few are called to prolonged fasting. They are sustained by the archetypal Guardian Angels watching over nations. Such extreme dedicated prolonged fasting is usually accompanied by martyrdom, as prolonged fasting invites the betraying, satanic powers. This occurred in the life of

Jesus in the desert in His prolonged fasting, and in the life of John the Baptist. Satan worked through Herod to murder John the Baptist, as he worked through Judas to murder Jesus.

Prayer during fasting has a particular significance in speeding the cleansing of one's karmically laden aura. Prayer on the knees is a posture producing an opening of the solar fire in the solar plexus. During prayer on the knees, the solar plexus opens similar to the shutters of a camera, enabling one to move out of the orbit of his ego intensity.

ASTRAL PROJECTION

During a period of dedicated fasting in some instances one becomes lighter than gravity, and sometimes free of gravity, whereby he may have the power of astral projection or etheric visitation. While fasting on the desert, Jesus had this power when Satan took Him to the pinnacle of the temple to look over the world. In the Bible the power of visitation was used by Ezekiel, Isaiah, and Daniel; in the New Testament the visitation power was used by Philip the Apostle.

Fasting can produce visitation-flight power while one is in a state of full consciousness. Around the heart's matrix are four atoms called the luminosity atoms. These lock man into his physical body. When they are loosened, the etheric body disconnects itself from the physical body. One is then free to travel. If this occurs in the daytime, it is called astral projection. If it occurs in night during sleep, it is called night-flight.

The silver cord etherically attached to the etheric matrices of the spleen, liver, heart, throat, and crown of the head determines how long one may stay out of the physical body during night-flight or during astral projection in the day.

Astral-projection techniques cannot be acquired through any form of occult mumbo-jumbo. This visitation power is obtained only by initiates who have practiced this art over many, many lives. Claiming to have this ability without factual evidence of its power is self-mesmerism. Many, thinking themselves to have astral-projection powers, have in reality a certain kind of telepathic receptivity stimulated by psychic overcharge. Such telepathy enables a person to penetrate with his mind places or persons at a distance.

Astral projection is actual visitation, reproducing one's apparitional or physical likeness to the eyes of witnesses, so that one is literally seen by other persons with their physical eyes. In true astral projection one reproduces his body through scientific knowledge of how to materialize his full presence to its total representation. In astral projection one is able to speak to those who see him and to be touched by those who recognize him.

A happenstance or accidental astral projection can occur when someone unwittingly stumbles over the barriers confining man in the limitation of gravity and time. All such instances being recorded or testified to are caused by cosmic overcharge of energy playing upon the etheric body.

On entering certain vicinities or localities, which act as magnetic polarity points in the earth, one can step out of the ordinary time-range governing the processes of the etheric-body velocities and the astral-core velocities. Many astounding stories have been written concerning the reversing of magnetic currents in certain localities. When this occurs, one can have an astral projection by stepping out of time. In this instance, time as an energy flow has been reversed.

Disappearance of objects and reappearance of objects in an unfamiliar environment is caused also by the reversal of time energy flow due to overconcentration of cosmic energy.

Psychics having resource to cosmic energy overflow are usually kinetic psychics. Little understanding their use of these powerful surpluses, they are objects of curiosity and wonder. Madame Blavatsky used these kinetic powers through memory mechanisms, as she had used levitation, astral projection and kinetic powers in an Atlantean time.

Many children during the years of puberty from the ninth to the fourteenth years, having used kinetic powers in a former life, due to the ripening glandular pressure upon the etheric body open the spectral powers of clairvoyance and clairsentience. During this time certain young persons are exposed to the elementals. The elementals are a life-wave kindred to man, yet never having taken physical bodies—existing in the astral atmosphere of the earth.

All persons having kinetic materializing and kinetic powers are assisted by their elemental friends until they have attained full-consciousness initiate-knowing of the utilization of these powers.

A person having an impure heart and knowledge of the elemental powers attracts to himself mischievous elementals. The fakirs of the East for aeons have known and utilized the elemental magic existences. Persons seeking the spiritual life must move beyond magical assistances. A spiritual person flexible to the unseen world is aware of elemental magical assistances existing in the astral world. Since the coming of the Christ to this earth, all spiritual initiates have called upon the angels to assist them rather than turning to the elemental forces for their helps.

There are good and bad elemental forces. Young people having intensive psychic magnification in puberty provoke mischievous poltergeist action into their environments.

The poltergeist action can be caused by elemental kinetic force or by the unseen dead. In the young it is more likely to be the elementals who stimulate poltergeist environments. In older persons inclined to mediumistic receptivity, poltergeist action is caused by the unrisen-dead kinetic unharnessed electricity.

Psychic force produces phenomena. Psychic force, using the energy mass in the base of the brain, in the solar plexus, in the adrenal glands, and in the etheric body, unites with the kinetic energies of Nature, and thereby produces moving of objects and the changing of chemical substances and of atmospheres. The power of mind over matter is made possible through psychic force used in conjunction with a powerful will.

Poltergeist action is the result of an intruding psychic force. One produces poltergeist phenomena through overcharge of psychic force within the astral core centered along the spinal canal. The display of phenomena is a psychic-force manifestation drawn forth from Quelle remembrance of levitation powers in ancient times.

Persons deliberately using powers of phenomena are primal psychics who project from themselves, automatically, untimely and unusual phenomena. Psychic phenomena seemingly unpremeditated occur in answer to a deep subconscious desire to be noticed or to call attention to oneself.

Psychic phenomena presently being researched in which mediums or psychics have the power to will objects to come to them, are hold-over powers from ancient times, and are the result of having formerly used etheric and astral projection.

The base of the skull where Quelle is seated at the level of the brain stem is a volatile mass of electrical and sub-electrical energy. To produce phenomena one must draw upon the primitive elan in one's nature. This requires an intense primal willing. Through drawing upon the adrenal gland's molecular center in the spine and the solar-plexus fire, a primal psychic uses a remembered Lemurian practice to lift objects and thereby produce startling and unusual phenomena.

After death, the primal projection levitation and phenomenal powers are unrestricted. If one who has died has a strong desire to communicate with the physical world, he has access to the use of primal etheric and astral energies, and thereby may produce phenomena in the physical world which are upsetting to the living.

If one has moved in his soul's evolvement toward the higher powers of his mind, he is unable to produce primal etheric or astral phenomena. Only in the life of those who have yet a positive linking with their primal natures can phenomena be produced.

All souls are working in their upward rise to use the transforming powers of their mind and the transcending powers of their spirit. Man in his most highly evolved state will be in command of all energies through the use of his mind. He will produce, however, another form of phenomena. As Jesus produced the phenomenon of changing water into wine, man will produce with full consciousness miraculous phenomena in the spirit of creation. Primal phenomena work against the forward progression flow, using the destroying principle. Spiritual transcendent power works with and for creation.

IX

THE PSYCHIC LIFE

OF CHILD AND FAMILY

The Early Years and ESP

ESP is the extra ultra gift or additional power given of God that man may be concerned with survival, with a will to live, a will to know, and a will to love — and particularly, that he may prepare himself for things yet unknown and unseen.

All children entering the world have psychic powers. Regardless of former-life karma and abuse of will, psychic power in a child is at first naive and unsullied until the child reaches his seventh year.

Previous to birth, one unites the psychic antennas of the soul with the primordial psychic force in the body of the woman bearing him. Before the soul unites with the soul of the mother to give him life, psychic forces are at work in the nervous system of the mother and of the embryo to be born. In the first four and one-half months of the development of the embryo, movements of the cells, heart beat, and life force within the embryo are caused by an inductive psychical evolutionary process.

In the first four and one-half months, the etheric vehicle of the embryo is fed by the interchange of intelligible psychical energies between the mother and child-to-be. In the last four and one-half months of his building and shaping in the womb, the psychical stimulus energizes the generation ancestral memory images drawn from the united sperm and ovum. These undergo extreme contest between the genetic strength or weakness inherited from the father and the mother. In extreme imbalance of psychical forces between the mother and the child, the mother bearing the child sometimes reacts in a rejection manner, being unable to retain the embryo; thus a miscarriage results.

Throughout the ages men revering birth of children have intuitively known of these forces — psychical, organic, chemical and biological — affecting the first period of pregnancy.

When the four and one-half months of gestation in the womb have concluded, the senses are incorporated into the embryo to be born; the soul and the senses in the embryo then fuse and unite. The higher aspect of the will of the child to be born begins to directly share in its own shaping and forming. Heavy karma between the soul coming to birth and the mother bearing the child is also reflected into the temperament of the mother in this time.

If the lower psychical impulses of the ego to be born are karmically alien to the mother's own psychic nature, a subtle allergy between souls occurs; during the time of gestation, this will cause the mother to act in a manner contrary to her own character and development. If a soul entering the earth is highly evolved, the mother can make spiritual and psychic union with the child-to-be and undergo a receptive, beautiful spiritual experience during pregnancy.

By making union with the biological processes of the body of the child-to-be, the mother intuits the physical needs of the child; and through spiritual union with the child-to-be, she intuits the spiritual processes of the soul of the child. She intuits his individual talents and strengths, that she might help him to develop the creative aspects of his nature while under her influence.

To thoroughly understand the psychical impulses moving into the emotions and the mind — shaping and forming the character in early childhood — one must open the book of reincarnation and assess the various facets of reincarnation, or of living many existences.

If the karmic debts of a child are in a state of balance, the higher psychical impulses in a child are uninhibited and unrestrained by the higher ego of the child. All children under the age of seven, regardless of past-life records, use a certain degree of uninhibited psychic power. Were it not for this psychic potential in the nature of the soul of the child, he would be unimpressionable to all of the shaping, forming, and training aspects of his tender years.

Psychic impressionability works in three manners in the child less than seven years of age. First, psychic impressionability constantly imprints inductively with intense magnification the growing, patterned, unfolding world of the child. Second, a psychic inherent reliance upon former-life attributes of strength or weakness of the child is experienced in a lunar-like reflective memory, as the sensitized mind and emotions of a child of these years come under the memory and suggestible influence of past lives. Some children are born acutely hostile to the world due to former emotional wounds inflicted in the just previous life. Some children come in accident-prone and fearful of moving objects and disciplining persons due to physical injuries received in former lives. The third stage of psychic impressionability of a child relates to a higher side of the child's nature — a free, pleasant, flowing response to the former-life soul evolvement and experience.

Children expressing this higher side of their soul's nature before their seventh year are imaginative in a pure and creative way, joyful and spontaneous.

Until the ninth year all children, unless there is a karmic affliction, remain close to the inner-plane memory of their before-birth experience. Parents training these children find little difficulty in disciplining them when they keep open the door of the child's mind to soul resources.

The parents' responsibility to a highly evolved and psychically endowed child will often open doors to their own psychic nature to thereby lead them into a knowledge of the greater spiritual realities. A more sensitive child should receive from the parent an authoritative presentation of things spiritual, absent from bigotry.

The naive wonder consciousness of the child stems from his present life's unformed psychical nature. Refreshed from his stay between lives, the child enters into each new era with open-minded wonderment and naivete.

As a plant is nourished in the ground or the earth through cosmic generative forces, protecting the seed from the harsh impacts of displacement, so is a child in the first phase of its life a precious portion of becoming and developing. The generating, pressing, psychical life-will in the child is influenced by the constant overshadowing and development care of the angels.

Children born to unmerciful environments, being close to heavy karma inherited from former lives, undergo intense aggravation and suffering. Finding themselves once more in the harsh physical world of judgments, they sometimes retreat into psychical fantasy.

The psychical nature and will in child or adult cannot be denied. This nature so astutely provided by God is a pressing force demanding some outlet or action in the child as well as in the adult.

Repeated fearful dreams of children reflect their psychical disorganization and their failure to accept the home environment or placement in life.

The first look or encounter between mother and child after birth reveals the will of the child, whether forceful or selfless. Parents understanding the psychical processes of the soul should dedicate to give right, firm, tender, and reasonable discipline from the moment of birth. Looking into the eyes of a child, a spiritually evolved parent can discern whether his child has come to be at home within his own soul or whether he has been placed in his life as a karmic disturber.

A mother or father having an immature attitude toward birth, and untrained sentiments regarding the raising and care of children, ignorantly waste the precious vitality and outflowing impressionable impulses in the psychical imaginative nature of their children.

Even the most hostile, karmically burdened children enter the world with the desire to begin again. It is the obligation of the parent first to seek to unite with the soul of his child, and secondly, to look for the karmic frailties or lower attributes of ancestral inheritance.

Blood inheritance is a blessing when the parent inwardly unites himself and the higher thinking attitudes of his ancestral origins with the soul of a child through acknowledgment of the psychical power motivating the life force in all persons. The greatest joy between parent and child may be achieved when parents having spiritual reverence recognize the psychical life-force to be malleable and sacred. Miracles may be manifested between parent and child when a devoted, evolved parent looks upon parenthood as spiritually creative.

The psychical influence between parent and child is delicate, sensitive, and powerfully dangerous when used to influence or shape the will of a child against the urgency of its own destiny.

Throughout the ages men have looked upon the inexperienced years of the child as the years of innocence. As men come closer and closer to the knowledge of the true meaning in reincarnation, they will acknowledge and accept the fact that some children enter the world retaining some of the cynical harshness of former-life experience, resisting life, resisting discipline. Surface psychology as yet gives but a fragment of the answers concerning a child motivated by manipulative or unharnessed psychic forces in former lives.

The soul's record of a child with soul-immaturity entering the life of a family makes its first impact upon the parents' life during the time of conception. A lustful or irresponsible act of procreation will attract to the parents a soul having a past-life record of undisciplined will.

The little understood pre-birth psychical selective soul-power, enacted during the time of impregnation and ovulation between the sperm and ovum of the father and mother —choosing and directing the particular gene to give embryonic life to the soul — is not an accident. The choice of genes is a decision made by the ego whose karmic pattern and selection determine the color of the eyes, the skin texture, the physiological and functional organism of the body, frame, stature, and chronic tendencies in health. In the moment of copulative gene infusion, all of the things related to ancestral karma and ego karma or soul-grace are decided by the soul entering the world.

The number of active chromosomes working with the genes during conception is determined by cosmic equation. The genes determine the ego's fixed field of fate through which he must overcome certain former-life and inherited ego-tendencies of moral and physical weaknesses while living in the world. Balanced chromosomes come under the influence of the celestial Elders or Hierarchy determining the potential of man's fulfillment in his spiritual destiny.

The higher and transcendental psychical impulses are sealed into man through the chromosomes. The ancestral canvas upon which one paints the story of his soul's sojourn is centered in the genes.

As children advance toward puberty, their dreams of the night, stimulated by psychical childhood fantasy, are extended and magnified. At puberty there occurs in the child an externalization of the psychic pressure force due to approaching glandular development. At puberty all children move from the naive side of dependency on parents and the angels, and come under the direction of their own will and ego. However, until the twenty-first year the ego is not totally centered in the mental will control of the consciousness; during childhood the ego is suspended *over* the brain processes of the child. In puberty the child begins to be an observer and weigher of his personal mental development. During adolescence his psychic powers are more uniquely personalized through the budding gland system supporting the astral or planetary life in his emotions.

In ancient times when men understood the laws of puberty, the puberty period in the life of a child was known to be initiatory. The great sages in those times took unto themselves these emerging egos, training them in the etheric ethic of life's unfoldment.

Because men have depended overmuch on their outer senses, rather than their inner sense perceptions, they think it best to seal away the vital psychic confrontation in this period in the life of a child. Too often a materialistically inclined parent reproves an over-psychically charged child, considering this aspect of the child's nature too burdensome to understand, rather than opening his own mind to a shared experience with his child. The remedy for psychical awakening and proper use of this voluminous energy during puberty is to insist upon the child's channeling this vital creative force and energy. During pre-puberty one should prepare the child for the impact of puberty; he should lead the child through ethical and moral techniques to use his imagination powers and to explore the world reverently and earnestly; but more, one should assure each child of a directing and supporting universal mind.

THE PSYCHIC POWER OF THE YOUNG

Men in the present age, experiencing the end of a mighty reincarnation cycle, are confused and bewildered by the unruly and riotous nature of the youth of this time. In the latter day of a reincarnation cycle, straggler egos or shadowed souls — irreligious, agnostic, and atheistic, having never known the Christ initiation in former lives — enter the world intent upon increasing their genesis stature. Yet, they are incompetent spiritually, morally and physically to incorporate into their souls the general theme of the upward rise in evolvement. Parents, failing to accept that they could give birth to a dissident ego, and failing to understand the ego of the child given into their hands, are helpless when exposed to these destroying egos.

In the reincarnation cycle of the present time, there are many Oriental and East Indian egos being born into the Western civilization. Such children, in their revolt against traditional Christian worship, crave the former bliss-state approach to union with God.

Inasmuch as traditional Western religion fails to encourage the personal-mystical life, masses of former Eastern egos are being born to stimulate and to expose the weakness in the structure of traditional Christian worship. Parents of such children, having lived up to the letter of the social side of traditional religions, feel a sense of betrayal.

A child comes to birth to his ego during puberty. At this time psychical energies — playing predominantly upon the gonads, the adrenals and the pituitary gland — stimulate an overflow of the subconscious in the astral primitive brain or Quelle. In this era of genesis rise, an ego having unruly psychical impulses from former lives, instinctively turns to aggressive and militant groups, acting out his primitive psychical force through riotous behavior. Such souls enter into this era or time as destroying egos.

Parents failing in the earlier years to encourage their children to follow religious principle and ethic, being remiss in their sense of religious obligation, sometimes seek too late to retrieve such children. Children in the phases of psychical overflow in adolescence are retrievable if there be grace. The period of adolescent psychism is a time of unrestrained inventiveness. Even though a child may desire to use his psychical energy to follow or mimic fallacious causes or persons, he can be retrieved through the higher grace aspects of his soul.

To turn an adolescent toward his talent potential, to teach him the ethic in the use of reasonableness, to give him a philosophy built upon sincerity, will free a child from the forceful psychical accumulation occurring in adolescence.

Children dare adults responsible for them to teach them. When their parents fail to teach them of true things, they lose respect for their parents. This disrespect is outpictured in society. Hypocrisy is the object of every child's hatred. To find it in his parents produces contempt, disrespect, violence and dissent.

The first seven years of a child's life are etherically, spiritually malleable. If the parent fails to make union with the soul of his child during this time, he will undergo a major estrangement between himself and the soul entrusted to him.

When a child enters into adolescence, he is exposed to unbridled forces in his own nature. If the parent has not built a flexible trust between himself and the child before this period, the child will cease to be united with him. Regardless of the psychic force in blood uniting all persons in families, the shattering of faith and hope is frustrating and sometimes crippling to the adolescent young.

The adolescent phase of an evolved child's life should be emotionally reverent and receptive to the cosmic overlaws generating life. During puberty the child has an opportunity to absorb into his emotions the devotional aspect of religion. If he fails to make God the primary center of his devotion in this time of his life, he is more likely in the future years to experience religion through his intellect rather than through his devotion.

During the first seven years of a child's life, a reverent attitude toward God as the Creator and director of life should be developed. From the seventh to the fourteenth year, the child's devotional attitude toward life and God as the Cause should be encouraged. From the fourteenth to the twenty-first year, his mental attitude toward God as the directing mind should be confirmed. If a parent fulfills these cardinal principles in spiritual disciplines, he will prepare his child to reverently use the higher psychical forces existing in his nature, and thus become a coordinated person, realistically meeting life with virility, expectancy and creation.

Genesis Trauma

In childhood's impressionable years, one blossoms into the self-image he is to identify with, to some degree, throughout life. If this image be molded by persons having unintelligent sentiments — such as parents, sisters, brothers, grandparents, and emotionally immature instructors who unknowingly suppress the true image and ego impulse of the child — the result is a sense of inadequacy, confusion and superficial values. In youth, one can suffer from faulty self-inflation stemming from a parent's prideful desire to see in his child the virtues he has been unable to personally express. The child, being suggestible and impressionable, responds to and fixes this image-picture into an egotistical expression, and the natural thrust of the ego and identity is distorted; and the emotions of the future will be expressed through a façade built upon unreality.

In the atavistic stages of childhood and youth, sisters or brothers often seek to inflict upon one sensitive brother or sister a sense of inferiority. The herd instinct of casting out the weak exists in all tribal-genesis and human-genesis families. Thus, a sensitive, spiritually inclined ego becomes the whipping boy for the overflow of hostility in the family-atom. This antagonistic instinct existed even in the family-atom of Mary and Joseph; the Bible states that Jesus was thought by His brothers and sisters to be "beside himself."

All persons, upon reaching adulthood, must encounter the instinctual etheric impulses sustaining the superimposed images built throughout the younger years. When one opens the mature and true self and begins to unite with his higher mind, he must overthrow all mesmeric, psychic expectations of faulty imaging, and stand forth in his own centered identity as earned from mental and spiritual grace in former lives and in the present life.

In youth, to be free of false self-imaging is to prepare to become a new man in Christ. All initiates, whether young or adult, must undergo the death to the superimposed self-image, and identify themselves with the reality of the spiritual image, rather than with the karmically created man.

The traumatic genesis scars are eventually healed when one sees all relationships as being equally purposeful under God. To bless is to heal. One moves beyond the reach of negative imaging impulses into a glorious and perfect wholeness through releasing, blessing, forgiving and understanding.

One on the path of spiritual life should determine to cast out any form of self-conceit, and should refuse to accept the hindering invented images gathered throughout the years. Strict and honest self-evaluation is the first step toward a life of spirituality. Blessed is he who is schooled in the reality school of divine rightness.

Some of the invented childhood attitudes contributing to a false self-image are: one is taught by his elders to believe himself to be faultless and that he cannot make a mistake; through inductive suggestion one is convinced that he is brave, infallible, beyond temptation or coercement; one thinks he is of a superior race, family, or religion; one feels he must excel his fellow associates, as he believes himself to be more resourceful, more qualified, or just better; one is compelled to maintain status and prestige by having a better home, a bigger car, a more fashionable dress or suit; one has a child who can do no wrong; one feels he has a superior intellect and a more advanced spiritual understanding than others; one feels that he is exempt from correction.

Invented attitudes from past lives building the self-image of the present life are: a false sense of values regarding possessions; a superimposed frugality; criticism of those having money and of how they spend it; an overzealous sense of austerity; a martyr complex, assuming burdens for public praise; a belief that one is born to reform others, and therefore thrusting forceful corrections on others; a hatred of authority, concealing a hidden desire to dominate; an inclination to castigate another in time of trouble; refusing to respond to spiritual ideas; being unteachable; giving to gain placement, and thereby acquiring authority over the minds and wills of others.

The Psychic Family Pattern

A spiritual scientist having made a covenant for self-realization does not look upon his family relationships and placement through karma or grace. He sees each member in the family first as a soul, second as an evolving ego rich with godly potential.

It is the ethic in all forms of association to begin with one's own correction and discipline. By unbiased looking inward, one sees his own flaws contributing to and supporting the negative separating aspects of tribulation and sorrow.

The psychic energy supporting the pattern in the family-atom sustains the etheric reflection of all ancestral negations. When one desires to extend and emphasize the negative traits in the family, the patterns of negation are given vitality and life; the wounds of karma in the family are increased.

In each family-atom there may be found one ego who, as the ancestral chronologist, bears the full intensity of the psychic memory of ancestry. Such persons usually seek to strongly influence the family as to tradition and duty, with often an emphasis placed upon kindred traits, religion, and the rearing of children. These persons keep alive the psychic stimuli and legends in the family-atom. Such egos are assertive egos, having inherited the primal psychic fire in the ancestral genes; these persons act as the ancestral conscience. The initiate desiring to live a spiritual life is often misunderstood by such egos.

Jesus understood the higher self-genesis ego. He knew that God seeks to reveal Himself to all persons. He explained this to His disciples in these words: ". . . Who is my mother? and who are my brethren? And he stretched forth his hand toward his disciples, and said, Behold my mother and my brethren! For whosoever shall do the will of my Father which is in heaven, the same is my brother, and sister, and mother." (St. Matthew 12:48-50)

The spiritual life includes a mediative ministration for the family and for all men in the world. Through mediation one comes closer to the spiritual reality in *all* relationships. Mediation gives a spiritual perspective. Ancestry is revered in the mind of the initiate as the means and not the way of life. To understand soul choice through reincarnation softens and mitigates the might of the curses and sins carried down the ancestral line.

The cleansing of the family-atom is kept alive and set into action by the spiritually evolved ego in the family. The soul placement, which so wisely directed him to the blood ties in the family association, contains an innate wisdom-strength. Therefore, through spiritual mediation the family may be translated from bondage to ancestral weaknesses into vital and spiritual strength. Through a conscious awareness of one's own ego requirement in the spiritual life of the family, one fullfills the first ethic of association: all are under God; God alone is the Source and Cause; all living under Him are of the Light.

Very often an initiate is sent by his soul-wisdom into other environments, that he may organize his selective spiritual strengths for the purpose of better serving the world-family. This does not exempt him from being a mediator in family relationships. Through loving mediation, one can be present while yet distant. The power of mediation is fully realized when one knows that soul ties are the only lasting and fixed ties in responsible association, whether of one's blood-family or of the greater blood-stream family — humanity.

Many initiates, failing to understand the infallible power of mediation, seek to ignore all family unpleasantness, thinking it to be out of the range of conciliation. As one evolves, he learns that all souls do not progress in the same rhythm. The laws supporting his own mediative life positively color and spiritually affect the lives of those correlated to his life in the world.

The Shadow Body of the Family-Atom

The family-atom expressing the higher self-genesis atmosphere is individualistic, ingenious, creative, and reverent. Higher self-genesis persons are rarely understood by lesser self-genesis persons, so few having reached this state of evolvement.

One may recognize with ease the lesser self-genesis person, as he is represented wherever there is psychological or psychiatric stress. The lesser self-genesis person is self-engrossed; he is personally centered in expectations of a successful life rather than in spiritual being. The higher self-genesis person is selflessly centered in the universal life. The predominance of self-seeking persons in this age generates a selfish society bent upon license and personal preference.

The weight of a collective lesser self-genesis evolvement is placed upon the moral and spiritual shoulders of advanced souls. Self-selected placement in a shadowed family-atom doubles the life burden of the more highly evolved ego; sometimes this produces potential sainthood, enabling him to lift by a supernatural love the souls sharing life with him.

Some egos, having reached an advanced degree of evolvement, deliberately choose, before birth, to expose themselves to the guilt or shadow action within a family-atom. Other egos less evolved, with heavy karmic burdens, are attracted by birth to a guilt-laden family-atom; these sometimes become corruptible, sensuous, apathetic, unmanageable — with tendencies toward criminality.

Into such guilt-laden family-atoms come less evolved egos who incarnate as drunkards, drug addicts, psychotics, dissidents, atheists. Condensed family-atom guilt produces heavy karmic involvement. The central figure or parent supervising these souls can be sustained by spiritual initiatory formulas. Negative combined souls are under their own shadowed guilt curses, set up by long ages of deviation from God and His Will. Only a staunch, unwavering soul centered in a shadowed family-atom may survive.

The strong, hostile currents in a family-atom in the lesser self-genesis age produce an unstable society. In the age of supposed reasonableness, vast numbers of lesser self-genesis egos demand indulgent panaceas for their indigent ways. A resisting mentality is an irritating cell in the flesh of society and of nations, and as such continues until some form of higher ethic is established. The spiritual scientist trained through initiatory formulas in the inner planes will work on the outer planes to produce a balance. It is the work of the initiate to strive to activate the living principles and ethics established by Jesus.

God seeks to utilize all effervescent souls. These souls come into the world to meet the rise in human crises. With spiritual fortitude supported by the presences of heavenly mediation, advanced souls take upon themselves the yoke of selfless service. Through initiatory formulas they work to purify a polluted society. Planted as holy fermenting seeds in irritated points of society, they scientifically conjoin their ideas, soul powers, service, and works to accomplish the demonstration of the spirit to calm the minds and heal the soul-sickness of men in the world.

Ancestral Grace and Health

The spiritual healing arts in lesser self-genesis require an enlargement in prayer, faith, and understanding. Lesser genesis egos denying the ancestral survival supports may be exposed to many health trials through the body, the emotions, and the mind.

Ancestral survival grace fails to completely support or sustain one who feels himself to be beyond the influence of the family-atom. In all intimate and rightful associations God has set a restoring principle through which one may conjoin something of his bodily and physical needs. Through associated interworking blood relationships, sympathy and empathy from blood relatives play an important part in all healing. When sympathy and the love of a mother for a child are repressed, this checks and nullifies the inherent interflow of ancestral struggle for survival and renewal. Should a mother fail to be sympathetic to her child, the angelic healing helps are thwarted. Where sympathy is lacking, the ancestral instincts fail to fully play their part in the survival of the sick.

Moving over the lesser self-genesis experience with love, respect, and reverence for one's origins and source of life, unites one more firmly with the angel of his body—the Luminosity Angel. To seal away by deliberation the flowing chain of ancestral survival helps is to shut away millions of years of upward survival instincts. Through lesser self-genesis callousness to unconsciously hate or deny one's origins is to mitigate or lessen the will to live.

Lesser self-genesis is self-deceptive in that one thinks himself to be beyond interior supporting human influences in things of the body, emotions, and the mind.

Science will discover in its research of the genes the necessity to retain the mysterious energy particle assuring survival. To break the chain of survival strength in any person is to outrage the Will-of-God compulsion existing in all sentient life in earth and in all worlds. When one closes the door on reverence for the source of his physical life, the survival impulses are reprocessed into destruction.

To retain the will to survive in sickness, one must return to love for those who gave him a physical form. One should seek not to worship the source of his physical origin, but to look with awe and acceptance upon those who struggled to rise that he might some day enter the world.

One seeking to open the door to the spiritual life should keep his mind open to the strengths and the inherent weaknesses in his human nature. He should assess his ego inheritance as being more than his ancestral inheritance, yet he should also acknowledge that he lives in a human world outpictured by countless relationships all interdependent on strengths and weaknesses. His soul and the higher aspects of his ego will come in time to unite him with his true parent, our Father which art in heaven.

Belief in the Luminosity-Angel body helps for bodily health will reinforce the will to live. Mantrams designed to unite with the Luminosity Angel give the power to merge the body impulses with the strengths of the best of inherent traits, both physical and spiritual.

> O Luminosity Angel of my body,
> If it is the Will, give unto me
> The grace strengths of my ancestral traits,
> That I may arise and do
> The Will of Him who healeth all.

THE IDEAL MARRIAGE

There are three fundamental reasons why marriage for the lesser self-genesis ego is generally imperfect: immaturity, untrained sentiments, selfishness. These three are rooted in unknowing.

The soul-record being obscured, lesser self-genesis egos enter the world seeking to mate due to race compulsion, karmic necessity, and soul prompting. Marriage provides self-amplification. Marriage burdens the immature, frustrates one of untrained sentiments; and, for the selfish, marriage is exploitation to further one's own interest.

An immature ego marries expecting to remain in status quo. One of untrained sentiment marries expecting perfection. The selfish marry for a sexual bed or a meal ticket.

Through self-control, self-reliance, and love, one may animate his life through the most positive of relationships — marriage. To deny and to demote one's selfish instincts, to think first of the one most close, is to engage oneself in an enterprise filled with satisfaction, harmony, and delight.

The first twenty-eight days of marriage set the sexual pattern in marriage; the first three months, the domestic reality; the first year, the parental and external influences. The third year determines whether the marriage is of karmic necessity or of the higher aspects of the soul.

If the marriage is of soul-grace, a family-atom of high order encases the domicile; and the persons directly involved — such as husband, wife, child or children — are insulated against intrusion from in-laws, from outward seduction and inferior associations.

If a marriage is karmic, the dweller or soul-debt reflection dominates the marriage; thus, a family-atom of a lower order encases the family. The marriage is devoid of sacred intimacy. Though a form of marriage may be maintained, the partnership is tainted by the selfishness of one or all members of the family. From this comes the cynical attitude that marriage is a relationship imposed by society.

In the lesser self-genesis age, less and less respect for human relationships is prevalent. The religious influence, so constant heretofore in domestic ties and family association, is obscured by competition between marriage partners. Agnostic attitudes and materialistic pursuits cloud the image of marriage. Amorality, divorce, neglect and indifference defeat the idealistic side and purpose of union in marriage.

It is the work of the higher self-genesis marriage to maintain the idealistic theme in marriage, to bind the wounds of the unknowing, to keep the vigil of constancy by pure example and show of principle, to instruct when required, to succor if necessary.

IN-LAWS AND THE FAMILY-ATOM

Marriage is the most exacting of all human relationships. It is also the most rewarding when two agree to unite in love. No man, situation or circumstance can separate or divide two persons whose marriage is fostered by grace.

In the quickened transition of the geneses, marriage cultures are being threatened and challenged. However, marriage will continue between man and woman until the latter days of cosmos-genesis.

One of the most idyllic prototypal stories in the Bible is that of the association between Ruth, the female progenitor of Jesus, and her mother-in-law, Naomi. However, not all in-law associations are so graced as to be harmonious.

In the present phase of man's evolvement, many are experiencing heavy trials within the marriage state. Often these trials are stimulated by unethical in-law intrusion. In the higher grace aspect of marriage, the wife has a Ruth perception, and sees a blessing through reinforcement of blood ties or in-law grace. Such women are strengthened through in-law association and feel secure in their relationship to their husband's family.

If the mother-in-law is reluctant to relinquish her son, she unconsciously, and sometimes consciously intrudes into the marital affairs of her son and his wife. When husband and wife love one another unequally, and the husband fails to free himself from the dominating will of his family, he will remain etherically tied to his father, mother, brother or sister. And he will be unable to assume the serious marital responsibility demanded in marriage. This also applies to a married daughter and her parents.

To intrude upon the formation of a family-atom offends the sanctity of marriage. To release a son or a daughter into marriage requires more than a protective parental love. The requirement is to look into the soul of the child one has begotten or borne, and to remember that after marriage the Father will henceforth direct him.

Many well-intentioned in-laws are frustrated if the wife of their son has had a casualty childhood in family-atom associations and the wife refuses to respond to their suggestions or helps. Parents of the husband come under heavy discipline; restraint and patience are required. This also may occur when the husband retains the hostilities of childhood in his thinking and feeling.

In-law incompatibility produces a bruised state in the marriage relationship between husband and wife, and prepares the way for future rupture in marital affections.

The etheric encasement giving resiliency and mobility to marriage is frequently subjected to in-law psychic bombardment. In-law telepathic expectations enter more often into the mind of the wife, as a woman is by nature subjectively telepathic to the pressures from her husband's family.

Responsible individuals have earned the grace to know that all human relationships — when founded upon mutual trust, reverence, sincerity, kindness, and respect — will flourish. When these precepts are taught in childhood and observed, marriage grace will lead one to the perfect equation between the three family-atoms — the family-atom from whence the wife comes, the family-atom from whence the husband comes, and the family-atom the newly married will activate to support the evolvement of their daughters and sons.

MARRIAGE SACRAMENT AND THE ANGELS

Marriage is a soul seeking a soul, a mind seeking a mind, an eye seeking to look into an eye. When two persons agree to respect and revere one another, the marriage contract is sacred. The betrothal, the marriage ceremony, and the connubial bed are blessed when two souls rise with the tide of their love.

When the helps of the angels are absent, no amount of analysis, psychoanalysis, sermons, or scoldings can set aright a marriage contract. Only when the husband and wife are in full agreement can the contract of marriage be utilized, and can they experience a marriage authorized by heaven.

All persons entering into the marriage sacrament should have full understanding of the nuptial ritual, the angelic supports, the sacredness of the vow in betrothal, and the promise of fidelity in marriage.

Father, mother, sister or brother should also understand the marriage of their child, sister or brother to be a sacrament between two people who will henceforth be changed as to attitude, personality and desire. To trespass upon the vitality of union in marriage is to commit an unholy offense.

Spiritual service may be rendered during the marriage service when parents and relatives enter into prayerful hope. A marriage ceremony overemphasizing pompousness restrains the angelic participation in the marriage. Marriages based on display are exhausting, costly, and often create hysterical and shattering situations sealing away the sacred helps accompanying the marriage sacrament.

When marriage contracts are entered into through the will of a parent rather than choice by the ones to be married, dominance is retained by the parents throughout the marriage.

When a marriage contract is superficially agreed upon, there can be little support, if any, from the angels.

When the wife or husband retains mental reservations as to leaving the single state, or clings in thought to any other attachment, the marriage will be penetrable to acts of adultery in some future time.

When any person enters into marriage thinking himself to be superior to his or her betrothed, the marriage will produce acute suffering to the one who is made to feel inferior. In time, the pattern will reverse, and the one considered inferior will prove to be the strength of the marriage.

Marriage has a sacred mystique when love and trust are present. This mystique increases with the days and the years, and creates a holy environment for the work of the angels.

PARENTHOOD AND THE RIGHT WAY

In lesser self-genesis may be found many persons seeking a path or a "Way." These are very often parents — fathers and mothers — who are seeking to lead their progeny into the *right* way. Parents in lesser self-genesis, trained in psychology and sometimes in the metaphysical or power path, often inadvertently neglect their children — priding themselves on giving their children the full *right of way* as to their individuality. They give to their yet untrained children the full use of their expressive minds and emotions. Such children are neglected children, using certain untrained liberties without ethic. Thus, parents who have found metaphysical logic to be sufficient unto themselves, often find themselves with disobedient, irreverent and precocious offspring.

The Western ego is inherently metaphysically inclined, reared in the idea that excelling or success is more important than merit in character. The present resisting youth may be said to be ripe karma for the lesser self-genesis parent in this age and time.

It is the work of all higher self-genesis egos and parents to present to the young the ethic of consideration. Character earned through former life family-genesis morality grace must be reinstated in each life with ethic. All educational procedures should begin with the culture of self-knowing based upon consideration for others.

To be a good parent one should rely upon the proven aspects of discipline, teaching his children the first rudiments and precepts of obedience to Universal Law. Each parent should recognize the individual soul aspect of each child given into his charge, avoiding partiality or bias, using the divine plumb line to keep the unshaped and untried wills of his children within the Will of God.

Mystically-inclined parents produce disorganized, unrealistic households. Untrained philosophically-inclined parents sometimes attribute to their children non-existent genius attributes. Spiritually realistic parents see their children as individual egos and know them to be under the Just Law even as adults are under the Just Law. Such parents fulfill their grace by supporting and fulfilling parenthood within the image and Will of the Divine Father in heaven.

THE TRUE PARENT OF ALL

Karmic overloads, when unresolved in family-genesis or in the family-atom, follow and repeat their lessons in the destiny patterns of adults. Regardless of distance or separation, there is a repetition and reproduction of unresolved weaknesses in the subconsciously motivated acts of the adult.

All souls come to birth in a particular family-atom due to karmic choice. It is destiny to find oneself in a particular nation, race, or family. The soul-record previous to birth determines one's race or family — to shape and to discipline, to mold and to build.

In the family-atom genesis states of the Western races and nations, where the knowledge of reincarnation is withheld, millions — having been indoctrinated in the idea that life on earth is an existence lasting for a brief period of years — lack an eternal resilience. Their perspective is shallow as to the flowing soul-theme in all human relationships.

The glory and beauty of human association seek to come to birth through Jesus, the Son of Man. Jesus saw the ending of the fixed paternal dominance in the family-atom. He also saw a new genesis coming to birth. With the ethic of love, He prepared mankind for these crucial separative times.

The majority of men think of love as being expressed only on the personal and physical plane. Failing to understand the law of reincarnation and re-embodiment, they seek to blame their environment, their family, their father, mother, sisters and brothers for their own shortcomings and weaknesses.

When psychiatry and psychology turn to the knowledge of the soul's eternality, they will extend their ethic and their service to man. The biased, unintuitive psychiatrist and psychologist will come up against an impenetrable wall in the psychotic states or abnormalities induced by the unrecognized, urgent pressures of the soul.

The spiritual scientist seeks through the Christ Light to instruct men as to their eternal inheritance. The Father of all life in this eternity is the true Father over all men. All states of genesis come under His provision and love.

The soul-debts of men cling to those who believe in resolution through human observances rather than Divine. The

Light of the Christ seeks to resolve the psychic, soiled energies within the family-atom. He who invites Him in, will be lifted into the higher states of self-genesis or holy individuality. His family will become to him a provident grace, rather than suffering and disgrace.

THE FAMILY-ATOM AND THE MATURE MIND

The central core of a family-atom generates a psychic field, forming a *psychic womb*. All blood relationships are united and reinforced psychically. The psychic influences in blood ties are life-lasting—and, of all relationships, are the most impressionable. Hostilities in a family-atom can never be rationalized mentally into non-existence. Only through the recognition of soul to soul may karmic relationships in family be dissolved.

Even though the dissolution of a family-atom may occur after the individualization of each person has been accomplished, one still retains the psychic impressionability of infancy and childhood. One may feel that he has overcome the jealousies, tensions, and rivalries of childhood; yet, when under stress, he will find them ignobly rising up within him. These psychic retentive influences of childhood are the reminders that one must yet mature, even though he may appear mature on the surface. Failure to assimilate and master inhibiting repressions of childhood limits the full expression of the ego.

In the demands of mature associations, a true and realistic approach to one's own self is necessary. Maturity evaluates one's own identity. The impressionable psychic negatives of childhood are put away when one knows himself to be of value under God. Over-evaluation of one's self, or magnified self-esteem, is sometimes a compensatory action; in this may also be found one's immaturity.

On reaching mature self-awareness one is free of the sub-jective psychical influences retained from childhood. The objective search within reveals the weakness of immature prejudice and judgment.

The Quelle spilling-out process through dreams and med-itation enables one to appraise, to magnify, and to dissolve the subtle, psychic segments intruding upon his evolvement, prog-ress and growth. Keeping a dream diary, observing the sentient memories of childhood in dreams, finding the rele-vant psychic symbols causing awkwardness and imbalances in one's spiritual progress — these give an internal health to the emotions and the mind. Being maturely honest, accepting the correcting aspect experienced in dreams, will speed the cleansing of the karmic soil inhibiting one's rise in the light.

The use of pre-sleep mantrams enables one to research his inner world and to develop the power of dream cognition. Thus, the memory of the night's action will rectify one's thoughts. This is especially true as to one's motives or motiva-tion; for the key to motivation holds the answer to one's peace of mind.

Family karma lasts as long as the tensions in the family-atom are stimulated by a non-spiritual atmosphere. Spiritual power cleanses and stills the psychic atmosphere in a family-atom. The psychic effluvia in the family-atom may be changed to holy magnetism when all in the family-atom rev-erently unite their souls' action.

UNIVERSAL SERVICE

The evolving initiate lives in the world; his life incorporates family, friends, co-workers, personal associates or friends, and sometimes one or more co-atom persons. He is shaped by spiritual disciplines to look upon all relationships as a part of a divine pattern or design. However, there are periods of extended and intense initiation when he may fall into the snare of thinking that one or more persons stand between him and the light. During this period, karma is accelerated between the persons related in this trial by fire. All of this is a vital and unavoidable function in the life of the higher initiate.

Should initiation occur on the family-atom level of evolvement, the initiate is inwardly made aware that he is rising to a higher degree of genesis to clear the path of certain psychic debris, that he may better serve the souls of mankind. The individualistic mind of the initiate must be free of all inductive psychic expectations of family, friends, and even of close associates.

During a cross-over in initiation, the initiate must adhere to spiritual principle in every step of the way, seeing only a resolution to the extremities of his anguish through the clarity of absolute faith in God. The initiate must identify himself as a person and an ego willing to render a world service. There must come into the life of every initiate the knowledge of his own spiritual identification rather than karmic expectation, whether on the level of family or of persons.

The process of universal initiation seeks to free the initiate to trust wholly in the unknown and the unmanifest, that he may move beyond the psychically imposed expectations of less-evolved persons.

Clearing the way toward higher qualification to serve in the light does not mean that one must sever or disconnect himself from relatives, friends, or associates. However, it is necessary for him to separate his thoughts from the possessively forceful aspects of the thinking of others, that he may become an individualistic identity in his own right, and thus incorporate the singular process within his own sphere of illumination.

Meditation, prayer, and contemplation are extremely vital in these periods. Even as Jesus was ministered to by the angels on the desert during one of His greater initiations, so does every initiate come to the time when he must support his commitment to God with total surrender to the spiritual tasks before him.

When anyone thinks it necessary to cease loving those who walk with him on the path — whether of family, friends, or associates — he is not an initiate. He is yet but a novice on the scales of initiation. All persons in the initiate's life are a part of the design producing his personal identity. These walk with him. Whether present or absent, they all share in the grace of his illumination and freedom. All who accompany the initiate also rise to the degree of their souls' expectation when a spiritual initiate rises to go forth to serve.

X

ESP AND THE ANIMAL KINGDOM

To better understand the powers of ESP and to be aware of the forces underlying one's own sentient nature, one should turn to the animal kingdom.

No matter how men may try, they cannot justify their actions of bestiality by comparing themselves to the beasts of the jungle nor justify their immoral sensuality, because their individual psychical nature makes them personally responsible. Men, being more intellectually sensitive and self-individualized, are united mentally with their senses. Their discriminatory faculties, plus reason and logic supported by the conscience attribute of the soul, place upon man the responsibility of knowing himself and of clarifying himself to himself. Through awareness and understanding of that which moves through him and works with him, he is a potential creator for God.

Animals—not having consciousness through reasoning and through the discriminatory faculty of the intellect—survive, live and die through the specie instinctual overdirection consisting of an intelligible effluvia envelope. The species' psychical etheric envelope encasing all animals protects and directs the mating, begetting and birth habits of the animal creature. The dying of the animal is also under command of the species psychical influences of the Species Angels.

The wild animal kingdom is intensely subjective to the Species Angels. Their jungle predator habits in killing to survive are controlled by the subjective psychical laws enforced by the Species Angels.

Wild animals and birds respond etherically to the lunar tides and the solar winds, using their psychical lunar-brain function to migrate in certain seasons; to mate in certain periods; to desert their young under certain laws of psychical enforcement.

When an animal is domesticated by man, one can observe that the animal is chameleon-like and takes upon himself the nature of his master. The psychical emotional and mental moods and the senses of a man move into the domestic animal. Man can see his own uncontrollable hostility reflected in his cat, dog, cow or horse—or he can also see his own higher nature reflected therein. In households where there is harmony and love, animals prosper and thrive. Where man's sense of appetite or taste is gluttonous, his animals reflect this trait. Man's brutal disregard for others is reflected in the animals owned by him.

Man's fear of other men builds a psychical atmosphere of distrust, fear and hatred in the home. The dog or the cat owned by such masters become semi-predators, often reverting to wild instincts rather than domestic.

Inasmuch as a man's passions, desires and thoughts etherically image and determine his own appearance and looks, a domestic animal will grow to look like his master through the psychical etheric interchange between master and animal.

Animals become telepathically, psychically attuned to the habits of their masters. They know the coming and going of their masters before the act of going or coming is objectified in the mind of the master. The animal intuits his master's desire or intent; he also knows psychically when his master's attention has waned in a situation.

The psychic-brain force in all four-legged creatures is centered around the navel. An animal is able to psychically gauge time, distance, and locations due to the solar and lunar energies moving upon his psychical abdominal or navel brain. The navel brain in an animal acts as a psychical gravitational compass. When an animal is lost, he can return to his former location due to the psychical navel-brain's gravity pull. The psychical currents of his former homeplace, playing upon the psychical brain, become a magnet drawing him to the exact location of his home environment.

Tracking animals use this same power through the psychical instinct of smelling. The animal can smell and track out the etheric effluvia of any form of life having sentient ether and also blood. The blood of animal or man, having its own life-identity tone, can be traced by a tracking animal through the use of his psychical brain.

Things or possessions permeated by sentient ether become important and necessary to a domestic animal, such as a favorite dish, etc. Such dishes and their locations become psychical points sacred to the animal; with continued use the animal builds an effluvia envelope to protect his sense of security within his feeding environment. He sets up his own protective insulatory field which protects him from man's bacteria alien to the health of an animal. All animals remain telepathically connected where their food is located through the action of their lunar brains. Thus, regardless of where an animal may be, he knows the moment when food and water are being placed in his feeding receptacle.

When men overdomesticate their animals and make of them fondled, indulged creatures, the animals lose their psychical inherent survival instincts, becoming totally dependent upon their masters. Something vital is lost in the animal when he is overindulged. As men more and more domesticate animals and prevent them from making union with the Species Angels, the animals will cease to function in their natural instinctual manners. The species will also die out; through too much inbreeding and indulgence of animals, total species of animals will become extinct.

The most healthy association between the psychical nature of man and the psychical nature of animal is a trustful, free, and wholesome association. An animal renders his best service to his master on the psychic planes when there is an escape way for him to return to Nature from time to time.

To spay an animal or to make him sterile is to upset Nature's laws. This nullification of the sexual instinct in an animal violates a great law of Nature, and will eventually break and distort the animal specie-chain supporting evolutionary laws.

When one has an animal spayed or takes from any living creature the right to mate, he must prepare himself for the mechanics of Nature to rebel. In the natural animal mating instinct, Species Angels watch over breeding, mating and begetting. When man usurps this authority from the angels, the animal becomes a different creature, unfamiliar with its own impulses, wholly dependent upon the impulses of his master. Thus, anyone sterilizing an animal or stopping the animal's natural response to the psychical laws of breeding and mating, will take upon himself certain karmic responsibility to the animal kingdom.

Should he neglect or give up his animal friend or companion through caprice or indifference or even necessity, he should think twice and even thrice before he takes this step.

The psychic relationship between man and animal places a heavy responsibility upon a dog or a cat or a little beast taken into man's environment. The psychical navel brain of the animal, being subjected to the emotional will of man and being under domination of man, feels the subtle undercurrents in man's emotions, and everything that man feels the animal intuits and absorbs. If man becomes sick and the animal is closely aligned with his master, the animal takes on the psychical negativity of the sickness.

The navel psychical brain of the animal receives and records domestic hostilities, domestic inharmony, and tensions between persons in the home. A loyal and devoted animal seeks at all times to unite persons he loves. If husband and wife have some severe disagreement, the animal is torn psychically between the two persons he adores. A dog being by nature extremely loyal to man — and being a hunting creature — becomes very restless and often uncontrollable in such situations. If he has been with an inharmonious family over a long period, he may become ill with mysterious diseases—losing his fur, becoming listless and unresponding.

Men having strong primordial psychical force need the companionship of animals. They instinctively intuit that an animal in some manner disperses and grounds psychical force and pressure. Animals kept healthy by pure psychical force in the home render great service to mankind.

A man being unable to live wholly with himself, and being unloved by other men, often overcompensates in his love for an animal in a domestic environment. When this occurs, the animal becomes a parasite, failing to fulfill its full nature or naturalness. Such creatures are the victims of man's own unexplored inhibited psychical will, and may be looked upon as an animal sacrifice for man.

When men lived in the first period of consciousness in this earth, they consciously used their lunar brains through the solar plexus. In that phase of evolvement, men were unable to totally control the vibratory sound into speech. In the animal, sound is concentrated first into the navel or psychic brain, and then is reflected onto the physical ears of the animal.

The sense of hearing in the animal far surpasses this sense in man. When the mentality of man was developed by degrees, he sacrificed a certain range of psychical hearing, that he might develop other degrees of perception in his thoughts, speech and mind.

An animal is therefore capable of hearing sounds un-registered by the ear of man. As protectors in the home environment, animals become the ears for sounds that man is unable to register. The animalistic psychical instincts of man have been toned down that he might utilize and make more sensitive the extended faculties of his ego and mind. The life of the animal is selflessly related to the life of man. Even though he cannot speak and cannot reason intellectually, the animal has certain noble characteristics, and his responsibility to man often indicates that he has certain attributes of courage, loyalty, and perception excelling man's.

The extended sense of man working under the system of duality — trial and error, cause and effect — seeks to make man's senses into astute and accurate instruments. An animal, not having the full play of the duality action of his nature through the use of intellect, has no division of loyalties, nor can he tolerate it in his nature. Thus, an animal will sicken and die if man puts upon him for too long a period of time a condition of division and separateness. A dog more than

any creature in the domestic environment is wholly loyal
to the human spirit.

God gave to man the domesticated animal as a unique
creature, a friend, and mediator between the kingdom of the
angels, of the ferocious animals and man.

In the animal kingdom — in both the wild and the tamed
— a sense of humor is present. Many believe this to be a sign
that the animal kingdom is in some manner intelligent beyond the understanding or knowing of man. It is true that
animals do find men humorous and delight themselves in
teasing men. With certain undertones of nuance and meaning,
an animal teaches man some of the greatest moral lessons.

The life wave of certain species of animals is under the
command of the greater cherubim angels. This includes the
porpoise and certain fish in the sea. The felines, the elephant,
the dog — all have a psychic hookup with the cherubim
kingdom. Thus, in the feline kingdom, the teasing attribute
is psychically imposed upon the cat. However, an animal has
never been known to ridicule man with his teasing or with
his humor.

Cherubic humor in the animal is pure, teaching man of a
kindly kingdom, understanding man's fallacy and limitation,
forgiving and ever-ready to give a second chance to the one
who most abuses him — man. Only man uses humor to ridicule, and thereby cheapens and makes less a most beautiful
and wholesome attribute of his soul.

When men are pure in heart — wholly concerned with
union with God — the angelic kingdom working through the
animal kingdom sends to him creatures of the animal kingdom adoring him. St. Francis of Assisi was one of these.
Something is accomplished in the physical world when there
is harmonious union between animal and man.

An animal having lost psychical contact with his master,
and with the human etheric envelope encasing the family and

the home, may respond to the destroying principle and thus seek to punish the family or his master by soiling the rug— or chewing and ruining some prized article in the home. This revenge aspect in a domestic creature only occurs when an animal intuits himself to be an object of indifferent affections from those responsible for his destiny.

Domestic animals suffer when they are left to their own resources. When their master sets a pattern of repeated absence, the animal must be reassured that such actions are to be expected. An animal senses when his master is psychologically disturbed, or behaving in an erratic manner. To deviate from the familiar rhythms of the household, upsets an animal. The more sensitive the tie between master and creature, the more heartbreak for the animal on being neglected.

Only one having inner sight can truly estimate an animal's revolutionary upsets in a household where sickness is present. The vicarious suffering of an animal is intense where chronic diseases or incurable diseases are present. The animal remains alert, tense, nervous, disoriented. An animal may seem to go his way when this occurs; this is not the case, as the animal disguises his tensions through use of animal anesthesias.

It is said on the inner planes that when our Lord suffered on the cross, the animal oversoul was alerted to man's suffering as never before, becoming aware of the necessity for all animals to make men aware of the need for charity toward their fellow man and the animal kingdom.

Animals reincarnate and sometimes return to the same master as a loving, claiming animal-friend. When a certain time lapse has occurred between the death of the animal and his new birth, he can return to his former master. Animals outliving their masters see their deceased masters as being the same as when living, having seen always the interior man; the master now in the inner planes appears no different. However, an animal knows death to be separative in the sense of the former securing physical aspects of association. The animal accepts with a certain fatalistic knowing, stoically accepting a second master.

To put a healthy animal to sleep for one's convenience, or to take the life of a domesticated sensitized animal, distorts the chain of specie control in the animal kingdom. As in the life of man, cyclic timing in an animal's life is also a part of the great economy of life. Taking a life upheld by a sharing consciousness upsets the inter-biogenetic chain of life. In premature death, the specie-life impulse of the animal kingdom is upset and out of balance on all levels when death comes to an animal out of timing.

Animals know this law, as may be seen in a herd of cattle when one is to be killed by man. An uncontrollable unrest possesses the herd, accompanied by a pitiful lowing and bellowing.

Through ruthless slaying of whole species in the animal kingdom, and through artificial means of preserving domestic animals, man is rapidly destroying the life-impulse rhythm in the animal kingdom. On man alone rests the responsibility for the return to union with the animal kingdom so as to keep alive the resurgent psychical impulse of animal life assisting the emotional life of man.

It is no accident that the great Rishis of India introduced a system of yoga for man establishing certain Hatha Yoga practices identified with the animal kingdom. The Rishis recognized the dependency of man upon the animal kingdom. Certain habits and traits in man, related to sense extension, are very closely related to the psychic aspects of the animal nature. Many Hatha Yoga exercises resemble animal postures, producing in man a union with the animal life-soul instinctual nature—thus enabling the yogi or yogini to re-charge the body with survival prana or cosmic fire.

Animal sentience is psychical. Animal sentience correlates to the clairsentient nature of man. Man and animal are bound together in a cosmic brotherhood. Their conjoined function can neither be ignored nor set aside. However, man does not stem from an animal, nor does he reincarnate as an animal to balance the system of karma, as taught by certain transmigrationist sects in India.

Death and Animals

Sentimental persons owning animals and losing them by death very often determine never to involve themselves in giving love to another animal. There is in the nature of each soul the need to link with the life and death principle existing in man and in the animal. The universal certainties supporting the ending and beginning of life on earth hold the key to one's own balance in the self and in his relationships with the world as given of God. To accept death and birth as a process of unity in the One, is to live in a state of eternality as a number one creator for God.

To dream of the death of some one or of some thing one loves is to research the cosmic reality of death. One must accept what his dream tells him of death and abandon himself to the Universal Soul of life as an eternal, confirming certainty. In any aspect of life one must see transition as a sublime wisdom keeping the harmony and the balance within the heartbeat and life in God.

All fearsome symbols in dreams contain in some manner covered or hidden death aspects. Sleep itself, a minor death, holds the key and the answer to the question of death and life. Through visions in the night, one is researched and measured. Pluto dreams, or when Pluto is well aspected on the night of one's dreaming, will reward one with the just and right vision as to the why of death. Persons having Pluto well placed in their natal charts need not the assurance of what death *is*. Their souls have long since opened the mystery called death. To these souls men must look and lean, that they may be healed of their fears of the greater night — death.

The Father in heaven overdirects the Specie Angels as cognizance-regents over the animal kingdom. Jesus understood this when He said, "Are not two sparrows sold for a farthing? And one of them shall not fall on the ground without your Father." (St. Matthew 10:29) The Specie Angels working under our Father in heaven are the supersensory knowers for the total animal kingdom. At all times the Specie Group body is aware of every heartbeat action and instinct of an animal. If man could understand this great truth, he would also understand how his own soul is embodied in the Divine One, or God-Soul who watches over the souls of all men.

The animal aware of others' compulsions in the psychic specie envelope endures, survives and dies without whimper or complaint. Man questions the why of obedience, the what of discipline; thus, he suffers. The intrinsic unity in all life is the first step toward the freedom or liberation into the life of reality.

XI

THE DIVINE EYE

The higher aspects of the Divine Mother or feminine principle maintain the balance between the involuntary nervous and muscular systems of the physical body, keeping alive the vital psychic powers functioning within the psyche or soul attributes of man. All psychical energy, force, and power generate vibration, energy, electricity. In higher conscious thought this reacts as light. In the lesser mind this generates a sub-electricity acting as a mental heat. When thought is wed solely with the dot-and-dash action of the voluntary nervous and muscular systems, this produces the forceful personal will.

The Divine Mother or feminine-principle influence upon the involuntary nervous system persists in life and in death. Divine-Mother life force within man is preservative as well as disciplinary. When the Divine-Mother action of the involuntary nervous system is channeled into the outer consciousness as selfless love, health of mind, body, and soul is assured.

To materialistically permit the senses full reign, places pressures upon the voluntary nervous and muscular systems; the Divine-Mother action then becomes a disciplining and sometimes retributive action. Spiritually surrendering to the Divine Mother's inductive suggestion and direction, of the higher unconscious produces a supra-sense perception or divine intuition. By this, one perceives the heavenly realities through the single or divine eye of the spirit.

Each physical eye has seven layers of ether. When one works with the Divine-Mother principle of persistence, harmlessness, preservation, and devotion, the etheric layers of the eye are opened, and one sees beyond sense or with extrasensory perception. In the initiate this is done spontaneously while he is in a meditating or a non-meditating state. When events tense or crucial confront the mind, and if one has the grace of open etheric-layer sight, the advanced initiate sees beyond sense, things physical and personal, and he also sees beyond time and space. Such seership or inner seeing is an etheric psychic perception through a seership of the etheric layers of the physical eye.

Seership of the spiritual eye or divine eye is developed over the ages. The portal of the divine eye is centered between the eyebrows where the upper portion of the nose joins the forehead. To open fully the third eye or divine eye, one must earn the power of revelation rather than the sensory psychic vision. Psychic vision when untrained appears in unexpected and unpredictable manners. Spiritual revelation occurs due to a scientific process initiated and consummated through soul-directives over many lives of spiritual instruction. What one sees with psychic vision in the partial opening of the etheric veils in the physical eye is subject to change due to the will of man.

All psychic seership is the beginning of spiritual seership and should not be abused or despised. Physical mind involved in sense limitations of man cannot interpret nor fully define extrasensory perception because of its unexpected or incomprehensible unpredictability. Only spiritual mind can accurately assess the enlarged depths and dimensions of psychic sense perception. Untrained psychic vision may occur as an act of grace or as an act of karma. The inner nuances of the clear and exact meaning in psychic vision can be clouded by the karma of the one seeing, and therefore are biased, falling upon the karmic fears of the one concerned. One having higher psychic vision unifies and fuses the seven eye veils of ether within the physical eye through past experience or clairvoyant practices in past-life soul sensitivity.

The psychic processes of the mind are rooted first in the lunar brain located in the solar plexus; second, in the Quelle matrix situated at the base of the skull or the lower strata of the subconscious; third, in the root of the tongue; and last, in the Divine Thalamus matrix or the subliminal unconscious residing just beneath the gleaming brain or spiritual brain centered in the pineal crown of the head.

From the higher subliminal unconscious centered in the Divine Thalamus, one masters the subjective instinctual, forceful reflexes of the lower astral mind.

All degrees of the Quelle subconscious and unconscious aspects of mind are under command of the feminine principle or Cosmic Mother, called by the Rishis of the East the Divine Mother. The subliminal higher unconscious is experienced through the taking command of the exalted functioning of the higher sensory system.

To tap and to blend with the higher subliminal unconscious of the Divine Thalamus, where one unites with the Father Principle, is to come to a blended, balanced, sublime peace during periods of illumination and meditation — and to later express a spiritual power on the physical planes, beyond the psychic.

Above the base of the skull at the conjoining points of the involuntary and voluntary nervous systems, one's thoughts during meditation flow upward into the unified or blended cosmic matrix existing between the Father Principle and the Mother Principle. Here one experiences the divine marriage, receiving the androgynous powers in a bliss union with God.

Miraculous healing, initiatory powers, spiritual gifts—all result from communion with this holy union of the subliminal power of the Cosmic or Divine-Mother principle and the imaging restoring will-life of the Father principle. When ones meditates, he must move beyond the lower Quelle psychic energy excitation into the exalted bliss of oneness with God. He does so by being initiated into the marriage of the Divine-Mother power and the heavenly-Father power within the crucible of his higher mind.

The voluntary nervous system functions within a slower range of energy than that of the involuntary nervous system. The voluntary nervous system is dependent upon the involuntary nervous system drawing its power from a master energy within the vagus nerve, that it might have a continued flow of spiritual vitality. The voluntary nervous system in an undeveloped person, being as yet not totally in harmony with the quickened and higher subliminal flow of the unconscious, responds in a dot-and-dash manner to the healing and revivifying powers of the subliminal unconscious. This accounts for the short sustaining of spiritual sight or vision. It is the work of man to sustain the flow of spiritual sight and cognition. To do this he must call upon a third aspect of vitality in the master vagus nerve.

Man's lower psychic nature is predominantly kept alive in the voluntary nervous system by the lower planetary kinetic energies, stimulating and energizing certain glands and the voluntary nervous system. These less refined planetary energies compel one to explore and experience through his senses all facets of the externalized physical world. The senses when extended work with the subjective instinctual will of man to produce a psychic power sometimes protecting and in some instances foreseeing the consequential results of action formerly set into motion in the physical life.

All men have the psychic power to foreknow the results of actions for which they are directly responsible. A psychic monitor dwells in all persons. All persons have a super-sensing faculty. Were it not for the Divine Mother working with the soul in an unconscious action in the background individualizing the explorative psychic use of the senses, men would lose touch with the cause of being and of life.

It is the object of all spiritually inclined persons to balance and utilize the higher kinetic manifesting psychic energies and powers through the higher sense perception. Jesus used these powers to manifest His miracles. The higher intuition, the offshoot of the feminine principle, is a commander and preceptor, a prompter superior to the senses. When intuition is followed or obeyed and given reign, one is free to express the Divine-Mother principle, and also to apply the willing and the disciplining laws of the Father principle.

PSYCHIC PROCESS OF THE MIND AND THE PSYCHIC MEMORY

The higher unconscious sustains the creative and prophetic aspect of memory. The psychical lunar brain in the solar plexus and the Center Q or Quelle located at the base of the skull control the instinctual atavistic and lower phases of karmic memory.

When one is emotionally distracted, obsessed, and continually self-interested, the lower instinctual functioning in the

lunar psychic brain produces a continual flow of subtle psychical thoughts overenergized and overbearing to others. The
psychic thinking of an undeveloped lunar-energized ego penetrates the mental atmosphere of others as a raw sub-electric
energy. Psychical telepathic powers of such persons are
demanding, forcing entry into one's peaceful auric mentality
and emotional privacy. Such psychic telepathy is devitalizing
and inhibiting to the receiver. The mental images supported
by karmic memory in the undeveloped lunar-brain psychic
person become fixed in the adolescent cycle. Such persons
rarely move beyond the fourteenth year in their emotions.
Regardless of their adult appearance, immature emotional
persons remain inwardly fixed in the mental and emotional
memory patterns of an adolescent. Such egos act as static
agitator karmic catalysts in the life of the family and society.

During the shift over in a genesis rise, or in a reincarnation
tidal wave, multitudinous egos having strong subpsychical
powers are born to the physical world still functioning in the
lower psychical aspects of their memory. Their karma, covering long duration or ages, has detained them in the anterior
astral planes for lengthy periods between births to the earth.
This makes them unequal to the physical-life demands of the
era or the age representing a crest-cycle of reincarnation.
Such egos seek to compensate for their karmic laggardliness
by the use of force or enforcement upon the lives of other men.

No one can function mentally as a mature person unless
he has in former times used rhythmically the three higher
psychical aspects of his memory. Maturity of soul produces a
coordinated balance between the lunar brain or solar plexus,
Quelle or the portal of the subconscious at the base of the
skull (the primitive, psychical memory), and the gleaming
brain, the portal of the memory of the soul's action, centered
in the crown of the head. In the more highly evolved, the
feminine principle (centered in the higher side of Quelle)

overdirects the higher memory, assuring such persons of a spiritual mental process in wisdom.

Quelle has two actions: the subconscious and the higher unconscious. The subconscious side of Quelle works to move all things into the higher unconscious, that man may be illumined. The Divine-Mother action works with both sides of Quelle, seeking to bring the ego into alignment with the Divine Thalamus, or Father principle.

The feminine principle, when stepped down into the psychical aspects of the intellect, gives a genesis retentive memory pertaining to physical occurrences of the past; pertaining to world history and to family history. The Divine-Mother action, or the sustaining of the higher cosmic psychical life-memory processes in the soul of man, assures man of his past spiritual heritage, revealing to the initiate past-life grace records, and reveals to him his coming fulfillment as a soul on earth. Divine Mother works threefold in all phases of the memory to teach and keep before each one the design for his inherent spirituality.

Psychic mental power absent from the spiritual becomes an offensive psychical mind force. Psychic mental power with spiritual *awareness* of the past, the present and of things to come is a divine precognition beyond instinct, beyond intuition.

A mind fixed or attached solely upon the reliability of sensual body sensations, is unaware of the higher psychical processes of the mind. Such a one short-circuits the soft guiding instruction of the feminine principle or the Divine-Mother wisdom. Divine Mother, or the feminine principle, involves her children in spiritual action. She stimulates their spirit of devotion to channel their energies toward the attainment of purity, chastity, and peace.

All magnification of the lower extrasensory powers stems from psychic lunar-brain pressure. One should determine whether extrasensory power stems from the lunar brain centered in the solar plexus, Quelle in the base of the skull, the astral brain at the root of the tongue, the Divine Thalamus where the Father principle is centered directly above Quelle, or from the gleaming brain or pineal crown at the top of the head.

All seek to reach the final step of illumination which is experienced in the gleaming brain or pineal crown. When the Divine-Mother principle is married to the Divine-Father principle, the pineal crown moves in orbital and spherical fashion — and one is illumined. The Divine-Mother and Father principles produce their progeny or children. Illumination is the progeny or child of the androgynous marriage or union.

Illumination flows from the pineal crown outward into the starry portal centered between the eyebrows. Flowing out into the world, the light of the higher mind goes into the world to teach, to reveal, and to inspire.

The head of man is a temple of illumination. The heart of man is a temple of devotion. All initiatory trials seek to make these two temples into one through continued dedication. Through acceptance of initiation, gravity-will is mastered; self-obstinacy is overcome. And man becomes an instrument to serve his God.

LUNAR BRAIN

Psychic power is innate in all men. Psychic power when selflessly motivated is used by the soul as a divine attribute given to all men through which God can act for Himself, through man and for man.

In one phase of the psychical process of the lunar brain, one may identify psychical action by *eye* action. When psychically functioning, the pupil of the eye seems to enlarge, widen and extend. Such a one gazes as in a fixed second of sighting. The body becomes set or rigid as one seems to function through a certain extended magnified perception and is temporarily withdrawn from his own personal ego will. During lunar-brain psychical perception one draws upon the earth memory in Nature—from the stone, the mineral kingdom, the plant, the animal and man. The functioning of higher lunar-brain psychical power enables one to sustain his inherent response to Nature through *feeling*. All scientists working with the forces of Nature experience some degree of the lunar-brain psychic perception. Withdrawing from their own mental egoic concerns, they eventually give to men a knowledge pertaining to the cause and effect of the natural processes of life sustaining the body and survival of man.

In men expressing consciously their psychic natures, there is an awareness of a certain withdrawal of the personality aspect of the ego, so that another aspect of one's being may perceive, discern and experience.

The higher ego, using the psychic perspective and reflective memory aspect of the lunar brain becomes ultra wise while accepting the tutelage of Divine Mother. One can perceive Nature in a reflected lunar light with an androgynous eye of vision and of revelation.

The hair on the physical body works for and with the psychical functions of the lunar brain. Each hair of the body is a psychical electrical antenna. Men are aware of danger first through the smelling sense; secondly, through an intense, increased warming of the minute and predominant portions of hair on the physical body. Unseen enemies, dangers to the body, obnoxious spirits of the unrisen dead are all sensed first through the sense of smell received by and working upon the hairy parts of the body.

At the nape of the neck, in the base of the tongue, and in hair covering the pelvic center and appendages of the body where hair grows, the protective, instinctual psychic alarms are set off in the pores of the skin and in the nerve and muscular functions of the body. These psychical sensing impulses do not always reach the intelligence or thought; however, they are registered as alerts upon the glandular system, the salivary glands, and also the adrenal system, conditioning and preparing the ego to act.

Such alarm symptoms cannot be compared with the pores of the skin vibrancy-crawls which one experiences with the acknowledgment of angelic truths or helps. The skin pores are additional eyes of the body or vision portals, and are used by the angels to identify their presence or assistances, or to confirm the truth of a spiritual statement. The pores of the skin become like little eyelids rising all over a particular portion of the body that one may know when he has heard a true thing. Of such is one of the tongues of the angels!

Quelle Thinking

The Quelle psychic state stimulated by the subconscious mind is presently coming under the scrutiny of all thinking men, as it is steadily being seen that there are underlying root impulses compelling the masses, the group, and the individual.

The Quelle psychic portal seated at the base of the brain contains in its etheric matrix all of the riches and the poverty of the human ego. Quelle psychic thinking is a subconscious knowing, a knowing aware of depth, breadth, length and height of man. Quelle holds the instinctual memory of man's beginnings and the key to his sanity of the present. Consciousness mind cannot conceive or contain what Quelle knows. Quelle acts as a knowing computer having a most profound memorizer and forgetter. By Divine Providence and intent, healthy Quelle flows into the conscious mind in preconceived timings and occurrences. Through dreams and meditation rhythms, Quelle mind projects, rejects, ranges, and prompts onto conscious mind one's own myth-symbols of comprehension and enlightenment.

Quelle in its most hostile state is the enemy of peace in the conscious mind, as a dreaded host uninvited. Quelle, when working to rectify karma, acts relentlessly to temporarily destroy and flood out of the ranges of reason all that has been established as right in concept, in thinking, and in acting.

The Quelle psychic state opened prematurely acts to negatively expose man to the destroying principle. Quelle under karmic pressure ruthlessly exposes weakness long concealed in conceits, vanity, error, sin. All persons opening the outer expression of the psychic life expose themselves to Quelle's inflicting action. Thus, the history of all chosen sages, prophets, and seers records the fiery trials accentuated by the unleashed Quelle fire.

In the spiritual state the initiate of the psychic life brings the Quelle matrix under the command of the *Divine Thalamus*. When this occurs, he opens intricate psychical analyzing and revealing aspects of his creative mind. From this comes spiritual genius. Working directly with Quelle to accomplish this, is the astral inductive mind which is fed and quickened by the planetary stimulus working upon the glandular system.

The Divine Thalamus is seated over the *higher dome* or the superior sensory nerve chalice situated in the higher portion of the skull directly above Quelle. The Divine-Father principle overdwells this energized mass of molecular sensing energy.

ASTRAL THINKING

The astral aspect of the psychic thinking nature draws upon the glandular system. Astral, meaning star-reflection, is a unique, unceasing, fermenting, mirroring and moving action producing in man a state of emotion, mood and inductive feeling and thinking. Each of the seven major glands of the body contains an astral counterpart or starry planetary center which is stimulated by the lower and higher vibrations of seven planets: Saturn, Jupiter, Venus, Mercury, Mars, Uranus, Neptune. The vibrations from these planets shape and subtly direct the individual ego, re-enforcing its expression.

One who thinks wholly with the lower astral nature is out of the range of higher self-awareness. One who thinks wholly with higher astral thoughts is prescient when the higher ego or self is in command. To think in total lower thinking, or astrally, one becomes a subjective psychic receiver. To understand and to use the resources of the higher psychic nature, one must objectify and command the glandular star-center higher velocities located in the spinal nervous system. These centers are stimulated by the solar and lunar fires working with the varying changes of planetary action.

If one is oversubjective, impressionable or suggestible — that is, plus-astral — he is not aware of himself as a whole person. He is content to emotionally respond to life; he is a fated vessel rather than an initiate.

The astral psychic nature in its lowest aspects produces the exploitative psychic, the witch, the mediumistic seer living vicariously through the magnified ectoplasms and telepathic compulsions of the unrisen dead. The harsh side of the moon or lunar tides works with the lower aspect of the psychic nature, using the chimera reflective lunar light rather than the higher direct *solar light* supporting the planetary or starry points in each gland. The glands of the lower psychic express the lunar astral nature; such psychics work with the gravity tides and the lower electronic frequencies of the earth and the lower vibrations of the planets intermingling with the magnetic belt surrounding the earth. The solar-tides initiate works with the higher astral refined, supercharged wave lengths. The sun or solar-light initiate is under the command of the Christ Spirit. The lunar astral-light psychic is under the command of the Race Lord, Jehovah, and the lunar and terrestrial angels.

Thus, a person of predominantly lunar nature is astrally psychic and is gravity bound to the acts of phenomena produced by the astral world. The contrasting tumults in the psychical lunar temperament, sometimes ecstatic and sometimes melancholy, are best analyzed by an understanding of the astral chimera variables, and by a comprehension of the intricate system of karma.

Solar initiates are spiritual psychics, having reached the fourth aspect of transcendental action. They use the higher astral psychic stuff (akasia) of the First Heaven and Second Heaven to rise beyond karma and to heal emotions and thoughts. They are fully aware of *all* of the psychical currents in their own thoughts and of the nuances supporting the higher psychic awareness.

ENERGY AND CONSCIOUSNESS

Man is a unit of universal energy participating in a universal cause. The mind of man is being particularized into an instrument of consciousness. As a being of will, he draws all degrees of energy into his mind and produces consciousness.

When man masters universal energy, he will be a superconscious being. The power of the psyche or the soul of man is the builder aspect in his nature. To live, man must build. In building he draws upon the psyche or soul, using psychic energy, psychic force, psychic power, psychic perception.

All energy contained in sentient life is a unit of consciousness. Therefore, all things sentient contribute to consciousness. All degrees of consciousness knowing or unknowing give off energy. Degrees of unknowing energy in consciousness are destructive. Degrees of energy stemming from a knowing consciousness are creative.

Mind as consciousness is a diffused light organized by a central intelligence, the highest of this intelligence being God. Mind absent from God is an egoist instrument dependent upon a subtler light supported by forces, strongly charged with raw electricity, subjected to static, heat, and pressure.

The lower psychic nature is inverted consciousness. Spiritual nature is an aware consciousness. Spiritual consciousness is the property of the higher mind. Mind becomes actively and creatively conscious when higher ego *wills*. The higher ego is the willing center of creative consciousness.

The psychic nature as consciousness is built from the consciousness of the past, a consciousness only useful to the present state when it plans for a spiritual future. A building consciousness is a creating consciousness. Only a building consciousness knows awareness. Only a creating consciousness is aware of the Spirit of God using him to build.

Psychic nature engrossed in sensation and inverted self-reflections, knows not the joy of building or creating. The lower aspect of the psychic nature is a self-engrossed intoxication, a mental toxicity, knowing only instinctual multiplication rather than creative simplification.

Psychic mind power builds instinctively upon the myths of the past as experienced by groups, masses, and persons. A personal myth, when psychically charging the thoughts, produces self-worship. One seeks to fulfill the hero idea; he is illusively separated from others, convinced that he is an exception. A group myth expressing thoughts of self-superiority creates cruel bigotry and separation. A mass myth projected from a sense of inferiority produces the psychic longing and hunger for a dictator; a mass of peoples feeling national guilt instinctively crave punishment, and subconsciously desire their final end, calling forth and submitting to leadership of a tyrannical and destroying ego.

A person having magnified psychic thought power projects his overcharged thoughts as an atmosphere. He generates his likes or dislikes as power upon the receptive field of the untrained emotions and thoughts of others. He becomes a karmic agent over the mental wills of others less familiar with the drawing powers of the psychic nature. Psychic instinctual persons when strongly self-willed can become revolutionaries and disorganizers of weakened systems, national, social and personal.

All highly evolved persons having the power to influence positively the mass thought patterns of men are psychically powerful and spiritually oriented. They are consciously organized to soul ideas and come to the world to save men during spiritual and national crises.

The glandular system determines the karmically motivated mental obsessions of man. Each man brings to life one key obsession. If he does not utilize this obsession level, his obsession becomes his adversary or enemy; he then may be said to be obsessed. Obsession is a fixed, one-pointed thought emanating a psychic energy repeatedly seeking to identify itself in the outer compulsions as a clue to the karma of the past.

Obsession thought clues and patterns may be traced in dream life, in day-by-day surface actions, in crisis actions, and also may be observed by those understanding the basic motivation elan ruling the exact and just system of karma.

Desire for power is the main and supporting root of egoist obsession. No matter how one may seek to conceal it, the desire for power exists in the human ego — power to possess, to command and demand. Power over things and persons begins with the infant in the cradle, as it began with Cain and Abel, and today it is embodied in masses of people pushing and pressing for placement in a crowded world.

Grace from former-life use of power will enable one to remain mentally rational and to absorb and utilize one's main passion-forte or obsession. The higher mind and will make one's obsession the servant rather than the master, and thus one obtains his heart's desire for expression. In dreams the initiate has access to an unlimited insight and foresight. The mystery mind portals in the human ego-archives open to the initiate while in the state of sleep, functioning as they cannot function in the waking consciousness.

If one seeks to express the full potential of his creative mind, he must be prepared to encounter the little understood aspects of the psychic forces and energies supporting the imaging process of his mind. To zealously guard one's creative thought is to inhibit creation. To live in a guarded state of thinking, when karma and grace aspects are ripely united, upsets the timing of one's creation. To freely create stirs the sediment layer or level of desire and emotions inactive and long restrained in the mind. Such sediments occur with terrifying intensity for the rigid mind. Fixed ideas concerning methods in creation frustrate the ripe flowing tides of creation. To truly become a whole creator for God, one must step aside from self and from all previous and limited concepts which do not coincide with his spiritual, natal inclination. Higher psychic creative nature must be recognized and acknowledged as a thrust of the supernal unconscious supporting the desire to create.

Higher psychic nature in creation enters into the reaches of the yet unmanifested, into memories of former-life perfected projections and methods, and into infinite approaches to the cosmic in creation.

Psychic nature, when spiritually free, assures the creator that he will produce ideas ingenious in creation suitable to the present, giving therapeutic and historical answers to the past. The high psychic nature desires to produce original

thought themes suitable only to what *he* can do as a creator.
No other person can do what a free ego can do. To depend on
lower psychic nature *alone* produces fallible limitations in
creation. To recognize the refined states of the psychic nature
and its creative nuances is truly to become a hierarch of the
creative mind.

Every ego has a story, a message, a drama and a mission
in the world. To find one's own is to become centered in a
plus-life filled with divinity. One is shaped from life to life,
that he may present his message. The drama of ego divinity
is fully expressed when the flow of psychic power becomes
impersonally channeled through spiritual purity and ethic.

Psychic nature for the creatively ripe produces an intuitive
insight in expression. All persons expressing new facets of
creation may be considered prophets, as the living and
immortal aspect of all skilled presentation is prophetically
looking into and anticipating a future yet unborn. Men not
creative are dependent to a great extent upon the invisible
theme of foreseeing by others having more envisioning
natures.

Psychic power is a mystery feared by the inexperienced, the
superstitious, and the unawakened. This does not, however,
mitigate the fact and truth that as psychic energy is dormant
and alive in inert mass, psychic force is latent and ready to be
utilized as a supportive vehicle of consciousness in all persons.

The degree of psychic power and its utilization is dependent
upon the refinement and sensitivity of each person. How it
is expressed is determined by the state of individual karma
and the evolvement reaches of the soul. Soul-power is creative
psychic power. He who creatively generates psychic power
must be responsive and responsible to more than one world.
The psychic nature is timeless and knows no limitation in
dimension. When pure psychic power is expressed by a highly
evolved soul, mighty things are materialized and manifested.

All creative persons united harmoniously to their psychic natures radiate light, power, and enthusiastic stimuli for the world.

UTILIZING THE PSYCHIC ENERGIES IN NATURE

The psychic nature of Nature works to give man a life body. The physical body of man and his etheric or life body is Nature encased in a body. All substances of the flesh body begin with and end with Nature. To channel the higher ESP powers, one begins with obedience to Nature's law. Obedience is impossible without the agreeing will-function of the mind. Therefore, the beginning of the command of the psychic life starts with mind and emotions as students of Nature—Nature as the laboratory and the substance of life, giving life.

The psychical energies in plants and mineral life are cosmic life energies awaiting the intelligent utilization by man. Through the ethical use of psychic force and the use of the higher will, man can draw to himself all of the substances of life rejuvenation and health. He can also draw to himself with the highest spiritual aspect of his consciousness the requirement for a sustaining way of life.

Ethical mind and will or the higher mind and will must be the director of all psychic energies, forces, powers. If the mind is sacredly aware of the life force, heaven on earth may become the reality for the now.

There is a Nature psychic life supporting man's physical evolvement on earth. Until man has produced a perfect will, a perfect mind, and a perfect creative consciousness, he will be interiorly served and exteriorly supported by Nature's psychic life.

To draw upon the higher resources of Nature, one must know himself to be generated by a moon and a sun regeneration. In the earth man is both an initiator and an actor. To understand oneself, one must see Nature's lunar and solar energy fire mirrored in his body. Through the lunar energy action, one is receptive and permissive. In Nature's positive solar fire, one is a projector and a builder.

Through the subjective processes of the mind one is responsive to the reflective lunar side of Nature. With the positive aspect of his consciousness mind, one is a mind sculptor using the solar cosmic plasmas of Nature.

During the night while asleep man's direct lunar brain, situated in the solar plexus, draws upon the banked solar or sun fires retained in his etheric and physical bodies. These fires are especially indented into the root of his tongue, flowing into his subjective mind at night. In the day he enacts outwardly the lunar-brain suggestibility of the night received from the retained solar fires in his body and in Nature. His desire to care for the body, his instinctual appetites, and his hidden hungers are manifested during the day; these are gathered from the night's induction working with the psychical lunar brain.

Healing comes in the night more often because the ego-will is made less willful during sleep. The primordial lunar fire of Nature functioning in conjunction with the accumulated solar fire at night acts with absolute knowing as to the need and care of the physical body.

Man uses Nature in the day as an object of careless regard. In the night, despite his unknowing, the solar and lunar fires of Nature work, heal, and prepare his body to better function in the world of the day.

God gave to man the ultra sense to make him a perceiver and an observer of the forces and functions of his body. To neglect this sense of intuitive awareness is to be sick and out of the range of the lunar and solar regeneration and recuperation laws. When one unites with a systematic process of study to make holy the processes of Nature, he will reinforce and activate the lunar and solar sides of Nature, and he will free the positive action of his mind, that he may work with Nature to heal, to restore, and to remain attuned to the life, or cosmic force supporting all life in this eternity. Therefore, man must devise a deliberate way of working with the cosmic lunar and solar tides of the body.

The lower etheric body and the physical body respond obediently to certain levels of negative psychical suggestion. To constantly analyze the functions of the body produces a neurotic expression of the body. The body goes out of normalcy ranges when this occurs. One thus defeats the wholeness of his cosmic awareness.

To be receptive to and put into action certain balancing processes for the body, such as cosmic exercise, walking, and rhythmic movement; to eat of Nature without greed or gluttony; to use the elemental resources, such as water, air, and sun for the physical and vital ether restoration in the body — will keep the wheel of regeneration and recuperation moving in a perfect unison with universal law. To work to visualize the perfection of the body and to consciously unite with the solar clock of energy-freeing at dawn, with receptive and meditative attitudes at dawn, noon, and dusk, will produce physical-body and etheric-body harmony throughout the day.

Lunar action in the lesser etheric body, united with solar energy in night sleep, rebuilds a vital spirit of joy and acceptance of the coming day. Before sleep the use of molecularly energized *archetypal mantrams* and suggestible techniques unlocks the accumulative healing restoring energies in the physical and etheric bodies, assuring one of a night of dream cognition, progression, and service to one's body and service to others in the night and in the day to come.

DRUGS AND PSYCHIC VISIONS

Persons born with unbalanced glandular pressure giving emphasis to the psychic fire in the pituitary gland are karmic-

ally laden with sense appetite memory. Being out of range of
the conscience flow of former-life ego will experience, they
enter the world with indecisive minds and sometimes amorality. If former-life memory indulgence still remains exposed in
Quelle, the result is a desire to experiment with drugs.

All persons taking drugs can reach only into the lower
astral planes with their visions.

The arc of life is spiritual, seeking to draw men upward,
but when there has been for many lives a downhill inclination
in the use of the senses, it is easier to lean in the direction of
seeking to extend the ranges of sensation through drugs and
eventually drug addiction.

The taking of drugs experimentally is due to the absence
of the discriminative faculty of the soul. Taking drugs deliberately to extend the amoral nature is a desire for death, or a
suicide-wish fulfillment.

Those who would heal the addict must be armored with
the understanding of the karmic laws and also of the redemp-
tive aspect under Christ. But as in the case of every form of
death-wish compulsion, healing can only be successful when
the one caught into the snare of self-deception desires within
the depth of his being to be retrieved and healed.

To seek to use drugs to enter into the psychic state offends
the flow of Quelle. The use of drugs to obtain psychic powers
penetrates the psychic nature through the back door of the
mind.

In Uranian-charged drugs stemming from synthetics, as in
the case of LSD, drug use destroys the protective etheric
covering around the lower brain stem where Quelle resides.
Hallucinations, crime, terrifying experiences are caused by
the use of the Uranian-charged drugs. Damage to the etheric
matrix cannot be healed in one life. Unless there is some
compensation in the balance of the brain's motor life, one will
suffer throughout life a magnification and distortion of the

mind's processes. Overstimulation of the subconscious flow cannot be equalized with the objective mind after extreme violation through use of drugs upon the etheric matrix surrounding Quelle.

Healing for the drug addict or experimenter in the enlargement of the primal psychic eye through the use of drugs must be placed totally in the hands of the angels and of God and of those under God. If there is grace, one will receive mitigation.

Psychic disorganization of the etheric matrix covering Quelle results in too much subconscious flow and not enough practicality of the objective mind. Self-observation will show the reformed addict his self-inflicted unbalance of psychic force requires constant diligence, that he fall not into depression, anxiety, uneasiness and non-creativity.

All persons using drugs are to some degree casualties in a decaying life theme. Resources to heal such persons, unfortunately, come to the world as hindsight.

Karma made from the use of drugs can be rectified through works of the future by which self-purgatory is expiated.

Karma is made by one leading another into drug-taking or by causing the addiction of another. This is a sin unto death. One cannot expect his prayers to be answered for one who entraps another person into the vice of drug-taking.

> If any man see his brother sin a sin which is not unto death, he shall ask, and he shall give him life for them that sin not unto death. There is a sin unto death: I do not say that he shall pray for it.

> I John 5:16

ILLUSION AND THE MIND

To say that phenomena's action is illusion or unreal is to lose sight of the why of phenomena. The perpetual pendulum of sameness and changing has a progressive aspect — and the clue to this mystery lies in the consciousness of man. Even though men seem to think that the restless and distracting world of phenomena is a world to escape from into a world of peace, there can be no peace for any soul of this earth until he understands the mystery of phenomena and masters the phenomenal world. Man must gather the essence of his confrontation with phenomena into a nucleus of expanded energy and accumulative power, that he may use the divine power of a hierarchy mind.

It is commonly believed that the dualistic aspect of the physical world is the only reality. Relativity supports are God-designed so that man may experience a certain kind of consciousness while dwelling in earth existence. From this he in time will become an initiate of the mind.

Dualistic atom energies support all physical phenomena. To unite with a third aspect of atom energy through self-realization and God-realization is to move beyond the phenomena aspects of chimera-like happenings in the world. With spiritual comprehension and overlook into the true and spiritual nature of man, one comes to understand the term *illusion*. One who lives in illusion, and believes the physical world to be all, dwells in a labyrinth of confusion. It is the design of God that man rise over the unceasing tumults of apparitional appearances. By the use of the higher mind one can move out of the dream existence into spiritual reality.

To the Eastern mind illusion means that which man has mirrored upon the psychic screen of the lower mind. Until spiritually awakened, man builds a chimera-like separative world. He believes that what he sees reflected in this kinetic mirror of the lower mind is the only world. Kinetic energy is psychic energy. Constant dependence upon psychic kinetic excitation processes of the lower mind produces pain, confusion, and bewilderment.

The spiritual initiate accepts the basic law governing higher metaphysics; that is, thoughts of any degree are creative. Archetypal metaphysics teaches that thoughts selfishly motivated build an overcharged mental vibrational field of psychic energy. All thoughts centered upon self-absorption produce less than perfect results; a self-absorbed person is a victim of his thought processes, never escaping from the lower and painful retributive aspects of karma.

Illusion living, thinking, and acting subject one to the lower aspects of the planetary energies, particularly to the disciplining planetary energy of Saturn, Neptune, and Mars. Illusion living, thinking and acting also slow down the rebirth cycles or return-to-earth existence, as the pattern of psychic kinetic force slows down one's return to birth to happier or more pleasing environments.

To be changed, to be born again through initiation to the mind, is to enter into the higher mind where the archetypal light of the Christ would give the new mind in Christ.

An archetypal thought is a pure undefiled idea as yet unpolluted by any human concept. An archetypal thought is a four-dimensional idea as yet unexposed to any form of competitive idea or comparison as to man's past thinking and acting. An archetypal thought enters into the pure thinking process in which love, pure desire, and receptivity are wholly dependent upon God's revelation.

Through regular reverent and receptive meditation upon God, one slows down the psychic kinetic field of the lower mind. To slow down the kinetic energy sustaining the lower mind is a painful process to the uninitiated. One should seek to keep all thoughts within the light, that he may avoid the downpull of the psychic repetitive illusion and awake to the calm of his own divinity within the light.

The use of violence of any kind—physical, emotional, or mental—unfailingly produces negative and painful results.

The psychic drainage from hostility and hate lies coiled in the Quelle portion of the lower subconscious mind, waiting to spring. When hatred has long festered, violence comes; grief and sorrow follow — and as the night follows the day, so does suffering multiply.

The psychic clusters of mental and emotional sentient energy, when overburdened, discolor the flow of the soul's desiring, and one can be actually imprisoned in a prison-like state of resenting and resisting in the lower mind.

The higher mind can be free to function only when the serpentine coils of the astral fire, forming and sustaining the lesser emotions and thoughts, are disciplined. One is disciplined by one or more aspects of pain — pain through extreme conflict in the thoughts, pain through being denied one's dormant wish fulfillment, pain through being suppressed by the harsh, selfish will of another person, or by some condition in life that is totally out of harmony with the conscience and the soul's expectation.

Violent persons, suppressing their own natural psychic flow with Nature, repressing their rightful wish fulfillment and expression of love, become deadly agents of karma. In the midst of peace, their violent acts and voices resound, disturbing acceptable ways of living.

One ego, when peace centered, can bring peace. One peace-knowing being can give to recalcitrant souls a look into the true, clear channels of peace residing within the souls of all men.

It is the work of the spiritual initiate not to preach to controversial minds, but to give through mediation peace reinforcing securities, not through vocal words falling upon the irritated, inflamed hatreds of unknowing. Through union the spiritual healer can still the dissenting agitations presently disturbing the creative interflow between the higher mind of man and the Divine Mind of God.

To condemn is to fix; to judge is to be judged. The initiate speaks through meditation the healing mantrams of love, seeing the union between all souls, seeing all minds within the enveloping love of the mind of God.

One may overcome and command the undertow and overflow of Quelle, or the subconscious mind, when he remains in a constant state of conscious awareness of God.

Man is an entitized particle sustained by universal cause, corrected by equation. Billions of years have been required to develop him to his present state. Billions of years are yet necessary to perfect him as he is imaged in eternality.

The soul of man cannot be unpoised, nor separated from his eternality. Sealed into each soul is a resounding spiritual tone directing him. Spiritual reality keeps the soul of man intact, though man often seems to offend cosmic law. Despite his striving and his unknowing, he rests in a suspended universal cradle harmonized by universal order, peace.

XII

SPIRITUAL EXTRASENSORY POWER

AND HEALING

Each man is a universe cosmically organized, functioning within a plan. It is the destiny of each man to behold his own creation as stemming from the creation of God. Only One knew this wholly and completely. This was Jesus.

Jesus came not as a builder of buildings, even though reared as a carpenter; not as a rabbi, even though versed in the Scriptures. He came to give to man a new mind through Christ. Jesus desired that man know himself not as a singular person but as a universal man. Jesus respected the will faculty of man in its individualistic aspect, giving him the right ethic for its use. He also revered the memory attribute of man, giving full credit to the lives of men who had preceded Him. And Jesus particularly colored His words and His deeds with a certain charisma of the imagination, telling men that His words would always abide with them. He knew in His practice of the eternal sciences that the will, memory and imagination are the eternal aspects of man's own being, and therefore the door to his freedom of expression.

Spiritual extrasensory power must draw upon these three eternal attributes in the mind of man. To see more and beyond the physical eye or sight, one must *will* to *know* what one is seeing or beholding. One must remember what has been seen in the past so as to compare it with what is being seen in the present. To manifest a perfect extrasensory spiritual power, one must have access to a vivid and powerful imagination devoid of glamor or falsity.

Jesus said that men would do greater things than He, knowing that as the years progressed, man's willing, memory and imagination would become more cosmically charged and directed toward universal issues rather than personal concerns.

Man has yet to learn that he is an image maker, a little hierarch in the making. Egotism is the enemy of one who would use the triune powers of his mind as intended under the direction of Jesus.

The sleeping fires of aggression in man keep alive his egoistic drives. Many persons think that the electrically overcharged ideas of the mind are evidence of a scintillating and brilliant mind. Ideas being a projection from the intellect, when charged with egotism, short-circuit higher extrasensory or spiritual powers. Thus, it is required of those who would truly be vessels for the light that they move out of the range of super-charged egotistical sides of their intellect. Through the power of spiritual self-suggestion one can slow down the egotistical drives of the mind, and make of his intellect an impartial, scrutinizing instrument.

Extrasensory powers can have no value when supercharged with egotistical opinions. The weighing process of all evidence of existing supernatural powers is a tedious process. Thus few in the world are as yet competent to remove their opinionated approaches to the reverent and beautiful aspect of the mind holding the clue to man's spiritual liberation.

Faith is on one wave length of consciousness; disbelief is on another wave length of consciousness. Faith produces superconscious or supernatural happenings. Optimism and enthusiasm are attributes of faith.

To be absent from gratitude for the good things of life, and to refuse to admit that the good things received are good, sells one into the loss of birthright. When one keeps open the artery of unbelief, living always in a state of sour skepticism, the energy body supporting the psychic mind becomes twisted and warped, producing a twisted mind and mental attitude. Emotions which should by spiritual right be the receptacle for enthusiasm and optimism are forlorn, empty cups of hopelessness when one seeks to enlarge his unbeliefs.

To be thankful for the smallest things is to build a healthy emotional body and a flexible mental attitude. Self-betrayal is the most grievous offense against life and God's Will for man. One betrays himself when he refuses to believe that God is the Will motivating his being and his existence. To downgrade gestures of hospitality and affection, to split in two or to reject the sincerity of others is a base and ingrate action.

Everywhere in the world one looks he may see misshapen bodies outpicturing non-conforming thoughts. In each life one builds his future appearance through his thoughts, feelings and acts. Especially in the latter part of one's life, he prepares the etheric mold for his next life.

On the face of an infant may be seen the disbeliefs produced by a past-life cynicism. Resistance to discipline in the babe may also be traced to a behavior pattern of resistance in a former life.

Psychology is beginning to observe and to recognize that there is a clairsentient pre-natal influence between the mother and the embryo. This is the first step toward recognizing coinciding reincarnation patterns. Psychology has entered Quelle through the back door of the mind, and will gradually come to the frontiers of the soul, and recognize the reincarnating tidal inferences in the life of human behavior.

HEALING AND THE EXPANDING MIND

Men now face a new scene in the play or drama of life. The curtain is rising on the play of the mind, the main actor on the stage being the energy masses stimulating life force and consciousness.

The first atom blast, shocking and upsetting the fixed lethargies and concepts in the mind of man, spoke many promising things to the alerted mind, many frightful things to the crystallized mind.

The science of space energies yet in its infancy will be enlarged into dimensions unbelievable even to those who are presently looking over the horizons of earth existence into interterrestrial relationships.

Men are always slow at first to recognize and accept the imminence of startling and new changes in their so-called organized environments. There is, however, nothing existing in the memory of man to which man can compare the new era of the expanding mind. Presently men are intuiting with a certain apprehension and even dread, this new age introducing unknown and unfamiliar patterns in morality and in ethic.

Too long man has shut away his cosmic sense and universal flow in consciousness. In the agrarian times men knew a certain peace gathered from harmony with the plants and animals. His sentient nature was fed by the first fruits of the earth. His span of life was short. He lived in a sentient mystic mood as a receptacle of life; rather than one who energized himself through his own ego will, he existed in the will of a life force. In this existence his karmic debts from life to life were less acute, less self-responsible. In each life he plowed under something of his wrongdoing where it sifted downward into Quelle as a sedimentized reserve, that he might in each life accumulate more conscience.

The brain of man is divided into two hemispheres. The left side of the brain works with man in his instinctual osmosis existence. Gradually as man began to be a little more than instinctual, he added the rational, decisive attribute to his mind. He began to develop individual conscience. He became more sensitive and more aware of himself as an ego. During this period, planetary forces playing upon his glands began to excite and stimulate the unused hemisphere of his brain. The extensive lunar or moon influence hitherto directing his thinking, adjusted itself to include specific planetary impressionability upon his glands and his mind.

Jesus' entrance into the world was timed exactly to coincide with man's birth to ego-individuality. Jesus, the Divine Master and Messenger of cosmic law and energy, came to this world to teach men how to use the full capacities of their minds. He came to transpose and unite the inductive faculties of man into objectivity. After Jesus, the solar and lunar light and the planetary energies working with the glandular system and etheric body of man began to hum a different existence tone and tune upon the ego of man.

In the divine order of all life, universal and personal, there are no accidents. Man's expanding consciousness must now behold universal cause at first hand within his own nature.

Because Jesus did come, men through the widening of their comprehensive mental skills will not lose sight of love. This divine element holding together and keeping intact all things in the universe of God and of men will not be taken from man.

Inhibited minds fear the scientific reachings into the consciousness of man. Explorative minds will seek to prevent cosmic innuendoes of the new insight into man and his place in the universe. Evolved men will keep apace with the interflow between the universal, the cosmic and the human, and thus become regulating ambassadors for Jesus.

Jesus knew that man on the physical plane has an indwelling spirit in command of molecular energies. When Jesus looked into a man as a soul, He saw him as an eternal being. When He looked into man as a body not yet fully aware of his soul-powers, He saw the molecular masses of the etheric body in one or two states. If the one standing in His presence was sick, weak, confused or violent, He saw these masses of energy disarranged, disorganized, underactive or overactive. If the person was mentally depressed, He saw these to be cold, alienating the cells of his body and brain, inviting a hybrid form of bacteria supported by the energy wave lengths of anti-matter.

All forms of chronic diseases He knew to be an offshoot of karma caused by unbelieving and depressive minds. In the sight of Jesus, these masses and coils of anti-life energy were resisting the creative life force, causing displacement and distortion of the identity pattern of the soul.

Jesus could see the powerful cosmic forces playing impersonally and impartially upon the body of man, and He knew that love alone was the remedial, stilling, rearranging, reorganizing of these energies in the etheric body. Jesus knew that man when consciously in doubt, in fear, opened the destroying wave lengths of life, and also that when he had through long periods of deviation offended karmic laws, he attracted to himself the hybrid anti-life bacteria diseases.

Jesus kept His own body in a perfect, organized alignment with His Father in Heaven through the power of Love.

Through wave lengths of love He healed, rearranged the molecular disorganized masses in the etheric body, bringing them back into attunement with the life force centered in the spinal canal working directly with the Father in heaven.

All healers working within the wave lengths of selfless love keep their belief, their faith fixed upon the great Physician, Jesus, following His ethic unvaryingly. The desire to be a healer does not make a person a healer. One comes to the world as a healer under Jesus, having earned these powers through training in the laboratory of cosmic reality.

There is no such thing as a "happenstance" healing. In the law of life force, some force of a higher order and some wave lengths have been set into operation to produce spiritual healing. The spiritual scientist through life after life training on the inner planes and through cosmic insight into the life forces of his own energy nature understands that right bacteria, when in balance, support the physical body, cells, and blood; balance and coordination of molecular energies support the life of the etheric body; the harmonious planetary energies support the life of the glandular system and of the ego mind.

To become a healer for God, one must realize that he should observe the rules, the commandments and the ethics as much as is karmically possible in the life of his own nature and being.

A heart consecrated to the love of God makes possible service to one's fellow beings. The akasic records of great healers show that they have in a sequence of former lives lived solely in the wave lengths of loving thoughts toward others. Their soul-records are colored with sacrificial acts, sufferings of the physical body, all for the sake of purification.

Many lives are required to develop diagnostic or intuitive powers to see clearly or clairvoyantly the cause of sickness.

To him who has healed himself of all manner of unfaith and doubting will be given the powers of healing the doubts and fears of others.

Jesus entered this earth free of earth karma. He therefore was out of the range of contagion. Healers yet having to attain the full powers of Jesus must by necessity suffer to some degree along with those for whom they would seek to open the door to healing. The only way one can avoid suffering vicariously through healing others is to become a mediator for God, knowing when to step aside and to let the Father in heaven work directly with him who is sick.

Love is a multiplicity power, uniting and adding to. A healer working to bring alignment into the energy processes of the etheric body does so by opening the corrective wave lengths in health through the power of selfless, mediative love.

All great healers representing the Great Physician have in some former life been alchemists, therapists, chemists, herbalists, masters of symbology. All spiritual healers have been aware of the functioning of the etheric anatomy as vital to the life of man.

Science of the present day has proved that this energy body of ether can be photographed. It is therefore not an illusionary fantasy idea stemming from a psychic mind; but the etheric body and its masses of energy supporting the vital functions of life, while not seen by the physical eye, can be identified and recorded upon the lens of a camera.

To see this body functioning through the eye of clairvoyance is to have X-ray vision. In this present age men will acknowledge more and more that in the etheric body may be found the reflected cause of sickness and also within the etheric body lies the cure or the healing of the sickness.

Extended sight into the etheric body will show that when one is overemotional, self-pitying, the etheric body gives off a cold moistlike atmosphere, depressing to those in the surrounding environment. It will be seen that such persons suffer from circulatory conditions, weakened respiratory tracts, thyroid gland malfunction, and some partial loss of hearing, more often in the left ear.

Research into the repository molecular masses of the lesser etheric body will show that these masses vary with the moods and progressions of the ego mind, that in no two persons do the molecular masses work in the same manner. Every ego expressing individual consciousness and sentient life may be found to have his own design and component patterns of molecular energy flow in his etheric body.

The more highly evolved a person is the more regulated the molecular energy flow. The more sensitive the mind's action is in the ego the more versatile the molecular energy flow receptivity to the incoming flow from cosmic energy, from soul energy.

The influence and the energy activity of the etheric body is reflected into the auric, egg-shaped envelope around the physical body. Through spiritual command, this auric envelope can be widely extended and magnified to touch, color, and influence persons in the world.

In the case of great seers, sages, prophets, the auric envelope reflecting the etheric body of a great personage can cover the earth. In the average person, the auric envelope energized by the lesser etheric body extends only into his personal environment of ego influence.

Every person has an aura, or a reflected sphere outpicturing his thoughts, his emotions, his feelings and desires. The pictures seen and reflected in the auric envelope surrounding the physical body are dependent upon the intensity and charge of energy sent forth from the etheric body. When a highly emotionally charged energy moves out into the auric envelope, it is seen as color. When thought fills an overcharged emotion it may be seen by a clairvoyant as a shape, as a symbol, a reproduction or a true picture of what has been sent forth from the mind of the one thinking.

When one is unprotected in his auric energy field, he can be influenced by the thought, voice, and telepathies from a stronger willed person. When protected, no outside person can impose upon the auric envelope or light of a person any image or picture or symbol. Each person seeks to be in command of his own aura. What is seen on an auric envelope by another person is the reflected picture of things existing in the ego of the person having the aura, and also the superimposed negative telepathies sent into the aura.

One's teacher, Master or guru can erase the karma reflected in the aura as a spiritual touch of grace, thereby lessening the burdens weighing upon the conscience aspect of the mind.

The average student and initiate works to purify his auric light through meditation, contemplation, prayer and mantramic speaking.

If an animal is in the environment of a highly emotional person, the animal receives the overcharged auric emotion as a form of violence upon his solar plexus. Persons sending forth from their auras a continuous stream of unruly emotion, overelectrify their environment.

The etheric or energy body not only pictures into the auric envelope what one feels and thinks, but the energy wave lengths of emotions and thought sent into the auric envelope seal in the pictures of feeling and thought. Thus a person carries the picture of himself as he is. To those less evolved a feeling of unworthiness reflected into the auric envelope is sent back into their feeling world as a form of emotional poison. Therefore, persons who carry with them destroying and violent aspects of their thinking and feeling are repellent.

This is one of the reasons why men should be guided by their first impression as to whether they are attracted to or repelled by a person. If there has been instant recognition and liking between persons, there is a co-atom or balanced equalness and a fusing of the auric wave lengths between such persons.

All healing is first activated in the etheric body, whether it be from medication, surgery, or through faith. When medicine is taken by a child with no understanding of medication, and healing comes, this is due to two things: the impressionable faith in medicine by the one who administers the medicine to the child, and the molecular energy wave length in the medicine being penetrable to the energy malfunction in the etheric body of the child.

In sickness, pain or suffering, the molecular energies of the body are imbalanced. Heavy self-centered pressures in the emotions and thoughts disorganize, break down and interrupt the cyclic flow of life in one or more cells of an organ, upsetting the balance in the cell chain reaction. In looking into the etheric energy body one can see that a sick organ draws to itself an overabundance or mass deposits of psychic energy, taking from one organ to restore another.

Continued negative thinking, fear, and concentrating upon the pain and fear aspects of sickness draw to the sick organ a mass of energy similar to bees actively working in a bee hive. When there is overemphasis of repairing and revitalizing energies around a sick organ, this becomes overconcentrated, and thus the organ rather than being repaired becomes malignant — and death comes.

Every sickness manifested in the physical body has its master counterpart in the etheric body. All healing to be permanent or lasting must reach the molecular mass of energies upholding the master counterpart of the disease.

Unless there is faith and belief in a restoring principle within the life force, the etheric body will not respond to healing for any length of time. There may be relief but there cannot be a total healing until one unites his believing with the restoring principle within the life force as given of the Father.

The breakdown of the etheric body and the disorganization of its energy masses come from lack of faith and disobedience to cosmic law. Long periods of disbelief, discontent and excluding oneself from faith in life are the source and cause of all sickness. There is no greater sickness than the sickness of unbelief.

Chronic ailments, malignant ailments, malfunctions of the body are accumulative karmic conditions. Many lives of unbelief, fear and disorganization in the process of conscience produce malignant diseases.

The disease called cancer is a karmic sickness paying off the accumulative debts of many lives. Man begins physical life in a single cell. The will to live from the moment of his being a tiny microcosmic element in a cell determines the cell life in his total life.

If the ego to be born enters the life stream, reincarnating unwillingly — fearing to fulfill, failing to respond to the sequential law of existence in earth — the result is a resisting and irregular functioning of the etheric or energy body.

If the soul-debts from a past life are heavy, cell structure can be disorganized, and one can suffer ancestral inherited ailments, past-life tendencies to be ill or ailing. The reading of the akasic records shows that some egos suffer the same ailment and die from it in more than one life.

The thread of destiny will not be denied. In each life an opportunity is given to rectify and to learn. To the highly evolved, the ailments of the body are not the main issue of life. They recognize the body to be still in a state of making.

They accept the flaws and frailties of their bodies, knowing the mastery or overcoming is given to them that they may in spite of their weakness fulfill their pattern, pay off their debts, leave something of creation to the world, and thereby attract to themselves in the next life a more perfected instrument so that they may better serve Him who has created all.

If a person has disconnected himself from the restoring principle through disbelief in a former life, he must reunite himself with the restoring principle in each life. All sicknesses work with the balancing principle in life. To have a perfect unison with the restoring principle in the etheric body gives the power to heal, to correct and to bring relief to the physical body. The Father in heaven is in command of the restoring principle. One must be united with the Father in heaven to be healed.

THE MENOPAUSAL YEARS AND THE PSYCHIC NATURE

All persons reaching the forty-second year begin to approach a change in the biological rhythm of their sexual currents, called by some the menopausal years. If one has followed the cyclic rhythms of his spiritual flow with acceptance and receptivity, he will enter into the higher aspect of ESP and he will experience extended spiritual powers.

Personal involvement in karma related to ancestral memory and to one's sexual offenses in a past life are more apparent in the depths of Quelle in this period of life. If there is any remnant of sexual deviation, perversion, Quelle is overstimulated during this period in the life of a man by pressure upon the gonads, the larynx and the thyroid gland; and in the life of the woman, upon the uterine system, the pituitary gland and the heart.

A woman between the years of forty-two and forty-nine, if emotionally immature, undergoes a psychic pressure both pathological and psychological. Past-life karma regarding motherhood, children and marriage will be aroused through the action of Quelle. Menstrual flow in these years becoming erratic will open certain lunar psychic forces in her nature. If karma is heavy, psychic pressure will cause her to fear, to distrust, and even in some instances to withdraw from her responsible activities in the world.

In this phase of a hysterical woman's life, psychic power is negatively magnified, acute, clouded with suspicion, jealousy. If a woman is highly evolved in these years, the menopausal state will be worked out in the mechanics of the etheric body. The processes of the sexual force will be sublimated into a higher range of mentality, assuring a superior degree of expansion in the mind. Spiritual experience will occur with clarity and authenticity.

Advanced women and men initiates work in these years to gain control of their sexual natures. The male initiate is biologically exposed at all times to race compulsions. It is his work during the forty-second to forty-ninth year to master the suggestible and impressionable race compulsions playing upon his sexual system. In these years the recapitulation of ancestral memory seeks to give to him the impersonalized racial impulses.

The Propagation Angels working on all men more extensively during these years play upon his glandular system seeking to compel him to beget and therefore bring additional offspring to the world. A highly evolved male initiate is not an exception in these years. Being more sensitive than one who has yielded to every sexual impulse, he will undergo severe trials from the racial sex compulsions. In the night hours through dreams he will be exposed to the subtle worlds where dwell the suggestible influences preying upon the chastity ideals of men.

All male initiates undergo these trials. At the end of the forty-fifth year certain mitigation occurs. As it is necessary in these years for a man to incorporate into his nature the higher aspect of the feminine principle, he may begin to change in his temperament, apparent in one of two ways. If less highly evolved, he will become hypersensitive rather than a balanced sensitive. If highly evolved, he will incorporate the higher feminine aspect of his nature. He will become spiritually sensitive, and thereafter render a balanced service in the world.

Psychic flow from a fallen initiate who fails to rise over the challenges in these years becomes degraded and shaded. ESP power gained by a male initiate in these years becomes an instrument for the light.

Male initiates in the present time are embattled in a war, that they may become avatars of the heart. In no time in spiritual history has the male initiate been under such intensification of pressure, that he might become a heart initiate and render service for God. To win this prize, initiates, both male and female, must know themselves, their motivation, keeping their eyes fixed upon the light and only the light.

OLD AGE AND THE PSYCHIC NATURE

On reaching the fifty-sixth year all persons return to an enlarged dependency upon Quelle. Psychic pressure formerly focused upon the sexual nature, now turns toward the absorption of a certain kind of memory. Memory flow when oversaturated with Quelle gives to the mind introspective moods in which the ego of a person, or the "I," functions by extracting perceptive and intuitive wisdom from life-force memory, ancestral memory, ego memory, and soul memory.

If one has fallen short of spiritual and soul interflow, and if he has failed to unite his actions harmoniously between his will, memory and imagination, and if he has failed to channel with purity the sexual fire within his life force, he experiences a psychic sub-charge of destroying molecular energies. In this period, inherent weaknesses of the physical body coincide with personal karma, producing chronic afflictions identifying the karmic cause of laggardness in the ego-tempo.

All ailments of chronic nature affecting a mature person enable him to receive from the depths of his subconscious mind or Quelle certain widened insight. In one who has persisted in a selfish, egotistical pressured way, Quelle seeks to introduce into the mind, heart and will a chastened spirit, that the person in a coming life may enter into the world with humility.

In the latter years of one's life, psychic energy no longer being fully focused upon the sexual, or that of begetting, in the highly evolved person sexual flow is sublimated into an illuminative side of the mind. In a person less than fifty-six years of age, all sexual life is under the pressure of psychic force and psychic energy. In the latter years this psychic force and energy should be shifted upward to the heart and to the mind.

The spinal fires feeding the higher mentality are more rightly channeled in the mentality of a highly evolved person. Thus, in the history of the spiritual life — with the exception of Jesus — all spiritual life is more perfectly manifested after one reaches the fifty-sixth year.

Only in highly evolved persons is the sexual psychic force completely equalized and balanced. By the normal rhythmic flow of spiritual events, all persons should enter into their spiritual interflow and command of their psychic natures on reaching their fifty-sixth year.

Ancestral psychic power is drawn forth and manifested in an older person as a family *knowing* and intuition; this knowing does not come from one's own knowing or singular experience, but with Quelle help this aged knowing psychic power stems from some extra or ultra flow of available ancestral knowledge.

In the latter years, persons who have access to psychic powers and desiring to spiritualize their motives, give invaluable help to the young and sometimes even to their adult children.

It is out of the order of the natural ancestral flow for one who has reached mature years to be estranged from his children and grandchildren. Only in extreme egotism and self-centeredness in certain karmic instances is a mature person separated psychically, emotionally, and mentally from those whom he has begotten or given bodies to for the world. Therefore, in the aged, psychic power manifests itself first in the recollection of ancestral strengths rather than weaknesses.

Quelle working with maturity produces memory of the present-life faults on the level of ego-karma. One learns in these years that he cannot erase this life's karma by merely saying "What is done is done." If he is spiritually honest, he looks upon the spectres of his present-life faults with a determination to rectify and balance in some manner weaknesses of ego-character of the lower mind and the lower will. He determines in some manner to render a selfless service on the level of friendship, man to man and society, that he may set into motion the mechanics of a better pattern for the next life.

The highly intuitive aged person recognizes within his own nature the necessity to regulate the flow of psychic force and pressure in his nature, to come to peace with life, its rules and its demands.

The erratic aged have the power through psychic force to agitate, to offend, and to curse the works and acts of the young. A selfish aged person using psychic power through cunning to gain extra unearned benefits for his aging years, for his comforts, at the expense of others in his family or society, makes himself in the next life improvident, poor. The survival instinct in the selfish aged becomes abnormal, overstressing certain aggressions out of flow with releasing love. Such persons set up forces of separation for the next life.

Spiritual soul-memory in the latter years produces higher ESP. From such persons come a true overlook and perception into a hope for the future. Writings, art, music produced in the mature years of one's life unite, blend, and harmonize the uniting points in the souls of men yet to be born to earth.

All egos reaching the mature wisdom of years foresee a future of promise in the upward rise of man, knowing that one life is not sufficient for all that must be done in the wonderful world of consciousness. They anticipate and invite the experiences of death as a natural portion and process of the unbroken thread of eternality.

Psychic powers in the aged can be astute, pure, healing, or they can be in reverse, cunning, deceptive, hallucinatory, senile. The senile aged mentality lives in the lower astral planes. Their fantasies are built upon chimera falsity. One who has developed senility through overpressured concepts of the mind, fanatical enforcements of the will, ruthless thrusting for place and power, is exposed in dream and in waking to the psychic chimeras of the lower astral world.

It is often the case that many persons living with senile persons do not recognize themselves to be victims of astral psychic pressure. It is also little understood why in dying some aged persons suffering strokes or paralysis enter into states of coma for a long period of time. It is not always understood that coma before death enables one to live on the inner planes while yet partially functioning in the physical body. Persons entering into coma before death, if in a state of grace from good works, experience something of the paradise to come. Persons having regrets due to negative actions, while in coma live in a state between agony and purgatory. Thus something of remorse prepares them for magnified introspection after death.

The Death Angels watching over both the negative and good in a dying state impress upon the mind of the one dying the need to rectify.

Psychic powers do not die or wither either in the living or the dead. Psychic energy in each life is gathered up and processed for the use of coming lives. Psychic power is encapsuled in the image of the identity to come.

Psychic power in the after-death life, not having physical restraints, can be disastrously used after death by an evil and revengeful mind. Psychic powers after death can be used by the pure to bless, to stimulate, to assure and to heal.

Medical science, through opening the door to the psychic processes and the energy fields supporting life will change X-ray techniques, the use of certain types of anesthesia methods and totally discard the use of antibiotics. Also they will refrain from the use of subliminal drugs affecting the mind of man.

Fixed ethics will appear in the medical profession regarding the two important factors supporting health and the human life. These ethics will especially temper and guide research procedures in the field of genetics and in the thought processes of man.

The new ethic pertaining to the energy age will give safeguards to the right of man as a willing and choosing individual. There will be a time before this occurs, but it will inevitably come.

It has been considered ethical until now to protect man from himself. In the future it will be considered ethical to give man the right to be himself. As time progresses and science leans more towards the ethic of mercy, the individual as a spiritual unit of God will be given the right of way to develop within the nobler and divine elasticity of his being.

Certain herbs and plants growing in the earth have tremendous psychic vitality. To discover through a selective palate and through the clairsentient gift of smelling what herbs or plants are conducive to the health of the etheric body will give freedom to the etheric body. It has long been known that sage, basil, rosemary and chamomile are psychically charged herbs. Cumin which is so often spoken of in the Scriptures has been known for ages to have a calming effect upon an extensively charged etheric body.

Psychical curative herbal arts open themselves to one who has spiritual grace. Nutritional laws are angelically oriented. When there is grace, the angels of the agrarian and dietary laws will open the clairsentient sense of smelling which functions also through the palate to the needed herb to give relief to the weaknesses in the etheric body.

Herbs do not heal the physical body. Herbs heal the etheric body, that the etheric body may set and direct the pattern of health in the physical body. One works with etheric preventive laws when he knowingly uses herbs to give a certain life renewing to the etheric body.

Psychical preventive herbal arts prove that each herb and plant of the earth has its degree or tone rate of psychical energy. Persons aided or healed by the psychical energies in an herb must have an equal tone rate or degree of psychical energy to the herb needed for the body that healing may come.

The clairsentient tuning fork of one's smelling and tasting will identify the psychical energy in the herb necessary for his healing and rejuvenation.

Unpolarized Energy in the Etheric Body

The power of psychic force generates more densely and strongly on the left side of the body in the unknowing or untrained psychic. When one is unbalanced as to psychic density, having less psychic energy on the right side of his body, he is weakened in etheric vitality on the right side of his body. Being unpolarized, he suffers depletion to the organs of the right side of the body.

When the psychic energy is more prevalent in the left side of the body, all psychic injuries are registered on the left side of the body, overcharging the organs on the left side of the body. When the spleen, the stomach, the left lung, the left kidney, the left side of the intestines, the left gonad are over-charged with psychic fire, the body goes out of focus or out of the range of regeneration.

One should seek to bring equalization to the psychic charges of force generating in both the left and right side of the body. He does this by meditation, contemplation, selfless service and creativity.

Overexcitation of any one of the senses produces an over-flow of psychic energy in the mind. Certain aspects of psychic thoughts generate excess power, cultivating the egoist side of one's nature. To remain at peace, one should unite with the polarized harmonies provided by *peace intervals* in the emotions and thoughts. Eventually such practice will bring a continuous flow of God-inwardness.

To polarize psychic energy and come to peace, one should begin by *listening* to the inward silence called the Hum in the Rishis' teachings; in the Bible, called Holy Ghost. "Be still, and know that I am God. . ." (Psalm 46:10)

POSTURE AND SHAPE OF THE BODY

One only needs to look upon the shape and development of the physical body after the age of thirty-five to see where psychic charge is more heavily concentrated. If the body turns more to the right through posture, shoulders, buttocks, or in the walk, psychic density is more heavily charged on the left side of the body. If the body leans more in direction of the left, psychic density is more active on the right side of the body. When psychic energy is equally polarized, one has an erect, flexible posture. A stiff unbending posture is the result of a fixed energy indicating its locality at the portion of the spine upholding the kidney structure. Such persons are unrelenting and unforgiving in their natures.

Psychic energy density settled more heavily in the end of the spine keeps alive the sexual aggressiveness.

To equalize the spinal fire controlling psychic density requires discipline, repetition of spiritual practices, and particularly devotion. One can through love change the etheric mold contours controlling his psychic energy fields, and thus give to his physical body better posture with more equalized vitality when he polarizes himself through cosmic exercises of the will, mind and emotions. This begins with mantramic sounding, prayers, creativity for freeing and commanding the psychic density charge, giving life to the shape of the body. The rhythmic breathing flow of selflessness with total love surrender to the life forces shaping the body will give health, beauty, vitality.

The appearance of the physical body, the life emanation dwelling in the eye, the shape, weight, the contours, the facial characteristics and features — all are self made through union or non-union with the life force dwelling within the etheric or energy body.

Uncontrolled psychic force in the etheric body produces disproportion in some degree in the outward or physical body.

Love animates and frees psychic flow, distributes psychic energy density, regulates health in mind and body. To love something, someone, and above all, God, is to build a body of grace appearance for coming lives.

When one is repellent to some other person as to appearance, this is caused by the malformation processes of the psychic force within the etheric body. All persons resent pressure and withdraw inwardly from persons having pressure. Psychic pressure causes repulsion, creates destruction, and to one exerting pressure, the result is isolation and death.

TIMING AND HEALING

Through spiritual union with the light of the Christ, the karmic cause in sickness is eliminated. The great spiritual Masters and teachers, and the greatest of all teachers — Jesus — are able to bend time, that one may look backward into the cause of sickness and gather its lesson. The Ancient of Days working with the Christ enables one to break into particles the energy-pressure time element, causing karma to be distributed according to one's strength and capacity. Under Christ, karma is instantaneously erased and the time condensation of energy is literally revised and reproportioned — and the past and present offenses against the body and the mind cease to register upon the senses, the body and the mind. One moves into the most high wave lengths of life and energy under the power of timelessness through Christ.

XIII

THE AURA AND THE HEALTH

Spiritual scientists recognize the body to be a marvelous, delicate, sensitive instrument imaged by Eternal Spirit. Throughout history it has been shown that men who have had a fearless outlook on life, an enthusiastic response to life and a hopeful vision for things to come, have refused to wholly surrender themselves to the frailties of their bodies. Being engrossed with the vital perception creative influences, their minds being stimulated by the ultra-sense values in their souls, they have lived beyond their pain and suffering and have set out a path for those who would understand and know the true resources lying *within* each person.

Stubbornly ignoring body ailments is not health. Refusing to admit one suffers is no anesthesia. There is something more to the command of the etheric energy body by the mind than the belief that one can *will away* pain or suffering by just willing. The pendulum action of cause and effect reveals

250

to the spiritual scientist that to seek to force-will away pain and suffering is to set up a stream of retaliative causes in Quelle.

Faith is not an act of will. Faith is an acceptance of an all-powerful law supported by the alchemy of universal harmony and spiritual love. Faith, in looking on sickness, recognizes a just law at work, a divine law at work. A mind saturated with faith evaluates cause, prays for guidance, right protection, acceptance, strength, wisdom.

A spiritual scientist, when faced with a malignant disease within his own organism, works not with self-accusatory thoughts beholding punishment for wrongdoing; the spiritual scientist blesses the divine law of exact and just correction. He sees any ailment of his body as being corrective and as a means by which he may correct, adjust and become more flexible and resilient in the cosmic scheme of existence.

A man sick with a malignancy is similar to a man caught on the ledge of a mountain between a steep precipice upward and a chasm below; he must either fall into the pit of despera- tion, or he must by faith scale a seemingly impassable height. So must one caught into the deep emotions and thoughts ac- companying the diagnostic fatality of a malignant disease, scale the height in his reach to God.

It would seem to the mind of the one having an irreparable condition in his body that he is surrounded by blindness, in- difference and a chain of ignorance, and that there is no human emotion around him capable of understanding the extent of his suffering. He concludes that he must turn either to total atheism or to a total faith in God.

To accept gives peace to the mind; to cease resisting slows down the mass of hissing velocities in the energies persevering in the destruction of one's body. His pause into peace and acceptance enables the spiritual wave lengths of the angels and those who would aid in his healing to reach him, to redistribute and to rechannel the molecular mass of energies clustered around the diseased portion of his body, that they may be slowed down and thus move back into other organs of his body from which this mass has been stolen. In this instance karma may be said to be ended and consummated. The accumulated debts from past lives have been resolved.

A person is in a state of grace when he has been born with great reserves of mass energy in his etheric body. Such reserves enable him to withstand the trials of his initiations and in some instances add to his years of life, or step out of the timing element, and thus serve God without break or interruption by death.

In the great Himalayas there are living Masters who have known the science of lengthening the years of the body. These great Masters are not only Masters working to initiate those ready for greater spiritual powers; such Masters remain in their physical bodies for hundreds of years so that they need not undergo the inconvenience of being born again.

All persons engrossed in the spiritual life gradually learn the science of timelessness, one of these being the reversing of the energy flow of time for those needing help in sickness. Through knowledge of the law of timing and timelessness, some healers and teachers rearrange the karma of their students or those they would help who are caught into fixed states of karma.

When a man dies, it is not how long he has lived that is important. It is what he has done with his years of living. One's achievement in the works of light is retained after death; only this lives in eternal time. All else can be reversed, changed, erased or rearranged through the ethical will of an initiate or of a Master.

In the mid-1800's some men in the Western world became aware of the occult side of learning, and until now the average person has more or less resigned or given over to the occultist the research into the invisible or little-known laws governing the inner nature of man.

Science now becoming interested in the biological energy phase of the psychic and unseen nature makes it possible for every man to discern and thus come to know this side of his being. Psychic nature always thought of as being a private world, a secret world, now men are engaged in experimentation with extrasensory motivation and its phenomena, and thus the personal psychic world will become more and more important to the individual. Every fragment of information, every look, and every phase of psychic intelligence and information no longer belong to the private person. All persons are to be informed, that they may learn more of the wonderful working and ingenious mechanization supporting all conscious life.

For many years persons working in occult research concerned themselves with the human aura. With inner sight or second sight some claimed to see and interpret the aura; among these were those who based their total research on the psychic nature through reading of the aura.

Scrying or seership is a versatile art. Any form of open sightedness or seership when used in a wholesome manner can be focused into any media, producing visions; for all forms, objects, or persons are maintained by ether. When clairvoyance is a perfected spiritual art, one can see visions in any object by fixing his gaze upon its mass. Auric scrying through the scientific use of electronic instruments can at present verify that man has an aura, that it is similar to an envelope of electronic energy, and also that it maintains the life of all growing and living objects, from plant to man.

The spiritual scientist will come more and more to see that the aura around each person, while egglike and totally encasing the body, is a most necessary vehicle complementing the energy processes of the etheric body, and is also a radiating vehicle for outpicturing and extending the emotional and mental processes of the individual.

The auric egg is a capsule of vital akasic energy. To believe that it is but a reflector mirroring the emotions and thoughts is to limit one's utilization of this knowledge.

The aura surrounding the physical body is a sounding board, radar system protecting man from the outer penetration and intrusion of overconcentrated cosmic energy. It also protects man from the heavier sound vibrations coming from the clamors and sounds in the world, giving insulation against the deadlier vibrational aspects of the planets and from the sun and the moon. This enables each person to hear the echo of his thoughts and his emotions, giving him the opportunity to have an afterlook into his conduct and thinking.

The auric energy field has a miniature universal and cosmic system of its own. It is neo-spiritual in that it retains man's thinking and feeling in reflected light and keeps it alive so that man can have access to it at all times as an aid to his memory and learning process. As the world-soul retains in akasic ether the memory of all things achieved in light by the souls of men, the auric neo-spiritual atmosphere keeps alive man's identity.

God planted this field of living reflection around man to protect him as an individual, that he might experience sacred privacy and make himself impenetrable to those who would infringe upon the soul right of his own evolvement; for even though men are communicable through their souls, God gave to each man his own green pasture of aloneness. This is the auric envelope and energy field around his physical body. This sphere of being belongs to him and to him alone.

In a great saint, sage or avatar, the ego having a magnificent aura of akasic purity sets no boundary to his aura, as he has mastered his nature within, and thus his auric field does not violate the aura of anyone.

In a person who is yet immature in spiritual evolvement, the auric envelope, while protective, can be an unyielding offensive separative obstacle to the communing with other men in the world.

Unbelieving men, agnostic men, atheistic men are encased in dense impenetrable auras. Their psychic lower minds engrossed in materiality give off only occasional penetrational flashes; this occurs only when there is some particular thing they want or desire.

There are sick auras giving off unhealthy atmospheres from persons who live in despairing mental energy climates. Such persons give off a cold wetlike aura, chilling and depressing to those who are near. Clairvoyant vision into a hardened egotistical aura sees fixed, rigid, unyielding thought forms stalagmitized and mirrored into the aura. The clairvoyant sees in the depressed auric light grey ghostlike vapor thought forms surging and resurging, giving off the feeling of unwept tears or the need for release.

A person of a psychically overenergized mind and emotion has a scattered auric pattern, disturbing to one who stands near and by sharing the personal environment.

To stand in the presence of an aura of a person pure in heart and purely motivated is also to receive peace and stillness into one's own auric envelope.

Until a healer has gained peace he cannot give peace. One has either instantaneous rapport with the aura of another person, or he has a withdrawing and repulsion to the auric light of another. This attracting and repelling law is infallible in auric proximity and association.

Some persons in the world having misused psychic laws in former lives and in this life have damaged the impenetrable cosmic ring-pass-not of the auric envelope. The outer rim of the aura is a mass encirclement of gamma rays collected from the sun. These rays act as repelling protectors to shield each person from intrusion, depletion, from forceful wills of persons, from the heavy cosmic charges of raw energies pounding upon man in every second and moment of his life.

Should man have abused the energy laws of his own etheric body, the ring-pass-not border of his auric encasement is broken open. He thus exposes himself to the raw elements of cosmic energy. The ring-pass-not can only be mended through the help of insulating angels and the work of a master spiritual technician. This requires long intervals of supervision, training and healing.

The breakdown in the aura is a catastrophe in life, requiring many lives to rebuild and to reconstruct the tenuous fabric of the auric envelope which is a delicate, intricate and superhuman task. Few in the world suffer such total tragedy, only those who have offended for long periods suffer this shattering of their auric envelope.

One can reverse the spiritual currents of his aura by wrong acts or long periods of amoral functioning. He can permanently reverse the reflected pictures in the aura back towards himself, and thus suffer extreme stages of agony accompanied by remorse. In this manner karma is burned out or expiated. It is a natural process for the auric reflected pictures gathered from the energy patterns of mind and thought to flow outward. To reverse and draw them inward upsets the natural flow of the auric light, causing pain.

Telepathy is a science of mind to mind in which one uses the same wave length of willing and sending his thoughts into the equal wave length of the one receiving his thoughts. Thought transference is made possible through the auric light.

The auric envelope or body is a pulsating and vibrating envelope and body. If one has looked into a boiling kettle and seen the pressure of heat upon water bubbling just before a violent boil, one can visualize exactly the state and movement of vibration in the auric light around the physical body.

The ego-tone of the mind, the heart beat, the soul's pulsation and the auric pulse, all should be at one. When there is excessive excitation the ego-tone accelerates the auric movement. An accelerated aura may be more clearly interpreted by a clairvoyant than a passive or sub-vibrating aura.

Reflected thoughts gathered into the auric light from the ego-tone of the mind are communicable, needing no will from a person to be sent or received by another. Thus, when a person is in a state of creation, with his ego engrossed, his auric vibration movement is intensified. There is an overflow of creation which can penetrate the auras of other men. His thoughts become automatically transferable to minds having equal auric creative pressure. So are ideas passed seemingly by accident from one mind to another. This is also an operative law for negative thinking. If one is intensively negative, he sets up the processes for others on the same chain wave length to become more negative. However, one can seal the aura away from coercive minds and forces.

The aura makes it possible for the thoughts of men to become mentally and emotionally contagious to one another. The radar system of the aura makes it possible for men to echo one another's thought. Either positive or negative thought processes are exchangeable through the reflected action of the human aura.

Some clairvoyants having been initiated into the science of the stars affecting the aura of man, his spinal system and his glands — having understanding of the astral core around the spinal canal — are able to read in the auric light surrounding the physical body the astrological processes of one's destiny; for in the light of the auric envelope is also reflected the mystic chart of birth, of past incarnations, and of life destiny. Persons able to penetrate the reflected auric zodiacal wheel can tell the second and moment of birth, as it is seen upon the auric envelope. They can also see with a perfect prognostication things to come in the initiatory processes as related to planetary aspects. Through reading what is called *constellation* in the auric light, one can identify the major steps of initiation to be set off by planetary action.

The aura is a necessary attribute of the memory. Were it not for the aura, the memory system of man would be inactive. The screenlike reproductions of remembered acts and thoughts are vital in the mind processes of man.

Quelle, the subconscious, enables man to forget certain things too painful to remember. The auric reflection enables man to remember as long as it is necessary to retain the impression of something experienced vital to the stages of his evolvement.

When Quelle timing is ready to lift the veil of forgetfulness, it is outpictured upon the living auric light, that man may return to it again and again until it has been neutralized into his stream of consciousness.

PROCESSES OF THE AURA

Many people dream of glass walls and windows in the night. This represents protection of the auric field.

A lunar psychic with the power of ESP perceives in the aura of a person the state of health first as color, secondly as vibration. From the color he knows the emotional state;

from the vibration he learns the cause. The tone of the ego in each person is in command of his body. The Word sustaining all life is the Eternal Spirit. In man it is individualized in the Stele, or sacred starry point between his eyebrows.

When the tone of the body is disorganized through past-life karmic pressures, the result is inharmony in the tone range of spirit in the body, and the result is maladjusted energy in the etheric body and an agitated pulsation in the auric envelope. Lunar psychics diagnosing through auric insight see this reflected disharmony and learn to interpret it. However, as no two auras are alike in their outpicturing of pain or pleasure, a person using psychic sight is always in a state of learning. While there is some symbolic similarity to identify underlying cause, the innumerable and infinite aspects of symbolic ideation limit each person having psychic powers to interpret what he sees with a different interpretation. Thus, though it is an aggravating truth, it would seem that no two lunar psychics agree as to what is seen in the auric light. This is confusing to one unfamiliar with the psychic arts and has been one of the causes for limited belief in extrasensory diagnosis revealing the unseen cause in health of mind and body, and has been used as a lever against research into extrasensory powers.

The primal etheric healer sees all things in the aura in a chlorophyll-like mist. He may be recognized by having an oval and partly obtruding eye, usually a rounded or high forehead and a general roundness to the upper portion of his head. He lives in a mystic light, being more often mystically shrewd rather than mentally practical. In his healing arts he draws upon the chlorophyll essences of Nature. He sees the auric light of a person through a form of moving vapor. He diagnoses and interprets the auric light first through the health band of chlorophyll residing inwardly alongside the gamma fire surrounding the auric envelope. This chlorophyll band registering health and vitality is a pure deep green, the color of translucent chlorophyll. It is needle-like, similar to porcupine quills, each quill being microscopic in size. A coiled mass of green energy exists in the outer encirclement of all healthy persons. Residing on the inward boundary of the gamma fire, it is a vitalizing green blood reinforcement of life, giving energy transfusions to the etheric body.

When one is anemic — resisting life, non-responding, noncaring — the lunar psychic sees this band of green to be bile green in color. The total auric light is colored by splotches of unhealthy green similar to solar flares in the auric light. In the time of approaching death, this chlorophyll band of life becomes brown, and finally grey, to disappear and fade out altogether. Thus, death can be predicted through the aura by the lunar psychic with primal etheric sight.

Some lunar psychics not having vision or second sight diagnose the auric light through feeling or clairsentience. In absence or in presence of sickness, they can draw into their own auric envelopes the condition as registered in the aura of another person, taking it into their own auras, even feelng themselves to be the person, taking on his personalized thought processes and attitudes. Such lunar psychics, when failing to use the ethic of detachment, take upon themselves the conditions, especially if in the use of their minds they judge or condemn the person. As a rule such persons have not understanding of karmic law, and thus judge with harsh judgments rather than releasing through the ethic of love.

Clairsentient lunar psychics are endangered psychically more than the clairvoyant lunar psychic. In clairvoyance one is not emotionally involved in what he sees. In clairsentience one is totally involved in what he feels. To give correct diagnosis through clairsentience, one must be emotionally involved in what he feels and intuits.

The magnetism in the auric light of a clairsentient lunar psychic can be stripped, devitalized. Such persons may become victims of their unknowing misuse of psychic power.

Until men learn to truly command and utilize the full capacity of their psychic resources in equal degree to their heart impulses and higher mind extrasensory impulses, they will be takers rather than givers. All persons experimenting with and experiencing and exploring the psychic arts must guard their ethic in their receiving and their giving.

The ego-tone determines that each person's aura has one signifying color. This is the major prismatic spiritual tone, called by some their own master color tone. This color tone permeates the auric light from the chlorophyll band inward, in no way interfering with other symbolic color forms flashing in and out of the auric field; yet the master color tone diffuses its color into the total auric egg or envelope. In the case of an aura being seen through inner sight, some persons may see an extremely sensitive spiritual person's auric field as a violet rosy color, and believe this to be the only color of the person's auric light. Indeed, it is the supporting color; however, with deeper research into the auric light one may see various colors and patterns forming and shaping as they are sent forth from the mind, the thoughts, the emotions, and feelings.

In the case of intense emotion, feeling or concentrated attentiveness in thought, all auras become diffused with one light — the blue light of akasia, indigo in color. This is caused by the innermost Eternal Spirit flame dwelling in the spinal canal around which the astral core is activated.

When a person is in a deep state of meditation, this akasia blue flame takes command of one's own master color tone in the aura. All spiritual persons seek to maintain as long as possible this blue flame in the auric light, as this blue akasia flame coming from the spinal canal has the power to erase all negative colorings, all negative reflected thoughts and emotions registered upon the light of the auric envelope.

All great Masters and gurus maintain this akasia blue flame of the Eternal Spirit in their auras. Thus, they are able to disconnect the rigid karmic reflections in the auric light of their chelas or disciples, and thereby release them from a chain of continuity in karma. This is the first step that occurs between the Master and the disciple. The blue auric light of the spinal fire of the Master literally consumes and burns away the first phases of karmic entanglement of his disciple.

It is necessary for the disciple to be free of the repetitious thought and feeling patterns he had used over many lives. The disciple is instructed by the Master through the mental love-circuit of telepathy how to meditate, to contemplate, and to keep open the Stele point between the brows where dwells his own identity command tone, so that he may sustain his auric light in purity.

An animal psychically interconnected in the point of his solar plexus to his master's aura is aware of the approaching death of his master. When the chlorophyll band begins to fade in the aura of his master, the animal becomes restless, confused, and anguished.

All animals are astrally and psychically attached to the auric light of their master's aura. The solar-plexus auric light of the animal is activated and reflected through the habit pattern of the master's auric light.

An animal's aura is centered around the navel and the solar plexus. Something of the solar-plexus fire in the animal dies when the auric pulsation slows down in the auric light of his master.

The aura of a human person becomes shell-like as a curved open hand acting in a radar fashion to an animal. When an animal is lost, the radar action in the aura of his master beckons and signals the direction of his return to the homeplace of his master. The animal is thus drawn back to his master by the radar pull in the auric light. This is also active between persons who are psychic finders of lost persons and objects.

If one has been murdered, his auric light remains close to his body for a period of three and one-half days. If a psychic is given the assignment to find the clues to an unnatural death, he should be given them during the period of three and one-half days, so that he may more perfectly penetrate and contact the life processes of thinking and feeling of the person who has been murdered. After a period of three and one-half days, the auric light having faded perceptively, one must depend upon another aspect of ESP, and this is communication with the soul-light of the one who has died rather than with the auric light.

Should the murder have been a karmic rectification — that is, if one in other lives had been a murderer and thus attracted murder to himself — the one who has died is unable to communicate knowledge of the cause of his death. Only in the case of imbalance in justice will the one dead reveal the cause of his murder and impress upon others the need to pursue its cause.

If there is unbalanced karma in a murder, the law of rectification will see to it that in some manner the murderer will be found. While it is not always known that the disclosure of the murderer comes from the one murdered, forces will be set up to put the finger of discovery upon one who has murdered as an instrument to balance karmic cause.

DIAGNOSIS AND KARMA

A clairsentient psychic feels his clues for diagnosis through the use of primal intuition. A pure and true clairvoyant sees his clue through the use of higher extrasensory mind. He recognizes it, and identifies the cause in karma. If his own aura is free of the particular degree of karma instigating the cause, he can set up forces of healing in the auric light of the one sick, but if the clairvoyant happens to have karma himself of similar degree to the karma of the one sick, he can diagnose, but will fail to heal.

The solar-initiate clairvoyant with extrasensory mending heals as he sees. Such healers are rare in the world. The solar initiate is both clairvoyant and clairsentient. If he desires, he can temporarily relieve the pain in suffering without pain to himself through a vicarious drawing into his own auric light the pattern of the cause of suffering. Through extended akasic light, he can fight and battle to dissolve the effect and adjust the cause.

Many persons having incurable and excruciatingly painful diseases are eased in the most anguished, painful side of their dying by vicarious anesthesias received from a spiritual healer of high evolvement.

DEATH AND THE AURA

All men survive death and live in some state of consciousness after death. Some sleep in swoonlike sleep for ages or aeons. The physical body does not survive death; however, the record of the body and its action in the earth is retained in the miniature etheric encasement around the seed-atom of the heart. When death comes, the aura is dissolved, and the essence of its record and also the soul-medallion's record flow into the etheric encasement of the sacred atom of the heart.

All of the processes of the aura, of the energy action of the etheric body, the functioning of the astral core, and the soul-medallion's action — all are retained after death in the higher etheric body, called the everlasting body. Nothing is lost out of the soul's sojourn on earth, that the good may be weighed against the negative.

After death, the pulsation of the soul, located in the center of the soul's medallion, becomes the heart beat for the everlasting body. The sacred atom of the heart is kept alive in a state of vibration through the pulsation of the soul. Like a winged angel fanning its wings, the pulsation of the soul keeps alive the spiritual processes of the everlasting body after death.

The higher etheric body or everlasting body does not have an aura. Only in the physical world does man have an auric encasement. The auric vehicle is a protective vehicle to protect man from the forces of gravity, the cosmic energies and the fiery pressures of the planetary energies playing upon the physical body, the etheric body and the astral core around the spine.

The auric light during physical life is a protective, absorptive and reflective armor, that the physical body may absorb the energies in a secondary action. The auric light acts as a radar system to reflect the unconscious forces flowing from the inner life of man, and to co-mingle these forces with the cosmic energies of earth and the planets.

In death, the auric light and its reflected patterns flow into the sacred atom of the heart; and man after death becomes dependent upon the *soul-medallion's sheath* or envelope, the everlasting body and the eternal atoms therein, and also the akasic fire he has retained from the astral core of his being to give permeability on the inner planes of life after death.

When one prepares to be born again into another existence or life, the soul's sheath of the previous existence becomes intensely active due to the quickened pulsation in the soul's medallion. Through the intensified vibration of the soul's sheath and the soul's medallion, one is drawn back to earth to be born again. The record of good written on the soul's medallion, and the errors recorded on the vibratory hum of the soul's medallion, draw the ego to where he is to be born, to the parents who are to give him birth, determining what he will do and how he will live in the coming life on earth.

The aura of one to be born is activated from the moment the soul plans to return to earth. And the pictures of former lives move towards earth existence, overshadowing the parents who give him birth. Ages before Jesus was born His aura was overshadowing the world.

When an ego prepares to enter the earth, the auric vehicle sets up its processes once more. If there should be non-acceptance of his coming, the auric vehicle becomes inactive. If his auric vehicle fails to reach responding souls to give him birth, he must remain on the inner planes until the timing in the physical world will prove more receptive to his coming to birth.

If the karmic records from past lives reflected in the auric light of the mother and the ego coming to birth fail to blend, there is a rejection between the mother's aura and the ego's aura; the result is a miscarriage or a stillborn child or a child born subconsciously aware of primal rejection.

In the life after death, depending upon the soul-record, one may be conscious or unconscious. If one believes that death is the end, after death he is unconscious in a womblike sleep, unaware of the processes of life after death and also unaware of his soul's selection to re-enter the earth. But if one is aware of the law of eternality, he looks upon life after death as a return to a world familiar to him in the processes of birth, life, and death. He takes up his soul duties on the inner planes where he left off in other times of having died. Such persons are united with spiritual reality, grateful to have laid aside a body no longer useful. After death, such persons review their previous life's action with impartial retrospection and introspection. Contrition for actions inharmonious to the soul's desire is undergone when necessary. Resolutions are made for coming life actions. A seed is planted for coming works of the earth. The one having died goes about his spiritual creations on the inner planes, that his inner-plane works may fall as blessings into the minds of those whom he loved and respected on earth.

Many persons seeking to understand the invisible processes motivating the soul, the mind, and the life beyond the grave are confused by terminologies, by fragmentary and fantastic ideas regarding life after death. To be wholly unbiased and to truly unite with the informing principle regarding death and life, one should acknowledge that he knows very little about life or death. He should, however, be grateful that he is seeking to learn, and he should be always in a state of desiring that he learn rightfully, and that his knowledge be uncolored by psychic distortions given off by fantasy.

One should never say to himself that the spiritual body, the soul and the spiritual life are incomprehensible to him. He must be just, giving full play to his understanding by remembering that until now he has had very little understanding of the physical-body processes, taking them for granted, using his physical vehicle without thought of its true origin. If he looks truly into himself at this time, he will see that he has little understanding of the body processes.

The spiritual body is far more intricately made than the physical body. To study the intricate processes of the spiritual body, of the soul, and of the spiritual life, one comes to understand more of his physical body and therefore learns to live a life of fulfillment while living in the world.

The knowledge of the etheric-body processes and the complex energy system of this body will widen the perspective and understanding of the worlds of the soul, the mind, and the body. Knowledge of these worlds is presently converging. The scientific ethic is never to deny that a thing exists until it has been proven not to exist; and if the scientists of this age are true to themselves, they will record the universal intelligence overdirecting the master plan supporting the life of man on earth.

In every era men give different names to God. Science will name Him and acknowledge Him. And through this, men will come to harness resources of the soul, and thus produce the mind as envisioned through Christ.

At the moment of birth, the zodiac is imprinted into the auric field of the one being born, the auric envelope being activated once again receives its cosmic starry message; the planets are configured and indented. Anyone having solar-initiate clairvoyant powers can turn the key into this wheel of the stars determining the underlying processes of the akasic-records compulsions, the soul compulsions, and the destiny to be.

No ancestral pattern in the cell of man can compare, challenge or make void the record of a past life. The record of former lives holds the preponderant or superior place over any ancestral inheritance. What man has been in other lives determines what he will do with his gene and ancestral in-heritance, how he will relate himself to them. If he has more soul-memory of eternal inheritance, his auric light and auric vehicle will begin its blessing on the first breath of his living. But if he brings to this world a record of violence, hate, hostil-ity, he will unite with all of the negatives of his gene inherit-ance, and he will scourge the earth rather than bless it.

The aura can become overcrowded by alien thought forms entering into the aura. These are intrusive thought forms setting up astral arguments in the mind. A negative particle of thought telepathically sent into the aura can reside there for a total life time, causing an inductive sense of inferiority to the person who has no knowledge of cleansing the aura. The aura must be aerated, shaken out and cleansed by the pure fires of prayer, mantramic speaking, contemplation.

The aura is a receptive indentor of thought forms externally sent from others and also internally generated by one's
foggy believing or unbelieving.

The energy field around the body, called the aura, gives off
an odor to one who is clairsentient. Astral soil as a psychic
fluid lingers in the aura, causing a stench or odor of evil to be
sent forth from a murderer—or an amoral person.

A dog senses and also smells the astral odors stemming
from the energy field or aura around the body.

The bacteria and germinal content of the flesh and cells
of the physical body is kept in balance when the solar fire
is in command of the auric field. When the solar-fire flow
in the auric field is uneven, the result is unhealthy distortions
of bacterial life in the physical body.

PSYCHIC DRAINERS

The solar-plexus magnetism is drained off by human
persons who are psychic drainers. The thyroid gland's vital
pranic energy is drained by entity intrusion from the unrisen dead.

One invites to himself some person or condition to drain
off his psychic vitality when he has repeatedly offended the
laws of psychic energy, force, and power. Psychic laws are
kept intact only through the ethical use of psychic energy,
force and power.

If the auric gamma fire has been weakened through disobedience, through the use of energy, that is, overzealousness as to work or emotional involvement or mental overconcentration upon a single idea, or if a person has been too
demanding of another person, using his will to manipulate
that person, or if a person displayed, exploited or over-
exhibited his psychic powers to gain selfishly, the gamma ring
around the auric energy field develops weakened, penetrable
openings to cosmic fire. The auric field generates a leakage

or devitalizing drainage. The solar plexus fails to insulate and protect a person from intrusion. A person is exposed to psychical, parasitical persons and events.

If a person has offended the laws relating to conscience, he is exposed to the sub-levels of telepathy from astral earthbound souls. The protective etheric portal around the thyroid gland is shattered and he has the misfortune to become a receptacle for unrisen-dead telepathies. Very often these telepathies pertain to sound and discarnate voices giving adverse guidance, misdirecting and confusing him. The damaged portals of penetration can be healed through yoga and cosmic exercises. Through mantramic speaking and through yoga headstand positions, the etheric matrix around the thyroid gland can reassume its normalcy.

The auric energy field and the band of gamma light can be healed by a spiritual teacher's assistance and also by the spiritual art of meditation. The hearing of music suitable to the ego-tone of a person can set the aura into a temporary state of balance. In time, the continued practice of meditation, spiritual helps and all of the spiritual practices protecting the soul's protective sheath can bring into the life of a person a mending and reconstruction of the auric energy field.

The spiritual scientist seeks to send healing sympathetic suggestible processes of mending light.

The aura when disorganized is a fiery self-antagonizing field of energy. Tension in the auric field produces suffering in the etheric body and physical body. One should work each day to keep the auric balance in the energy field surrounding his physical body.

Man does not have an aura after death. The aura is the product of the emotional and mental energy flow in the lesser etheric body. The soul's sheath becomes the reflector for after-death emotions and thought in the state of death.

Each time one is born to a physical body in the earth, he builds a new auric reflecting field of energy. Due to the energy processes of his growing and developing, the auric field is necessary for the relief of overtension and excitation in the etheric body.

The auric field serves as a recorder, a reflector and a protector; as a protective shield from external energy processes; as an internal reflector of energy processes; and as a mirror to reveal what has been thought and felt and what is being thought and felt. The aura is an image recorder. The aura energy field is a receiver of sound from outer space, mitigating the full wave lengths of sound, that the vibrations carrying sound may fall harmlessly on the human ear.

The aura is a radio telescope. Very much is to be learned in the scientific age concerning research into the versatile processes of the auric energy field surrounding the etheric and human body.

XIV

THE SOUL-SHEATH

The soul's sheath is a radiance sheath. The soul's sheath in a child is a pure translucent vehicle protecting the inexperience and naive aspects of childhood. The soul-sheath is very close to the physical body, and may be seen by the clairvoyant as a rim of incandescent light around the physical body. The soul's medallion situated around the head sustains this light of the soul's sheath around the physical body.

When a child reaches puberty, it is determined by his former-life grace or karma whether the soul's sheath will become a radiant sheath, expanding to engulf the auric light, or whether it shall be submerged and obscured by the karmic soil of a past life.

If an ego is highly evolved, the radiant sheath or soul-sheath becomes a visible body of light. A person standing near one having a powerful soul-sheath is engulfed by a holy magnetism emanating from the soul-sheath and the soul-medallion.

The auric envelope is a reflecting, vibrating body. The soul's sheath is an emanating and radiating body. The auric vehicle and the auric field are supported in their life by the soul's vibrational field centered around the medallion of the soul. The soul's sheath is sustained by the centered velocity of the soul's pulsation.

When a person is rejected, ignored, or resented, and sealed away from others, it is due to the auric field around the physical body and the negative life recordings upon the vibrational field of the soul's medallion.

Spiritual persons having a powerful soul-sheath are received and accepted by all persons containing the light in their consciousness and in their souls. However, persons with darkened conscience and perverted wills fear and avoid those having powerful, radiant soul-sheaths, recognizing in them their adversary. Desiring in themselves to remain in darkness, they often become violent enemies of persons having a powerful spiritual soul-sheath. Thus, the good are persecuted from time to time due to their soul radiance.

The grace record of man permeates and emanates from the soul-sheath. His virtues, his good and his purity are radiating, healing, spiritually animating powers. Good needs no advertisement or announcement. Good is, as God Is. There is no greater ring-pass-not of protection than the radiating encirclement of soul-sheath powers stemming from good.

As the gamma-ray ring around the aura can be perforated and weakened by abuse of psychic power, so can the soul-sheath be devitalized and evaporated by wrong use of spiritual gifts or mystically blind use of grace.

It is God's plan that man increase his soul-sheath in each life. To ride along the power of one's grace without earning or seeking to earn in each life is to overdraw one's grace, and therefore deplete the reservoir of grace reflected in the soul's sheath or radiant ring of soul-light surrounding the physical body.

After death the soul-sheath becomes the aura for the one who has died. If the soul-sheath is made inactive because there is no good to bring from the life just lived, the errors and negation are reflected in the lower emotional body shell. This shell, recording past wrong earth works, must be consumed through sub-electronic sound waves within the lower astral planes. Such dissolving is called purgatory.

The emotional shell when not dissolved after death by contrition and conscience becomes an *energy-floater*. An energy-floater is a floating mass of low-grade emotional energy. This acts upon the living in mesmeric or hypnotic action and is one of the mesmeric phases of ESP. Before one may render service for God with the higher ESP, he must be free of mesmeric and subtle guilt-laden influences on all levels — in the world of the dead and in the world of the living. After death each person should face up to his lower emotions and thus dissolve the emotional shell.

An energy-floater has no intelligence; it has no soul; it has only sentient energy. An energy-floater cannot be exorcised by ordinary means, nor will it respond to prayers. It can only be exorcised by forming a reverse-energy, or by building a vacuum between oneself and the floater. Thus, by energizing one's own thought and emotional field with thought symbols of a higher order, the floater fades away and is dissolved. One renders a service to the one dead who has generated such a field of hate and hostility, as the one dead may rise more quickly to his own instruction on the inner planes.

If the one who has died reincarnates *before* the energy-floater or emotional-body shell is dissolved, he will be born

with certain phases of psychotic mentality burdening his mind
and emotions. Many persons having mediumistic powers contact an energy-floater thinking it to be the entity of a soul
previously living. A certain kind of information can be gathered from these contacts with the undissolved debris energy
mass. On further or deeper contact it will be found that such
knowledge gained has no living verity or lasting satisfaction.

One who refuses to purge out his evil acts through rendering service while living in the world can, if he will, mitigate
and thereby rearrange his pattern of karma through being
purged after death.

Each after-death experience, even for a resisting ego, enables the ego to return to the earth a little lighter, less
burdened from wrongdoing. However, no person undergoes
hell or purgatory save his conscience agrees. Persons without
conscience, being in a comatose state, are not aware of purging after death. Their wrongdoing is recorded in their soul's
record in the same manner as for one who is aware of wrongdoing. However, engrossed in justification for evil, such persons are not consciously aware of the purgatorial state, and
their wrongdoing is sealed away from their conscious mind.
They must balance their wrongdoing through Quelle's action
in the next life.

Persons having a blind side to conscience experience their
purgatory in the physical world during physical life until
finally, through recognition of a just law existing in the world,
they make union with their conscience and begin a slow and
tedious climb. Through frustration and suffering they find
a pathway once more to God.

As one increases in spiritual stature while in the world,
the soul-sheath overpowers the auric reflections and their
activity. Gradually, the soul-sheath takes over the auric field.
The high initiate works that he may enlarge the soul-sheath,
moving out of the range of the reflected patterns of karma.

In doing this he is assisted first by the Masters, the angels, the saints, and the great blue akasic flame within the Master's aura. By gradual degrees he widens his soul-sheath.

All initiates must come to a timeless state, mastering the triad action of time — the past, the present and the future. When the soul-sheath becomes more powerful than the auric reflected light, one may be said to have mastered the triad time complex in human life.

A person with soul-sheath freedom sees through sight or visions not the frailties of the past or the wrongdoing of the present, nor the consequence for the future. He steps out of time and therefore out of karma. He sees things through the eyes of Jesus. And he moves those whom he would heal into wave lengths of light exceeding pain and suffering. From his own mental atoms he sets the time clock to read in eternal timing, and thus, healing, initiation and illumination become as one in the minds of those whom he would heal.

ESP AND THE MYSTERY OF THE EUCHARIST

In taking the Eucharist, or holy communion, the soul-sheath is the body of receptivity through which one partakes of the wine and of the bread. When one is in an intense state of receptivity, reverence and desire, the primal breath in the lungs is taken over by the akasic pranic breath, and one absorbs into his soul-sheath one of the atoms of the body of Jesus which feeds him with the bread of life.

The highly spiritually charged atoms Jesus used in His physical body while living in the earth are in the earth's atmosphere waiting to be received into the bodies of mankind. One can draw to himself during the sacred moment of the Eucharist the very atoms which once lived in the body of Jesus.

Ministering hands using transcendental powers during the Eucharist draw from the cosmic akasic atmosphere the atoms once living in the physical body and blood of Jesus, enabling the one taking communion or the Eucharist to receive the true body and blood of Jesus. When one knows and experiences this sacred reality during Eucharist, he henceforth is truly redeemed.

The higher ESP powers are transcendental powers. Through a belief in supernatural powers or the extended capacity of the work of spirit, through a state of holy expectancy, the higher ESP powers function beyond the wave length of ordinary mind, ordinary feeling and ordinary acting. As long as men fail to understand the powers Jesus used in transfiguration, in transubstantiation, they will be kept in primal darkness, blundering, forcing, pressing.

THE THIRD EYE AND THE SOUL-SHEATH

The gift of inner sight holds and contains the promise of infinite illumination. The eyes, the center of self-consciousness, are vehicles of light. Many think of the eye as being merely an organ for looking upon the world. The eye is the transmitter of spiritual light. The two eyes act in dual fashion to serve the third or inner eye situated within the pineal gland.

One born blind to things of the Spirit has in some way neglected in a past life to unite with the prismatic light of the soul. There are seven layers of ether in the physical eye. Each layer of ether is a vehicle for one of the prismatic wave lengths of light. When man has but three etheric layers of an eye open, he lives in a three-dimensional light. He responds only to what can be seen on the level of physical perception. He seals away the four more sensitive degrees of sight.

The physical eyes are orifice portals for the third eye when one is spiritually evolved. One having used etheric sight in ancient times sometimes retains the primal living function of the pineal gland. Such persons draw upon kinetic energies to see more than is seen in physical sight.

If one has moved beyond primal etheric action of the pineal gland and has been initiated into other dimensions of sight, he will first see through the reflective lunar light, which gives him the power to clairsentiently see in the dark of the night. He can move in a household knowing as much about the objects around him as if it were daylight.

Persons who have the misfortune to be blind use the lunar sight. The pores in the skin of the body and the nerve portals close to the skin take over the work of the eye. Persons with natural physical sight whose eyes are open to the wave lengths of lunar sight see into the auric light of others in a form of mistlike seeing.

Solar initiates having been initiated in many lives through meditation and contemplation upon God as light see through the power of illumination. Using the third-eye function of the pineal gland, they penetrate extended dimensions within substances. Through the power of attentiveness, concentration and contemplation, veil after veil of dense matter is lifted.

It is said in the physical world that no two persons on observing an object see the same thing. This is also true of initiates with inner sight. No two initiates see in exactly the same way. What one sees in higher clairvoyance is dependent upon the content of light in the soul's medallion and in the soul's sheath. The ego centered in light is familiar with the functioning of the third eye.

Any person having higher ESP clairvoyance also is aware that he never sees a vision in exactly the same way every time. If he were to do so, he would be seeing a picture of a thing, an object or a condition rather than a living thing, object or condition. Thus, a seer identifies what he sees through living and animated vitality.

If a seer sees repeatedly an immovable object placed before him as a center of observation, he knows it to be sent to him through telepathy visualization from some other mind. It is the work of the seer to determine *what mind* is sending a pictorial idea or object. A pure seer is aware that he can be mesmerized or hypnotized through the vision sent telepathically from another mind. It is therefore his work to identify or qualify that which is seen and observed.

Hypnosis is more prevalently active on the astral wave lengths of the mind than on the physical sensory wave lengths of the mind. A true seer must rise above the lower astral wave length of thoughts and emotion. The most clear and true visions experienced are those received by an ego initiate having total sense detachment.

The subconscious mind or Quelle is similar to a cup containing voluminous accumulative psychic energy. If one cannot move beyond Quelle's action into the world of visions, he cannot unite with the third eye. Quelle energy determines that he sees all things astrally regarding things physical and personal.

As long as the Censor in Quelle shields away one's entry into the greater dimensions of vision, one will approach ESP powers through a feeling of fear as to what he sees and intuits.

Seership has no lasting value unless it is accompanied by the *informing principle*. The solar initiate sees, knows and understands what he sees. The lunar initiate feels what he sees but cannot give it logos or words to interpret it. The lunar initiate more often interprets what he sees through a sense of feeling, dread, punishment. A death prophecy coming from a lunar psychic is not always an infallible prediction.

Lunar psychics are influenced by the moon's rays. In dreams the imaginative processes of their minds are unleashed. They touch the wish-level of dreams more often in their dreaming, bringing back to the waking world dream fantasy memories.

Solar initiates experience the daytime of the soul during sleep. All persons having dream cognition should seek spiritual instruction as to their dream symbologies. When persons have solar-initiate potential, their souls will not be denied in the night. They dream in dramas what they refuse to see in the daytime. Thus, all persons seeking spiritual evolvement should minutely record their dreams.

The eye as a physical organ is an undeveloped organ. And the pineal gland according to physical research is an unfunctioning gland. However, more interest is being directed toward the functioning of this mysterious miniature organ placed in the center of the skull.

The lunar initiate works with Quelle through the pituitary gland to receive his sight. The solar initiate uses both the pituitary gland and the pineal gland to open higher sheaths of the brain, thereby activating both hemispheres of the brain during spiritual experience.

Intense psychic pressure at the base of the brain where Quelle is centered is generated by six molecular stations located along the spinal canal.

In the base of the spine there is a coiled action of energy utilized for outer existence. This life force generates the sensual life. The brain system is directly connected with the base of the spine. Spiritual scientists seek to bring upward this powerful complex energy system, that it may unite with and magnify the brain's processes. In intense reverence, emotion, desire, prayer, contemplation and meditation, this energy flows upward rather than outward. Cells in the brain unused in physical sensory life are activated. The spiritual student seeks to rhythmically unite with this upward flowing current of power.

The pineal gland cannot function until the upward current's flow is even, non-forceful, peaceful. The etheric matrix supporting the pineal gland opens as a flower, described in the East as a thousand-petaled lotus. Thus, one makes union with dimensions of light, and the sight of the physical eye converges inward to become a perceiving, single eye, revealing, teaching, assuring.

It has long been believed that the eye is the window of the soul, as indeed this is the case. Seers having solar sight can diagnose the condition of the physical body and its health through penetration into the iris of the eye. The akasic record may also be read through *eye scrying* or penetration into the iris of the eye of a person.

The identity of a person, the self consciousness, the emotional, mental and physical state flow out of the iris of the eye in wave lengths of light.

In Egypt the eye was considered by some initiatory schools to be the portal through which the etheric body moved out of the physical body. However, the Atlantean schools and all true initiatory schools taught that the etheric body during dreams and after death moves out of the body through the crown of the head.

The all-seeing eye, a common symbol in mystery schools and initiatory schools, symbolizes the eye of God ever upon man. It has been observed during meditation that many novices of seership first see the all-seeing eye. The all-seeing eye is a confirming archetypal symbol that the one meditating has made alignment with the Father principle.

Spiritual science teaches that one should prove all things in the laboratory of his own nature and being.

A seer seeking to progress rhythmically in the spiritual life understands the law that he can retain upon the screen of his consciousness any symbol to which he feels an affinity; that is, he finds it to be constructive and helpful, after he has seen the all-seeing eye, to re-visualize the eye in the next phases of his meditation, so that he may make union with the coordinated processes in his rise and evolvement. He will find that if he does this, other visions correlated to the greater archetypes which stem from the mind of God will enter into his mind. Thus, there is a difference between symbols received from a human mind, or an astral mind, rather than from the mind of God. The seer learns to discern the difference.

In all seership powers the wave lengths of the heart and the wave lengths of the spiritual mind must be equal. If the heart is out of focus — desiring something for self — psychic-mental and psychic-astral vision will be the result.

CLAIRAUDIENCE AND THE AUDIBLE SOUND

In the Far East, Buddha is sometimes portrayed with enlarged ears. This symbolically portrays the extended sense of spiritual hearing reaching into dimensions of sound little known by the outer sense of hearing. The ear is structured to record vibration and sound that the mind of man may respond to the great audible sound used by the Holy Ghost.

When one unites with the audible sound, he is said to be clairaudient, or he is a clear hearer of the Word. The novice begins alignment with audible sound through shutting out the clamors or the sense aspect of his hearing.

Through mantramic speaking, prayer, contemplation and meditation, one who has heard the inner tones of spiritual dimensions in former lives will make of the bones of his body and of his skull a finer tuning fork. He does this through remembered postures of meditation. He opens and makes perfect his clairaudient powers by yearning and longing to hear once more the inner voice assuring him of his divinity.

A person yet in the psychic stages of evolvement very often is frightened by tones and sounds which he cannot define as being within his mind or in the outer and objective reactions of his other senses. All senses are interdependent upon one another. When one concentrates upon the psychic aspect of his being, it is difficult to define *how* one is hearing.

To some, clairaudience is a fearful aspect of the psychic nature, because what is heard seems to come from some other source than from one's own being.

Increased psychic tension in the etheric body can produce psychic hearing. The superstitious mind untrained in the mystical life looks upon the psychic aspect of hearing as derangement or hallucinatory.

History records that great seers have had the power of see-ing and hearing acting as one, voices and sight being fused in the spiritual experience. Initiates know that all of the higher ESP powers of the senses must blend to produce infallible perception of things spiritual and physical.

One should not fear the inner voice, but should research its source whether being received on mind-to-mind telepathic vibratory wave lengths, or whether it is coming from a nega-tive suggestible source, or from the spiritual informative source.

Sound of any nature, physical or internal, is distracting to the mind when inharmonious to the tone of one's being, even as an antagonistic color can set up an alien arrangement of the energy masses in the etheric body.

Sound first plays upon the astral core located along the spinal canal of man. Any sound failing to coordinate with the ego-tone wave lengths of a person is disturbing, upsetting and irritating.

If one has grace, sounds received in the etheric aural cavi-ties of the ears, when inharmonious, are muted out by Quelle's action working with the central nervous system of the body. However, if a person has not protection in the gamma-ray band around the auric field and the lunar light encirclement of the solar plexus, he is exposed to sound coming from the cosmic energy wave lengths of Nature. Being exposed to this sound endangers his physical-body coordination, his emotional peace; his thought assimilation is disoriented.

If a person has offended the psychic laws in a past life, he has a weakened auric gamma-ray protection. He is therefore subjected to the subtle sounds of the astral world and the hypnotic voices from subtle minds in that world. Only in a karmic state resulting from psychic offenses in a former life and abuse of the psychic arts in the present life is this possible.

One heals and strengthens the gamma-ray encirclement of his aura through mantramic speaking, through making union with the audible sound situated between the eyebrows.

When the higher energy flow between the pineal gland and the pituitary gland is united in meditation, the starry door of the audible sound is opened between the eyebrows. The flowing power of the Holy Ghost flows outward. And though one does not hear the audible sound with his physical ears, the sound is the Word made flesh, flowing forth from the higher mind. In this state of spiritual quickening, one becomes a manifestor creating for God.

St. Paul in his initiation in the Third Heaven heard "words unspeakable." His senses being sealed away in the physical world, he concentrated wholly upon his experience in the Third Heaven. He heard the archetones in the greater archetypes and knew no words in human language by which he could interpret to the unknowing mind that which he heard. He had touched the Greater Unmanifested which man was not yet prepared to receive. This is so in the life of all persons uniting the audible sound or the Holy-Ghost powers. Unless one has earned the three powers of the adept, he cannot always articulate that which he hears. Even so, he cannot always give forth what he hears to unripe or unready ears. The three powers are true seeing, true hearing, and true speaking. To achieve this, one must have reached timelessness in his evolvement.

Through union with the greater archetones, the seer of hearing reaches the very core of union with God. He unites with the hum or the great Alpha and Omega tones working with universal cause. He moves out of the causal time limitations of the physical world, and thus experiences universal cause.

All seer-initiates work to remain in union with and make clear the audible sound. The audible sound current can be felt as an outgoing, expanding, pulsing, ecstatic joy emanating from the eyebrow center. When the triune powers of seeing, hearing, and speaking are activated, the physical senses are muted and made quiescent. The lower aspects of the senses become as lowered flames in a lamp, while the innermost light of the mind sees, hears, and speaks of the Real.

True inner hearing has not been perfected until one can hear the sound in a seed, in a leaf, in a tree, in a grain of sand, in a flower, in its fruit, in a mountain, in a rainbow, in a drop of rain. When one unites with the archetone giving life to all forms of life, he unites with the cosmic music of the universe. Finally, one unites with the tone of his own direct star from whence he came.

HEALING AND SOUND

Science is presently exploring the unknown wave lengths of energy existing in the bodies of men. The study of anatomy will no longer be dependent upon flesh, sense, blood, cell, muscle and bone for diagnosis and analysis. Science will penetrate the motivating processes sustaining physical, emotional and mental states of man. Science will open the knowledge of the therapeutic wave lengths of sound, using them to heal, to cure, to dissect, to operate, to mend, and to relieve.

Surgery without blood, removal of pain during surgery, the calming of mental and emotional distress will be made possible through the discovery and use of cold, sub-electronic wave lengths for certain diseases and also certain wave lengths of energy producing a super heat beyond anything presently known.

Many persons in mental institutions today are classified as mentally sick when in reality they are psychically disorganized. Ignorance of the psychic nature of man and of the dangers of overcharged psychic force in the etheric body has been the cause of many persons being incarcerated needlessly in hospitals for the mind. The new reach into psychic nature and psychic force by science will produce correction methods for the disarrangement of psychic force affecting the mind.

Through sound treatment, the overcharged force pressures of psychic energy in the etheric body, overstimulating the brain of man, will be rectified and equalized through the use of cold, sub-electronic energy.

In the case of blood diseases, infections and malignancy, sound-wave therapy will be used according to the degree of the sound wave lengths coming from the organ affected. Discovery will show that wave lengths coming from cosmic energy stepped down into plant energy and mineral energy will respond to and master the wave lengths of sickness emanating from a stricken organ. In every seed producing a plant is a sacred atom emanating a tone. In the plant containing the answer to a sickness or a disease is an affinity wave length to a disease.

Initiates know the law of drawing forth the sound wave lengths from plants, minerals, atmospheres physical and etheric. Spiritual persons having pure auras record as transmitters the wave lengths of sounds holding the secret to the health and vigor of their bodies and of the bodies of others.

All things existing in the world of man relating to his maintenance of life and poise within the life forces conditioning him to life are maintained by light, tone, ether, akasia, vibration, sound, energy, color.

Breathing rhythmically with awareness of cosmic-energy flow fills the auric light around the physical body with revitalizing, cleansing, and reinvigorating sound waves of renewal and life. The spiritual scientist draws upon the wave lengths of sound through rhythmic breathing. He breathes into his aura a renewal of the life force — and the life force most relating him to other persons in the world is magnetism.

The exchange of magnetism between a healer and a person needing healing can only be accomplished by the healer having a more highly charged magnetic aura than the one sick. One emanates excessive magnetism of a pure nature when he remains in a regulated rhythmic state of union with the cosmic forces of life, and of the Spirit of God working within him.

Positive, healing magnetism is more prevalent in persons who have used the healing arts in other lives. Persons highly charged with rarified magnetisms of holiness have a certain charisma in their natures, an outgoing, loving emanation, enabling them to come into the proximity of sickness without danger of devitalization. It will be found that all healers using spiritual powers, having a high rating of magnetism in their auras, also have radiant soul-sheaths. Such persons live close to their soul-medallions, to their higher selves, and therefore are attuned to the spiritual rarified wave lengths of the higher mind. The radiant body or soul-sheath from life to life can be extended when one renders the highest service to mankind—and that is the spiritual art of healing.

All animal life is responsive to cosmic energy and sound. The birds flying overhead respond to cosmic-energy currents and radiations through which they are directed, from season to season, to migrate. The animal life in the world under the specie angels is controlled by the cosmic currents in its mating and reproducing of species. Wild animal life and domestic animal life are forewarned of storms, catastrophic events, such as earthquakes, floods, fires, and hurricanes, due to the cosmic energy music playing upon the solar-plexus center where resides their intelligence.

During eclipse periods between the sun and the moon, the cosmic-energy sound currents affect all life. These sound currents play upon the atoms supporting the plant life centered in the root of the plant. Every tree and plant responds to a cosmic knowing intelligence due to God's Overmind directing all life in the earth.

Man is governed by the same cosmic laws governing the plant in the field, as Jesus said, "Consider the lilies of the field, how they grow; they toil not, neither do they spin." (St. Matthew 6:28) Implanted into man's body and into his mind are portals of energy recording Nature's flow and also the communicating wave lengths of cosmic energy existing from mind to mind.

It is no accident when some men are intuitive and clairsentient as to change of weather, approaching storms, imminent earthquakes or tidal waves. This cosmic-energy responding to life-force intelligence is in all men. Even though some men due to city life are sealed away from the cosmic-energy intuitions, these primal instinctual powers still exist in their natures.

Due to overmechanized living, man is presently smothering Nature through asphalt streets and highways. Through congestion in living conditions and through pollution in the air

and in the streams, he is presently threatened with sub-
merging the instinctual cosmic-energy responses in his own
nature. To those more highly evolved, it is seen that this ab-
normality will be met by the retaliation aspect of cosmic-
energy life force. Men will be forced to return to Nature
through cataclysms in the earth, in the water, particularly
coming from the polar regions. Convulsions of a cosmic
magnitude will become more and more apparent to the
perceptive. Gradually, the emerging age must be confronted
by three vital propositions: Nature's revolt, man's rapid
mental expansion, and interterrestrial space knowledge.

There has never been an age demanding so much of man
as will be demanded of him in this new and phenomenal era
now overshadowing the world.

CHEMISTRY AND THE ENERGY AGE

Scientific medicine will be able to reproduce chemistries in
the physical body carrying their own antidotes to bacteria as
yet unknown to men.

The energy age and change of rate of vibration in the
earth's energy, due to mass atomic blasts of the past and of
the future, will produce latent bacteria unknown presently to
the science of medicine, chemistry, biology, and pathology.

The science of chemistry will discard synthetic substitutes
in the future. Chemistry will open wider doors to Nature
through energy processes.

Chemistry is in its infancy. In the new sciences, chemistry
will emerge through agriculture, through nutrition, through
right use of fabrics, through human-tissue therapies, through
interrelated knowlege of genetics, through knowledge of
sexual harmony as related to the hormone wave lengths existing between man and woman, through pollution of water and
of the atmosphere.

Chemistry in the next fifty years will influence mankind to act with new germinal foresight and insight. Chemistry will come to recommend a new assessment of union in marriage. Through measurement and adjustment of the hormonal wave length between persons, a balanced fusion in the sex life will produce stronger bodies and better minds in progeny or offspring.

ELEVATED PSYCHIC POWERS

In preparation for new eras through which men rise in the world, many egos are born to the earth with elevated psychic powers. Being aware of one's psychic power or having powers of thought exceeding the thinking process of average man, more often relegates such egos to a lonely existence.

Persons having extrasensory powers at the end of an era, having been used as genuine instruments to foresee the coming events of great new eras, leave to the world a heritage. Men remember them through the startling events in their lives and in the manner of their deaths. Three such egos still remain close to the memories of men in that each demonstrated certain parallels in their extrasensory powers. However, each one came into life to fulfill a certain soul-task and to leave to men the assurance of the omniscient power of the soul.

Socrates was said to have had a daemon whose voice over-directed his life. His influence upon the philosophical outlook of man lives today.

Joan of Arc communed with the Archangel Michael; hearing her voices changed the course of history between England and France and eventually the world.

Nostradamus' hearing of voices was stimulated through a cosmic union with the planets. He united himself with the logos angelic voices of each planet. His use of a woolen garment with a moistened hem and a bowl of water at his side, defines him as a perfected lunar psychic. All psychics using water or moisture as a medium for their extrasensory powers are lunar psychics. All psychics using light are solar psychics.

Joan of Arc's extrasensory powers identify her as being a solar initiate, as the Archangel Michael, the master of solar light, initiates all solar initiates. Joan of Arc in her life was united with her nation's archetype. All initiates having a soul-task which destines them to preserve or save their nations are solar initiates.

All persons, such as Socrates, whose soul-task destiny is to preserve the memory of a philosophy or certain ideas for the world, are Saturn initiates working to maintain the ethic of the use of the mind for mankind.

The lunar psychic powers of Nostradamus foresaw into centuries ahead. His power of clairaudience enabled him to hear the audible sound current through which he wrote his famous canticles. Nostradamus' soul-task was to look into the political revolutions facing mankind, and the change-over from monarchy to democracy. Hidden in the canticles of Nostradamus are great initiatory formulas beyond the prophetic aspects of politics and government.

Initiates of this age on the same wave lengths as Nostradamus will open the door to interterrestrial knowledge concerning the planets and their relation to the earth, and will also give to man certain cosmically charged ideas related to the galaxy in which this earth system dwells.

XV

TELEPATHY AND SUGGESTION

The word "influence" is one of the least understood words; however, it is one of the most important and relevant words in the subtle worlds. Subtle-psychic powers range from power-charged minds on the physical planes, power-charged occult minds existing upon the stuff of the lower astral planes, and occult minds thinking through the lower astral planes.

Telepathy is a spiritual art when used to heal, to reinforce the positive aspects of one's faith and hope. But when used to intrude, pollute, violate and defile the mentality of another, it is an act of sorcery and an agent for the evil.

Entity-possession has been recognized and understood by all great teachers of the inner sciences. Among these was Jesus. To come under the influence of an imposing telepathy from an earthbound dead, is to endanger one's own direct rational flow of the mind.

The new open concepts of science interested in the functioning of the mind of man will come to understand that suggestible communication between minds on the physical plane is not only an actuality, but is an absolute contribution and necessity to the advancement and progress of the mind of man. Mind-to-mind communication is vital to the survival of the mind of man. For one to be a successful sender and receiver of spiritual or mental telepathy, his thought must be highly charged with selfless emotion, containing a volatile attentiveness; one's emotions must be highly charged, yet impersonal and dispassionate. Intensity of feeling in the thought sends an unobstructed thought to the receiver.

The receiving telepathic set of man is centered in the area of his heart where resides the life-force sacred atom, called Atma in the East. The sending telepathic apparatus of man is centered between his brows where the eyebrows meet. This center is the door to the higher unconscious aspect of the mind.

To receive a telepathy from the living or from the dead, one must be in sympathy with the sender or with what the sender stands for; he must have a certain rapport or likeness to the texture and substance of the thought being sent. One must have within himself a willing receptivity to the ideas, thoughts or images sent, and must have some agreeing, expecting and accepting in the processes of his inner and outer desires. He must have a similarity or agreeing aspect in his mental nature to the mind of the one who sends. This agreeing aspect or suggestible complying may be in the subconscious mind or Quelle, or it may be in the ordinary intuition or thought process of one's everyday wishing, thinking and desires.

One cannot receive telepathy into his mind or consent to the will of another through mental suggestion, save he have in himself a receiving susceptibility to that which is being sent.

A fully-centered ego is not susceptible or suggestible to unrisen-dead telepathies unless he is in some manner sympathetically in rapport to the sender.

A subtle mind sending negative telepathy selects the sub-electronic wave lengths and mental cables of fear to send to the one he would subdue and mesmerize.

Persons filled with guilt are hypersensitive telepathic receivers of subtle earthbound-dead telepathy. Their heart stations of receptivity have no barricades against subtle minds seeking to penetrate their minds and wills.

All telepathic currents existing from mind to mind, living or dead, are kept alive by the flow of the unconscious mind. No one can receive any form of telepathy—spiritual, mental, or subtle—save Quelle consents to open the suggestible side of the unconscious action of the mind.

Telepathies from some source, cause, person, entity, or spirit may remain banked in the matrix of Quelle and in the auric field around the body for a period of years, beginning first as small or minute suggestions planted in the fertile receptivity of the Quelle matrix. If such telepathies are from a subtle source, one may react and portray in his outer world these suggestions during periods of despondency and depression.

The interflow between mind and mind will come more directly under the scrutiny of science in the latter part of this century. In the energy age now approaching man there will be placed a great emphasis upon discovery of the mental functioning of man. All the former biases concerning man's own inclusive and singular makeup will be scrapped and discarded.

It will be seen that man is a potential mental giant using pygmy powers of the mind. The halting stride of science has offended much in the soul of man by overscrupulous identification. However, it is inevitable in this era that certain egos devoted to the field of science will plunge into the cosmic aspects of the mind. The energy-scale thought processes will be weighed and measured. Ego-identity will be classified, gauged; and it will be confirmed that each man does exist as a thought identity. That which crosses the path of every scientist who is a lover of truth will be that man is more than can be conceived by rules, weights and measurements made by man.

Insight, intuition, foresight, foreknowledge, precognition, and all aspects of the mind's unpredictable transcendence will now come to be measured with new eyes, new attitudes and new acceptance.

The receiving set in the heart of man has been built over the ages through inductive processes little known to the average mind. The etheric matrix upholding the heart and the sacred-identity atom in the heart makes him a tuning fork for all life. It is not by accident that the mighty Scriptures state that man must go to the door of his heart to open the door to understanding.

The heart is organized to bear emotional burdens. It is intricately designed to withstand great surges of emotion. It is replenished continually by the sister and brother planetary generated gland system. It is also sustained by biological tides of sexual drives and procreation fulfillment.

The heart process and the soul process work directly together. The center or pulsation point of the soul located directly over and in the brain, sustaining the ego-mind, works in direct unison with the heart beat. Should the interflow of the ego-mind and the interflow of the spiritual mind and the outgoing flow of the physical processes of the mind be out of tune with one another, one may be said to be in a lower psychic state, using the heavier or dense aspect of his senses and of the lower atavistic compulsions in his personalized nature. In maladjustment, the energy fields of the etheric body become overcharged and something explodes beyond the psychic resiliency in one's temperament, emotions and mind. In time, the etheric body cannot receive or be fed by the flow of pure psychic plasma. It may be said, then, that the etheric body becomes anemic, subjected solely to a more dense psychic fire. When this occurs, one is exposed to the telepathies of the lower astral planes where dwell the unrisen and earthbound dead.

Disappointment, frustration, failure to meet the standards of society, of the family, and of one's own expectations make the heart vulnerable and contagious to unholy atmospheres in thinking, willing and feeling. Invertive feelings, moods of depression, recurring thoughts of bitterness, anger, hostility, and hardness of heart seal away the benign telepathic influences seeking to move into the heart.

Man is communicable to what he is. His thoughts attract thoughts on the same wave lengths gathered from his own thinking. His feelings draw to him persons having exact range of desire equal to his own desiring. Telepathy works within an exact law supported by unfailing equation. What man sends forth from his feelings and thoughts will be returned to him upon the plane of his mind and of his body.

The most certain way to attract opposing, intruding, and disturbing telepathies from the subtle minds of the earthbound dead, and to come under the influence of these subtle unrooted minds, is to open the subjective psychic currents through negative thinking and living. Long periods of depression, feelings of guilt, and a general dissatisfaction with one's fate, and being untrained as to the laws of karma and refusing to accept one's state of karma, will yield up one's

birthright to irresponsible and dangerous deranging forces
of the mind.

Scientists in their study of the energies of the planets will
learn that there are periods when persons who have had oversubjective exposure to their psychic natures will be responsive
to the gravity undertow of the planetary energies working
with the lower aspects of the psychic nature of man.

Entity possession is a reality. The tantric teachers of the
East spoke of entity possession. Masters of the psychic arts,
they used these powers through magical rather than spiritual
formulas. The greater teachers in the Rishi line of gurus and
other schools of thought, understanding the inviolate sacredness of the will of man, have taught that man must fight to
possess his own soul, his own will and his own mind, and that
the right to his own identity is between him and the Will of
God, and that any source taking from him the divine right to
his own choice, decision and will, profanes his own identity
within the Will of God. However, to witness and to see the
degeneration of the will under the superimposed will of another is a pitiful and abject spectacle.

Entity Possession

Persons dying to the world — atheistically inclined, forceful
by nature, believing in no after-death existence — find themselves in a vacuous state unable to unite with their angels.
Unable to orient themselves to a higher astral state, they are
dislodged, unrooted, floating, limbo souls refusing to believe
in the more heavenly state of existence, feeling themselves to
be in danger of extinction.

All of their hostilities, hatreds and reflexes of feeling and
thinking still being intact — and having no longer a physical
body to give them expression — these earthbound wanderers
of the nether regions seek to implant themselves into the
astral envelope of magnetism surrounding the spinal canal

and nervous system of a victim in the physical world. By degrees, they send forth charged tentacle-like currents, threadlike, toward their prospective or future habitation. They begin by drawing upon the effluvia within the spinal nervous system of their victim. By degrees they build a network of psychical cordlike penetration, breaking down the will system of a subjective person. Over a period of time, the subjective ego inhabiting the body is dispossessed. The dispossessed ego is similar to a man caught in a revolving door. He is going nowhere; he is getting no place.

It is observed by the spiritual scientist that clarity of decision and judgment are the first things lost by the victim. By degrees the subtle entity, taking over the brain impulses of his victim, moves into the house or body of the ego he is dispossessing, until outwardly it may be seen that a total change of personality has occurred.

An ego consenting to be possessed remains out of his body still connected by his silver cord until the time of his normal death, when he and the possessing entity are separated.

The pain and suffering of an ego subjectively receptive to possession is a form of hell. Exorcism of a possessing entity is possible only when karmic laws have been fulfilled.

If there is grace in the life of one in danger of being possessed by an entity, previous to dispossession, prayer, reading of sacred Scriptures, rendering a service beyond the call of duty, in which more than sweat is involved, will distract and root out any offending, intruding force of the dark.

The unrisen dead cannot draw upon any memory in his death state of consciousness except the memory he has known while living in the physical world. His whole thinking is geared to remembrance of what he has known while living in the physical world. Thus, he can prey upon the conscience of one living by making the living more aware of a pattern of neglect or wrongdoing which concerned him (the one dead). The unrisen dead uses scenes of the past in flashlike telepathic fashion, to keep the telepathic wave lengths open between him and the living. If some unresolved pattern of life is concentrated in the mind of an unrisen-dead person, he keeps it continually before the conscience of the one he would possess.

The way of escape for one who has an overexpansive sense of guilt toward one having died is to set up totally new rhythms of creating, of thinking, of acting. These patterns must be unfamiliar to one who would possess him beyond the state of death. The unrisen dead, having no way of entering into the new pattern set up by the exorcisor, floats away into limbo existence where he attracts to himself the help of the White Brothers and eventually his own Guardian Angel.

The truest and most effective way to exorcise an earth-bound entity seeking to intrude upon a person is to refuse to think on the past as related to the one who has died. One must wholly shut out all memory of past associations, particularly if there be any feeling of having failed the person who has died. It is the duty of all persons to use the present to its full capacity to set up wave lengths of creation, to move forward with life; to lean always toward the past with a sense of guilt is to betray the present and the future. Jesus understood this law when He said, "Let the dead bury their dead."

The risen dead do not offend the life of those whom they love. Their telepathies are powerfully charged with over-directing processes. The risen dead use one-third of their after-death experience to bless the living.

The unrisen dead use kinetic electrical forcefully charged energies after death. Unconsciously they burn with a cold fire those whom they would contact. Their presence is felt as a form of coldness. The presence of the risen dead may be known by warmth, healing and reinforcing joy.

All initiates should determine that they will observe the ethics, the rules and the commandments as given by Jesus, that their minds will be at all times close to the succoring, preserving, and protecting powers of the angels.

It can be seen on the physical and subtle planes that will and willing are mighty forces. For one to yield up his will or right to worship God in his own way, his right to love where he would love, his right to create in the way his soul would have him create, is to lean toward an enslavement and abuse of one's own birthright and divine heritage as given of God.

Some persons who have died having had an obsessive desire to possess a person's full attention on the physical plane, and believing there is no life after death, unwittingly commit psychic murder, finding themselves on the lower astral planes. Such entities after death concentrate all of their thought power upon the one they have desired to control while living in the earth. Having freedom of the mind in a forceful and concentrated way, the dead find themselves more powerful on the lower astral planes than they were on the physical planes. These have the power to draw to them any sympathetic person they would seek to have join them in the world of death. Their powerful thought projections set up destroying currents in the life of the person on earth.

If a person is subjective to the will of an earthbound dead in any manner in thought or emotions, his life, his future, and his survival are at stake. Into the mind of the one living begin to flow concentrated thought thrust concerning death and dying, failure and uselessness, suicidal thoughts attracting accidents. It may be said that such concentrated telepathic morbidity is responded to in approximately a thirty per cent ratio.

Needless to say, such earthbound ruthless willing has a karmic result. Persons dying determined to hold onto possessions or persons at any cost must return to the world in future lives in some form of malformation. Misuse of will on the physical plane and in the subtle planes offends the laws of trespassing, invoking rigid and imprisoning karmic situations.

Revengeful after-death persons must be caught into the snare of their own hatred-nets. This is God's perfect justice: what one does in consciousness lives and cannot die. The afterdeath state is a state of consciousness even as the earth state is a state of consciousness.

Blessing telepathies come from the higher planes of the risen dead in the astral world and the higher echelons of heaven. To receive these telepathic blessings while living in the physical world one must believe on God's perfect law of mercy, justice. He should know that life is deathless and eternal. He should seek to fortify himself with all protective measures of the soul. It is a divine gift to know that the transcendental processes of the mind and soul are communicable. To make union with God, His love, and His mind through Christ, is to keep the peace-ramparts of the soul steady, poised in a perfect light of communion with all souls in the light.

Spiritual, inductive telepathy is a touch of bliss, reassuring man that he is immortal and eternal. One should claim the royal way, the middle pathway, the golden way, and stand centered within his ego-will within the Will of God.

TRANCE

There are several ways in which one may look upon the entranced state of consciousness. In Biblical times it was commonly thought that to be entranced one must prepare himself through rigorous fasting rituals, states of prayer, and separation from community life in caves or on the desert — and thus, by subduing certain aspects of one's senses, become a holy receptacle for God. Speaking to the group conscience through the spirit of God, such prophets and mystics of old would begin their statements by saying, "Thus saith the Lord."

As men have moved away from communal life into higher degrees of genesis, the state of trance producing prophetic, authoritative powers has shifted towards another form of mentality and consciousness. As one advances in genesis, he becomes more and more aware that each man has ESP powers, not in the sense of group consciousness, but in a sense of individuality and self-discovery. However, in this modern age there are many persons who still follow the theme of entrancement, invoking upon themselves the state of trance through inner concentrated self-suggestibility; some experience trance by outer suggestion or hypnosis.

The states or phases of trance include relinquishing one's own body and consenting to possession by spirit-controls, producing mediumship. Some persons in trance in this manner are partly conscious while being in a neutralized state of consciousness. The entity speaking through them and acting through them works through certain charged sub-electronics, etheric currents or waves. This very often exacts a heavy penalty upon the biological processes of the physical body and leaves a karmic scar upon the ego.

All mediums using trance powers for the sake of service to good are to some extent martyrs, as they willingly consent to sacrifice and give up the full and rightful ego-evolvement demands in their lives.

Prophecy through trance mediumship is not clear unless it is absent from fear. Total trance in which the medium is unaware of what is being said through the entity using his body, speech and mind is absent from fear because the medium is not using his own consciousness mind.

In trance a medium is anesthetized by the overcharge of psychic energy coming from the entity taking possession of his speech and mind.

Mediums while hypnotically entranced are not personally involved in their predictions. When mediums are placed into trance by hypnotism, they are exposed to the suggestible levels of Quelle, their own lower subconscious minds, and to the suggestible mind of the one hypnotizing them and to levels of the astral world. Therefore, some of their information is not wholly formulated.

Entrancement through spiritual ecstasy and the power of meditation is the only true and pure entrancement for the spiritual aspirant. In mediumship one works with the laws of suggestion and hypnosis. In spiritual, ecstatic trance one enters consciously into the state of trance or ecstasy by making union with finer and finer degrees of light. Through intermediary formulas he makes more sensitive his spheres of telepathic and ecstatic alignment.

Mediumistic powers give off sub-electronic magnetism. Spiritual mediation ecstatic trance powers give off illumination, light, revelation.

Trance for the spiritual aspirant means one-pointed concentration and attentiveness upon thoughts of union with God. The lesser self becomes still, and the higher self is merged and fused in union with God. In mediumistic trance the self is insensible. In spiritual trance the self is totally aware and at one with the All-Mind. The self is not set aside in spiritual trance, for union in spiritual ecstasy produces memory and recollection of all things experienced. In mediumistic trance, there is neither memory nor recollection of what one has done or said while yielding up his body and mind for the sake of spirit or hypnotic control.

HYPNOSIS

Suggestion is one of the most powerful influences in the aspects of the psychic nature. Quelle is outraged — and punishes the offender and offenders—when hypnosis suggests that one do something to disorganize the converging interflow of will, memory, imagination and conscience as stemming from the ego-identity and ages of development. The theme flow of the ego, when interrupted, must be corrected and come to adjustment and realignment with the directing ego-ray assuring each person of his own identity.

Quelle works with suggestions which flow and blend with will, memory and imagination of the one being hypnotized or entranced. Timing is offended when hypnotic suggestions do not flow with the intent of Quelle and the soul.

Centered in the core of the Quelle matrix at the base of the skull is a Censor determining that man fulfill the flow and the design of his destined spirituality and also that he assume and take on the responsibility of a fate decided by certain karmic irresponsible acts in former lives. The Censor faculty of Quelle keeps balance between destiny, spiritual impulses and karmic-fate compulsions.

The will of man is as a thread seeking to weave a new pattern and design in each life. The Censor of the will of man determines how much will-thrust a man may spend or expend.

Hypnosis, upsetting the time clock of the akasic-records flow, is intrusive and penetrates the etheric encasement surrounding the Quelle matrix. The Quelle matrix may be compared to an egg encased in a shell. To one slow in evolvement, the outer covering of the Quelle matrix is as the hardened shell of the egg in which the subconscious function of Quelle is operative through sparse recollection of dreams. To the unripened or unawakened soul, this is protection.

The spiritual fire in the spinal canal through regular and repeated selfless meditation dissolves the outer shell and penetrates the inner white of the egg substance, finally reaching the yolk or the core of the Quelle matrix.

When one consents to hypnosis or to come under the will of another person, he gives over into the hands of the one using certain suggestible will-techniques the power to penetrate the integral or innermost center of his compulsions of being. Should this be done through curiosity, through the will to dominate, through senseless exploration or through exploitation, or through use of drugs or alcohol, Quelle is violated, and the result is retaliation by primal forces existing in the subconscious nature of the subject or the one being hypnotized.

The Censor faculty, timing and guarding the action of Quelle and the revealing of its secrets and its powers, when invaded, will reveal only fragmentary or partial knowledge as to its function.

When Quelle is probed through hypnosis to recover the memory of past lives, Quelle automatically uses a veil of forgetfulness distorting the flow of reincarnation memory. As a distorted computer, it will give off partial and disarranged places and facts; but with a sort of wry sense of humor will disclose enough romantic and dramatic leading points of truth to tantalize those who would probe to discover or to learn through the back door of the unconscious that which should be learned through the divine interflow of initiation and also from the healthy aspect of the forward processes of all learning.

Quelle keeps the time clock of evolvement. To seek to go back out of timing and to recover past feeling, past motivation and past thinking through the superimposing of one will over another gives but a minute hint of the reality of the soul

under scrutiny, and fails to give the interconnecting relationships between feeling and thinking.

Hypnosis has been used as a psychic art even farther than
the memory of the mind of man can reach. The first state
of hypnosis to be enacted on earth occurred when man using
gravity sense, and thinking it to be more than etheric, hypnotized himself into thinking that he was the sole regent of
the earth.

The law of dual will in one's own nature, of willing to
believe and willing not to believe are the left and right hands
of suggestibility. When one has been unbelieving over a long
period of time as to God and His Will for him, he becomes a
victim to the forceful will natures of those who would externally exploit his labors, his love and his creation.

Spiritual suggestibility from pure, non-intrusive minds is a
powerful blessing and reinforcement. Adepts in the inner
sciences use the art of suggestibility through prayers, through
mediative visualization, and through the spiritual healing
arts. Suggestion on this scale is a hierarchy power. It is known
by all ethical persons of the spiritual arts that one must visualize and give suggestion to one who believes himself to be
sick. The suggestion of a perfect body pictured in the mind of
a spiritual healer is neither hypnotism nor hypnotic.

The angels, of all Beings under God, have the greatest
powers of suggestibility. The total range of angel flow is suggestion, that man forget not his spiritual identity as a co-
creator for God.

In this period of scientific interest in the psychic nature
of man, it will be found that man can best be healed by reinforcing his faith and courage, and by also teaching him
that the psychical causative laws supporting the energies of
his body and of his mind are *within him*.

XVI

SELF-SUGGESTION AND ITS

NEGATIVE AND POSITIVE POWER

Self-suggestion begins with insight, inner sight and visualization. In the ordinary sense projection of sight, man records all he sees and perceives through the aid of the vibrations and prismatic wave lengths of the solar rays.

Through the lunar reflected rays residing within the lesser etheric body, the solar plexus, the etheric heart matrix, the root of the tongue, and the innermost point of Quelle, one records and remembers all that he sees. This memory function enables him to use the power of self-suggestion whereby he can regenerate his physical body during sleep and draw upon the lunar reflexes within his own nature. To visualize in a unique way through the use of the suggestible arts, one must know that suggestion is the right hand servant of Quelle and of the soul.

When sight is expanded from the physical objective state of seeing into an inner functioning of visualization, one can reach a phase of clairvoyance or clear seeing unrestricted by what one assumes to be true by appearances rather than what *is inwardly,* where dwells the origin of the true. The visualization power of self-suggestion, when used ethically and correctly, is a free and freeing power. As free as one rightfully desires, Quelle will respond unfailingly.

Self-suggestion is successful when one unites with the true picture of himself and of the plan for him. To seek to force Quelle to produce anything out of alignment with that which is the true intent for a person is to manifest a regurgitation unpleasant and sometimes disastrous. One should distinguish between what he wants or wishes and what is the *right desire* for him.

Suggestion is the power of inverse willing. To create an outer condition flowing in accordance with the need of the soul's expression, desire and suggestion must work hand in hand with Quelle.

Two things are asked of the ethical initiate in working with the miraculous functioning power of self-suggestion: (1) that he approach Quelle with utter relaxation devoid of force, pressure or coercement; (2) that he give over entirely to Quelle, knowing Quelle to work as a first-hand operative agent for God. Placing his desires on the most selfless levels of detachment, one may visualize improved actions for a coming day, improved vigor of the physical body, more responsive coordination in health of the body, and of all manner of things, conditions and situations through which he may be improved, always remembering that he is commanding and visualizing these things that he might better serve God.

Before sleep one may visualize through self-suggestion to his lesser mind that the lower mind perform with a willing spirit on the coming day, and that the lower mind have more love and consideration for others. In time, the power of self-suggestion will be operative in the daytime hours as well as in the hours of sleep.

Mighty believing, unwavering faith in the mystic projecting and manifesting power of the subconscious will produce a more orderly life, a more constant sense of awareness on a higher level, and give to man a feeling that he is directly participating in realistic universal laws.

All healing arts rely more than is understood upon the suggestible supports of the subconscious mind or Quelle. Man is his own physician, if he will. Through the power of spiritual visualization he has command of illimitable powers. He must, however, remember that force or pressure or precociousness or seeking to visualize anything out of timing to the Will of God for him will offend the rhythmic accord in his spirit and the cyclic law of his human nature.

Mantramic speaking is a form of self-suggestion, producing results beyond expectation. One can through pre-sleep mantrams quicken the motion and movement of Quelle, and thus accelerate himself out of the boundaries and fixities in karma.

Through intense inner picturing of right visualization, cells in the body will realign themselves to health rather than sickness. The blood stream will be purified. The muscles of the body will become obedient and relaxed structures supporting the physical, skeletal frame.

When mind, desire and willing are selfless, receptive vehicles of light and love, one can work directly with foreforces, prolonging the physical years of life that he might better serve; and he can also magnify and extend his senses into a powerful extrasensory perception of a high order.

Every time a man believes himself to be a fool, he has planted a seed of self-suggestion, preparing himself to be a failure. Each time man knows that he is using but a part of the nobler and more divine side of his nature, he has made suggestible abstract patterns come alive in his own nature.

Man must believe that he is a divine being implanted into a materialistic atmosphere to make it divine. One can, if he will, instantly change the current of disbelief into belief, and thereby set into operation the higher side of his suggestible and creative nature.

To use true self-suggestion is to become more spiritually sensitive. To use self-hypnosis is to become a fanatic. Self-hypnosis is egotistical suggestibility, and cannot produce living, creative, lasting things. Self-hypnosis comes from what one *wants* oneself to be or to have, and is produced out of an overwanting, an exaggerated self-importance, self-glamorizing and self-assertion.

A certain power metaphysics produces self-hypnosis glamor-pictured environments, lasting only in a chimera fashion until karma becomes the lever or checkrein to balance self-will enforcement.

Self-suggestion is soft, gentle, non-intrusive. It is wafted upon light waves of love, gently penetrating the true destined aim and goal, precipitating it into a loving, creating and perfected placement.

The way one may recognize whether he is practicing right self-suggestion or if he is deluded into forms of self-hypnotism, thinking it to be self-suggestion, will be that he thinks he cannot make a mistake and that he is always perfect. This is self-hypnosis.

The scientist of self-suggestion knows that he can err on the physical plane and also on the inner-plane sciences. And he also recognizes that the flow of suggestion is not dependent solely upon his own knowledge of this power, but that he is being prepared always through intercommuning powers of suggestion. To become a better scientist of his inner being, one should ask that he become each day a better interpreter of these great suggestible forces speaking to his inner being and that his higher sensory powers become fine and flawless instruments, thereby making him a skillful worker for God.

FEAR AND SUGGESTION

The downpulling forces of negative suggestibility are fear, anxiety and depression. To fear is to suffer. To fear is to hate. To fear is to be separate, to doubt. To fear is to betray oneself and those whom he loves. To fear is to veil oneself away from God. When fear is the prompter of one's suggestions, one builds a pattern or habit picture excluding him from all of the better things of life. To use self-suggestion while fearing is to etch a course of life assuring unhappiness.

Fear must be totally absent in the use of spiritual self-suggestion. To truly picture and to manifest good things, better things, one must be fearless, nor can one for one second use any form of disbelief or doubt in the science of self-suggestion.

Fear is a gravity downpull of the mind. What man fears will assuredly come upon him. To jealously fear that one will lose his beloved will in time set up forces of suggestibility whereby he will be separated from his beloved. If his beloved is money, or position, or creation, through a period of time fearful suggestion will manifest what he fears.

Fear of one's own body regarding health will manifest conditions of sickness. The opposite of fear—faith, trust, belief — are the three angels of power to uproot fear, producing courage and hope.

The prudent side of self-preservation does not stem from fear. To be fearless does not mean that one should be foolish, seeking to bend the laws of Nature. Fearlessness is courage in the midst of disaster, in the face of death, and in the face of banishment. One who is fearless will ride out the tide of disaster, and find a fertile homeplace in desolate places.

The most high compensatory value opposite fear is a love of life, giving off a continued radiance and vision of good, recognizing in the countenance of others a trust.

Habit patterns of fear are inherited in families. Mothers pass on to their children their hostilities, hatreds and fears. The mother in a family is a more suggestible instrument, impressing her hates, her hostilities and fears upon the absorptive suggestibility of her children. Using unconscious inductive suggestibility when fearful, she sets a course of regression for the future of her child or children. A hostile woman produces a fearful offspring. Hostile and separative family traits develop into antisocial attitudes after children reach maturity.

Psychic influence between mother and child, if the child comes heavily laden with karmic debts, sets up a cyclic chain of inference in the life of a child. On reaching adulthood, such persons must contend with hostile suggestible inference implanted into their emotions during childhood.

The psychic atmosphere of the home is absorbed as a mood theme in the back of the mind of the child, and comes forward in adult consciousness in a mood fashion. Persons given to black moods may trace such moods to childhood receptivity.

As men are educated to their psychic natures, they will be indoctrinated as to how to wear away morbidity stemming from inductive suggestion. Inductive suggestion may also be received by any person with whom one may be associated, particularly if one person has a strongly charged desire to dominate the mind of another.

The subjective person receiving an overcharge of disapproving psychic energy is made to feel guilty or uncomfortable, or experiences a suggestible feeling that he has wronged the person from whom he receives the inductive suggestion.

To be overexposed to a person having heavily charged dominant suggestive powers is to exhaust and devitalize one's capacity for self-expression. To protect oneself from such persons, one should move with deliberation out of their environment for intervals of repletion and recharging.

Fear is the basic and root cause for agreeing to accept suggestible inductive dominance from another person. One must search himself as to why he has attracted such persons to himself.

The power of attracting and repelling is a psychic power. In karma, one is attracted to persons who hold a key to his karma. In grace, one is attracted to persons who hold a key to his grace. When one comes to see that he has within his own nature spiritual and psychic forces upon which to draw, he learns that his dependence is not upon the will of persons but upon the Will of God.

It is necessary that one be conjoined with other persons and dependent to some degree upon their companionship. This fulfills a law of interflow between souls. However, no one should give over his total will to another. Having a will of his own, he should assure himself that his will is a right will by giving it over to the Will of God.

The greatest of teachers teach their disciples to fear those who would cast a shadow upon the freedom of their souls. Jesus taught that one should fear such persons above all others.

In all human nature there is a desire for balance, and there are balancing universal laws determining that this desire shall be fulfilled. In time, man will balance all of the forces of his psychic nature, and give freedom to the spiritual impulses of his higher mind and soul.

On the level of fear and its great impact upon the suggestible mind or subconscious, one should be alert that he does not take into his hands the harmful aspect of the dark side of balance, or that is, retaliation. Revenge in the hands of man invokes self-disaster. Very often one who is overfearful seeks to blindly strike out at those whom he feels to be the cause of his fear, when within his own nature lies the cause and the remedy.

Retaliation brings back to the revengeful person more than the bread on the waters. Acts of retaliation bring home to him a just justice. Through fearful suggestion man becomes his own enemy. In time, his fears become a fungus eating away the vital spirit of life in his own nature.

To repair and give relief to a fear-distorted mind requires patience, loving suggestible words of kindness, implanting into the sick mind a desirable sense of direction.

A divine intuition is required to see beyond the mass deposits of accumulative fears. To reach back into Quelle depths to heal, one must speak to something beyond the outer mind of a person incarcerated in a hell of self-made fears. One must with his own divine nature resort to divine resources of help. These kindred spirits of man are the angels. Of all Beings under God, none have greater powers of suggestibility than the angels.

The sense of smell in an animal, a serpent, a bird or a naive person is suggestibly receptive to fear, anger or hatred in a person. An animal will attack a fearful, hate-filled person. Sensitive children instantly know through communicable suggestibility whether they are liked or not, loved or not loved, wanted or not wanted.

In the very womb before birth the one to be born knows whether he is wanted. A child unwanted lives in the physical world always with the memory of womb unwantedness. The power of Quelle suggestion is communicated to the embryo in the womb of the mother. *Suggestion is older than the power of the senses, and therefore works before the senses.*

Through hypnosis one can be suggestibly influenced to see things not seen with the physical eye, hear things not heard with the physical ear, smell odors not existing in the physical atmosphere, taste food on the vine before it is manifested on the palate, touch objects or forms at a distance. Thus, suggestibility goes before the physical senses, and in a magnified degree is an accompanying phenomenon to extrasensory perception. To be successful in any form of extrasensory power, one first uses suggestion.

All desire works with the laws of suggestion. The desires directed by the lower senses will take one where his karma wants him to go. The flow of one's high or low desires determines his fate and destiny in each life. If one chooses to be a vehicle for the spiritual life, he must scrutinize his desires first and determine from whence they come — whether from a pure heart impulse detached from possessiveness or from psychically-charged fixed emotions desiring excitement and sensation.

The path to the spiritual life has long been described as the left or the right hand path. When one comes to the higher desire aspect of the spiritual life, he must enter into the middle way or the doorway so small that it is often invisible to him who would seek to open.

In healing suggestion powers, one should remember that health is a state of belief, and that mind is the agent through which beliefs are extended. The psychic mind or lower mind desires to tell one that he is uncomfortable, displeased, irritated, feverish. In suggestible helps, one who researches sees that each vehicle or body — the physical, the emotional and the mental body — has its own unique degree of health. The mental body can be hypnotized by false registering of the senses; and the emotional body, the suggestible understudy for the lower aspect of the mental body, can be coerced into feeling pain and suffering.

When the three bodies of man which he uses for earth experience are more psychically charged than spiritually dynamic, the energy body or etheric body mirrors and reflects the disorganization and lack of coordination between the three bodies.

The etheric body outpictures into the physical body the negative beliefs of the psychic mind or lower mind causing one to believe that he is in a state of dying. The three bodies should be as three harmonious friends, all working together in a synchronized action, that they may be in unison as servants for the spirit ruling the body.

When an ego comes with heavily charged karma from a former life, the psychic energy fields in each body are out of tune with one another. The result is weakness in one or more bodies — the weak body resisting the other two vehicles.

To heal and bring into balance through spiritual suggestion the nonalignment between bodies, one must unite with the directing higher will in the higher mind. A person not having connection with the directing will of the higher mind is like a man hanging on a rope frayed on the ends. Suspended above the earth or reality, he sees things out of proportion.

Persons not understanding the infinite and illimitable and higher power of the directing will in their higher minds, also may be said to be clinging to the frayed rope of their lesser wills. They are exposed to outer circumstances and external conditions which toss them ruthlessly about. Eventually pain, discomfort, extreme suffering lead man to the door of understanding. Flailing about, resisting, being pushed up and down, becoming no longer bearable, he ceases to resist; he becomes quiescent, accepting. It is then that the directing will in the higher mind unites with the great healing resources of God.

The ministering angels come forth, though not always seen by the sufferer in his outer sight. Their suggestible emolients of love give peace and a gradual wisdom to the mind. Psychic mind has been used by man for aeons. It has a mechanistic action in that the habit patterns in former lives seek to be used over and over in each life. Thus, if it were not for the divine mind of man there would be little progress for each life. Despite man's development in civilizations, he still retains the mechanistic psychic force reflexes of unintelligently directed aggression. Thus man, even in spiritual environments and in the name of religion, can still do violent things to other men and to himself.

The psychic habit pressures active in the etheric body and the lower mind are mechanically assured of survival from life to life. However, they may become generators for the divine life when one uses his higher mind in the Will of God.

A person giving himself over entirely to the lower psychic mind unites with the destroying forces when he meets an obstacle coming against his wants and his wishes. If he is approaching the beginning or the sunrise of a more divine mind, psychic pressure yet unfaced produces suffering in the dense lower vehicles — and sickness is often the door to spiritual initiation. However, when one is not evolved more sensitively and desires solely the sensual way of life, he becomes a psychic destroyer towards others, standing between them and their evolvement.

The directing will of the higher mind contains a shaping, a visualizing, and a manifesting power. When one uses spiritual suggestion with the help of the angels, the angels release manifold powers for him who sees the good and the true and the right for that one who has unknowingly set a snare in the path of his evolvement.

Jesus forgave men for their sins, understanding that they were often the victims of their own unknowing. He knew that great cosmic laws supported the psychic mind. He recognized that man could become a victim to unleashed and wild forces in his own consciousness when in a state of egoism and unbelieving. He asked only that men wholly believe. To be made well and to be made whole one must believe that universal cause supports his life in all states, in all places, and in all worlds.

Quelle is mistress of the night, and works at night upon the psychic nature to set aright the errors of the day. When Quelle is free at night, suggestion of the night produces improvement on the coming day. Pre-sleep mantrams give freedom to Quelle in the night. Before sleep, to suggestibly visualize a plan for tomorrow, a health for tomorrow, a courage for tomorrow, and a creativity for tomorrow, is to free Quelle's flow.

Mass Fears and Suggestion

In the present breakthrough by science into the psychic states of consciousness, men having a desire to contribute to the world and also group-bodies influencing men will find it necessary to understand the psychic functioning of the mind. The world is presently undergoing an accumulative exposure to the collective unconscious. Mass fears in mankind will be studied by scientists so as to learn the cause of fearful conflagrations, tumults and wars.

The new science of man will see that war begins as an accumulative hypnosis following a cyclic course and having as its root impulse a masochistic overflow of guilt in nations and in mankind.

Throughout the ages men have purged communal conscience through the horror of wars. Mankind now entering a higher degree of genesis, scientists concerned for the fate of the world will seek to prevent wars. Whereas in the present time, psychology approaches the individual through analysis and research, there will be included in the forthcoming world court a scientific clinical effort to establish an ethic between continents, and a probe into the cause of wars and their prevention. The world court will emphasize this phase of its activity.

Generations and eons of men living in the world have lived and died in the midst of adversity and danger, being in danger from the laws of Nature, from infectious plagues, from disasters, from wars. They have always had near them and within them the spectacle of fearsome things confronting them in the physical world. The memory of these terrifying mirages is reflected in the darkened side of Quelle. In certain periods they rise up into the senses of man, causing him to be hostile, to have hatred, and to have fear.

If Quelle has not released these banked fires of atavistic fears through natural processes — such as, being needed, serving and creativity — the result is that there is in the mind of the individual a thought and feeling process always tinged with dread and apprehension, or a smokelike screen over the thinking process, veiling away the keener aspects of the mind.

As men progress more and more in their belief that they are civilized, they repress their aggressive adrenalin-charged instincts, refusing to encounter and face their fears. Fear is thus driven back into the murky caverns of Quelle, and sooner or later Quelle will spill out hidden hatred supported by repressed fears.

When masses of souls in the earth reincarnate simultaneously during a new era of consciousness — souls having unresolved karmic debts and heavily laden with self-guilt — the result is fear and distrust of life, of their fellow man, and of their personal associations, and distrust of their own qualifications and self-worth. The overflow of Quelle in such massive proportions produces a disordered and inharmonious atmosphere among men. However, God's law produces in these times remedial grace, that such souls, if responsive, will benefit by compensatory conditions timed under the Will of God. This gives to man, if he will respond, a way to escape from the senseless pattern of negation and pain.

ANGELS AND SUGGESTION

If man understood more clearly the nature of the angels, he would build around him a hexagon psychic frame of invulnerability. At the expense of his experience and sojourn in materiality, man more often is compelled to live in the lower psychic side of his senses. This side of the senses has not the capacity to weigh, measure, intuit or see the angels. The lower psychic nature is the servant of the egotistical nature. Self-engrossment makes heavy the atmosphere of self, excluding conscious angel awareness.

The subconscious mind of man is aware of the angels. And man does draw strength in the night or dream state from the angels assigned to help him since the beginning of this eternity.

To open the angel doors, one must in desperation break through the confining walls of egotism, and must know himself to be yet in the making. He must accept that he is assisted by godly communing preceptors, teachers and angelic builders.

Awareness of the angels, rather than glamorizing the ego, expands the naive aspect of reverence in man. The ministering angels work with man in initiatory trials. To call on them is to become like Jesus during the time in which He was confronted by Satan. The angels ministered to Jesus and fed Him on the desert, that He might be prepared to withstand the greater initiations to come.

Angel suggestibility seeks to enter into man's beliefs and faith. Beliefs are like small soldiers on a battlefield. The angels would take this army of beliefs and use them to build creative mansions of the soul. Faith being the commander or authority over one's army of beliefs, the angels would use the power of faith to take and to hold spiritual territory, lands, governments and districts unseen by man.

Belief and faith are the two golden attributes the angels use that man may command his instincts to shape them into radiant extrasensory particles of light.

The great angels of ascendency grace seek to shake out from time to time the soil shading the soul. They move upon the mind of one in the distress times of initiation to assure him that paradise and heaven are a reality, and that earth must return to refinement and receptivity that men may use the higher aspect of their souls rather than the lower or psychic aspect of their senses.

Angels have little difficulty in suggesting to children that the world is a dear place. Only corrupt souls are slow to respond to the angels. One may extend angel suggestibility atmosphere to a third sort of atmospheric breath, whereby one is recharged continually with God renewals.

There are no walls or barricades to shut out angel flow into the consciousness of man, be he evil or good. Conscious belief on the angels will bring visions of the angels. Angel suggestion can mold the sight of man that one may see his angel. Sometimes an angel form is seen as a mass of blue light, or angel suggestion in thought may occur as it did to Paul on the road to Damascus. Angels through suggestion penetrated the consciousness of Paul, and thus made a fertile receptivity in the mind of Paul to receive the light of Jesus and to hear His words.

Angels do not yield or give up in a needy proposition. Perseverance is an angelic attribute. Man persisting has much to learn from the perseverance of the angels. Angels suggest to man that he continue to knock on all the doors closed against his prayers or praying.

To think of only one angel is to stint oneself of full enlightenment as to the angels and their helps. Angels come in companies, legions and armies to succor the needs of man. One should make wide his whole belief in the angels that he may invite an angel company into his suggestibility, that he may ride out the tide of his involvement in pain.

One should open the doors of his believing as a form of passion and accelerated faith with a look toward the angels as agents and messengers of God to help him mightily, perfectly. One should not analyze and decide how the angels will come. As each atom must find its own affinity in a molecular mass, so will the right angels in the right moment touch the painful spot, place and condition and soothe it with a perfect angel glow.

To heal through the help of the angels one must believe and have faith that he can speak to an angel and receive response. No other tongue save the tongue of love can an angel hear, nor will any angel respond to any tongue save the tongue of love.

To heal one who stands in a crisis of sickness, of weariness, of confusion, one remembers his own angel as a messenger ready on call to go forth and to deliver a message of love to the one sick. One addresses his angel, knowing that his angel will know and do rightly that which must be done in the name of love.

With a loving heart and a mind fixed on light, one asks his angel to speak to the angel of the one sick, that he may be made well in right proportion to the law and Will of God. Thus, one speaks an Angel to Angel Mantram to see miracles at work.

Suggestible healing powers minus love when used from mind to mind intrude upon mind and will, offending the ethic of healing. A mantram delivered by one's angel to the angel of the one sick fulfills the ethic of healing suggestion and mediation.

THE SUGGESTING ANGELS AND THEIR HELPS FOR THE SOUL-LIFE OF MAN

The personal angels watching over man's personal life work with suggestible angelic induction, not as man works with suggestible mind. The angels of the body, emotions, mind, and destiny cease not in their suggesting reminders to man, reminding man that he is a cognitive creature learning and earning within a phenomenal world. The body of man is seen by an angel differently from the way man sees his body. The dearest angel to man, who loves and serves him, is his emotional angel, or Angel of Pure Desiring. The Angel of Pure Desiring emanates a continuing effluvia of love suggestibility, making him more competent to extend love, to receive love, and to be loving.

The treasured Mental Angel stands by the mind of the mental initiate. As a perfect angelic penetrator, he works to keep his protege's thoughts on God and upon the plan of God. He keeps before the mind of the initiate that God is One spirit, One life, One mind in all. The Mental Angel initiates the mind of man into the mysteries of mind, and keeps the unfathomable riches of thought awake to spirit as creation through mind.

XVII

RISHIS AND THE CHRIST

The higher gifts of the soul are now ready to be harvested and to be used in the upward thrust of man's expanding mind. Should the Western world fail to respond to this most urgent need to increase its capacity in self-understanding, should it fail to avail itself of the new and acceptable techniques of psychic research and application as used in other prominent nations, it will have failed to rise on the crest of advancement. Through a perverse narrowness it will have stepped aside from taking hold of the link in the chain required to receive the full effulgent blessings in the scientific age.

In the next twenty years in the Western world, Western psychology, psychiatry, and religion will decide whether to permit the stepchild ESP or psi to be recognized and utilized.

Men in the Western world will either isolate and separate ESP power as being something to be dissected and shelved, or they will incorporate the knowlegde of ESP into all of the sciences — organic, human, and abstract.

Persons using ESP powers with knowledge and ethic throughout the years have lived by necessity under the shadow of indifference, ridicule and sometimes extreme persecution.

Knowledge of the psychic nature if ignored will be the same as though this nation had ignored the creative power of the atom. Knowledge of the intelligible flow of energies in the body, of its healing therapeutic suggestibility, of its necessity to energize and give vitality to the religious and spiritual life, also knowledge of the psychic phases of the unconscious—these are presently available and are essential in all forward-looking people, regardless of race, nation, or creed.

The Western mind is more often concerned with what one can do with psychic power or with what *it will do for him.* The Eastern mind has used the suggestible psychic power for ages, and has proved it to be an invaluable extension in the processes of the mind.

So often the Western person downgrades the Eastern philosophies, comparing the archaic financial patterns of the East with the materialistic success formulas of the West. The door of spirituality is now beginning to open to the soul of man in the West. The philosophy and life-force knowledge of the East is being offered once more to many souls in the West.

A Western initiate is so organized in his energy body through certain reincarnation progressions of the past that he very often does not understand that the Eastern practices of meditation and contemplation, when used by the Western ego, cannot produce self-realization in the same manner for him as would be produced for an initiate of the East. The spiritual or eternal atoms residing in the higher etheric body of the initiate of the West are more cosmically generated with individualistic energy than the eternal atoms of a person who has reincarnated into Eastern bodies for many lives. In the Western initiate's lower etheric body this is caused by the undisciplined and unruly kundalini fire from the waist downward, emphasized especially upon the fire of the adrenal glands.

Men are souls throughout the earth. Polarity or placement of a person is an act of destiny. All souls living in the West have at some time lived in the continents of the East. India, the cradle of the aesthetic side of the psychic life, has kept alive for ages the Rishi heritage. These truths abide in the eternal cradle of illumination. Men of the East have been the receivers of this wisdom and its infiltration into all forms of their personal and inner life.

The great Rishi-sage directives are stylused into the soul memory of man. These return inductively to men whenever there are uprising phases in the evolutionary progress of mankind.

In every continent there are highly evolved initiates. The Western initiate cannot reverse the clock of his reincarnation progression. The Eastern initiate remains content to be nestled in the familiar effluvia-fire supporting his spiritual life. The Western initiate today under the Christ Spirit looks again to the East that he might better understand the purpose of the coming of Jesus into the world. Behind the scenes of the West and the East there is now occurring a fusion of these two great resources of spiritual power. India representing the feminine principle and the West representing the masculine are to be married; this fusion of ideas, ideals, and spiritual philosophy will produce the scientific-spiritual child of the future.

Man of the West being unaware of the necessity to lift the lower kundalini fire into the receptacle of the heart is presently engaged in an overself-positive state of willing.

In the Eastern meditative practices the emphasis is upon the heart and the pineal gland. These two chakras or centers are the doorway to the portal of illumination.

The Western initiate failing to channel the kundalini fire through the heart puts an overpressure upon the vagus nerve system and the adrenal-gland psychic energy portal.

Physical ailments prominent in the West are more often due to the need to use techniques of suggestibility as used in the yoga practices of the East. Stomach ulcer, the hypertension sickness of high blood pressure, and heart ailments so prevalent in the West are due to lack of union with and command of the flow of emotions in the energy body.

The Western initiate lives in a world of outgoing demands. He has little time for meditation or contemplation. Engrossed in the outer world and its competitions, he is unaware of the marvelous world of the life-force within.

Everything in the Western initiate's life is achieved in his consciousness through movement, excitation, stimulation — all externally experienced. Yet, the Western disciple — despite the clamor, the glamor, and the force — is achieving a certain sort of consciousness necessary that he may eventually master and come to know and use the universal energy processes on a cosmic scale. In the space age facing man he will first harness and master the energy forces within his own body, and he will come to use levitation on a greater scale than used in the time of Atlantis or the early dynasties of Egypt.

The solar and planetary energies in his body will be harnessed to give him a levitation and locomotion power over gravity. With a simple compass-like directing apparatus attached to certain portions of his body, he will draw upon the solar fire of his etheric body. He will glide and move above the ground or earth by mechanically drawing upon the solar energy stored in his own body. He will also develop levitated cargo routes above the ground. This will come when man finally looks with open eyes upon the psychic regeneration aspects of his nature and mind.

Long before man used electricity the potential was all about him to light his environment, and thus he was able to move out of the prolonged sundown in his mind.

The expansion of energy processes will absorb man in the coming century. The psychic nature of man holds the key. The door will be found in the Western world by those holding the key.

The Eastern world has possessed the prize of soul and mind illumination for ages. Their peace and ancient Rishis' healing powers are still active for the more sensitively oriented egos of the West. Their power is inductive. In the present phase of its life the East may be said to give to the world inductive wisdom, and the soul of the West now seeks to objectify this wisdom uniting the world upward as one family of souls.

Jesus is the Saviour of the world. He is the Supreme Avatar of this earth system. The Christ Spirit in the mind of Jesus is the light of the world. All of the greater teachers linked into the guru line of the East recognize the sovereignty of Jesus and of His uniting mission in the world between the East and the West. It is the destiny for all men of the world to eventually come under the light of the world — the Christ.

The most recent records of the guru line in India reveal that in the Himalayas is a great teacher whose longevity grace enables him to encourage disciples and chelas both of the East and the West to make union with the Christ. Western disciples and initiates in this time are in their higher unconscious linking with the Eastern guru-Rishi line, seeking to fuse their Western Christ heritage with the Rishi heart rose of illumination.

Many of these are not aware of this in their outer spiritual manifestations. However, their hearts are hungering for the interflow of the Christ light and the Rishi intuition. Some have knowledge of the Christ and Rishi blending in their hearts' receiving center. These are presently absorbed in researching the stronghold confirmation of enduring verities to which they are heirs.

The refusal of the young to accept an over-compressed, unliving picture of Jesus has turned many advanced egos now living in their younger years to look to the East for instruction. In time, the more highly evolved among these will make union with the divine light of the Christ, and experience Him as the ultimate transcendental Being of Light, and will recognize that all paths of truth and light lead to the Christ.

The careless, soiled minority of young egos who seek the fantastic side of the psychic life through Eastern practices will fade out. These soiled neutral-field young persons can be identified by their lack of responsibility in relation to their persons, their habits, and their attitudes toward their elders and society. There are, however, a majority of young persons who will mature during the upward rise of the spiritual vitality now entering into this earth. These are the leaders and forerunners of the cosmic scientific era.

Religion, education, medicine, engineering, space projects and interterrestrial discoveries will be made possible through the unison of advanced egos who will see with one vision as with one eye the need to return mankind to the basic spiritual realities without which all projects, all inventions would be in vain.

In the world today there are clusters of initiate egos having interior communication with one another, often never having looked upon the physical faces of those whom they know so well and so deeply and dearly on the inner planes of consciousness. These radiating souls are in the world standing in their polarity station as servers of light. In former lives their souls have been tossed, stirred, pressed and tried in the crucible of the great initiations. These initiations occurred in Atlantis, in China, in ancient Egypt, in the great Andes, in the Eastern portion of the United States, in Persia, in Greece, and in Judea.

The crucible of initiation is a womblike encasing vortex holding together the interconnecting relationships between novice initiates and disciples, higher initiates, masters, and adepts.

When one is exposed to genius of a significant kind peacefully and quietly rendering service to the freedom of the dissolving of human and personal karma, one finds a higher initiate.

Some initiates come to free mankind from one faulty idea or concept which has inhibited the pure flow in nationalistic evolvement. Some high master initiates come to free demeaning and restricting social systems in continents. Some come to bring to the world great music, and unite man to the great healing euphonious energies or musics concealed in Nature and the atmosphere. Some master initiates come to teach the Word. All are unself-motivated; united with the audible sound currents of the Holy Ghost, they produce freeing ideas and appear in the world to prepare men to receive such ideas. They are, as Jesus said, rejected and scorned and often-times persecuted. It is sad that of all of the loves man has in the human world, his love fantasy and intoxication with outmoded beliefs is the most prevalent and obstructing. Thus, all advanced egos are resisted. Particularly is this so in the Western world, where man believes life to be most satisfying when demanding and aggressive.

India, the mother crucible for the world inductive mind, has given master formulas for a way of peace within. Jesus came to bring the greater archetypal ethics, that men might find a way of peace within and without. With the timing of Jesus new lands yet unseen by man were waiting to become the cradle for another step in the rise of genesis. High initiates at the time of the birth of Jesus lived in the world. Through anticipation of His being cosmically materialized for the world, these great egos began their forward look into a new era of life, a new way of life, through which the masses would begin to use the higher aspects of their mental atoms, and thus produce a marriage between reason and intuition.

Jesus was a master craftsman of transubstantiation. He understood and used the great cosmic energy laws; they were obedient to Him. He understood the heart of man, and He understood that man's mind was still in its infancy.

THE TEACHER

The more one evolves spiritually the more he must learn that there are no barriers to the soul of man unless he himself erects them. To be a whole person one must recognize all kingdoms — from the mountain to plant and animal and man to the angel. All come under the Supreme Spirit dwelling within.

The outer consciousness mind of man is fed by a psychical-life current indwelling as a wellspring upholding his higher ego and mind. The soul works continually to utilize all cosmic forces, energies, and intelligences. The soul desires with a compelling desire to use and to utilize to the uttermost all things offered in cosmic existence.

The power of extrasensory perception in man is ever present. It is the intelligible life-force energy compulsion linking the ego and the soul to perceive all aspects of life on the physical, emotional and mental planes.

Exposure to conscience is inevitable in initiation to spiritual nature; this may prove traumatic and painful if the initiation has failed to keep pace with the philosophic and wisdom aspects in evolvement. It is primarily of the first nature for all persons interested in harmonizing and utilizing their psychic natures, that they are instructed in the fundamental ethics in philosophy and in metaphysics. Overemphasis placed upon any one philosophy or upon any one metaphysical system can also be harmful, producing a sense of superiority and a skeptical mind. Overengrossment in a biased or a slanted system of metaphysical study emphasizing success of the ego builds addition to karma, creating unbearable tensions in evolvement.

True and pure psychic power is experienced in progressive stages, leading one into door after door of initiation until the spiritual aspect of initiation is finally fulfilled.

All initiators, teachers and gurus of the divine line of teachers warn of the dangers of the hypnotic glamors of the psychic world, and seek to protect their proteges from the pitfalls of being detained on the subtle, psychical plateaus of consciousness. These divine instructors understand the meaning of the suggestible effects of the sensory phenomenal astral planes, and seek to guide their novice charges over the lower precipices of delusion and derangement.

Obedience to the teacher and to what he teaches — the teacher as a representative of God, the One — will in time lead the novice initiate toward all of the joys to be had from the higher psychical state or the spiritually illumined mind.

When the timing is ripe, a pure soul prays to be found ready and worthy of his teacher, so that he may walk within the framework of the higher enlightenment, for he knows the sorrow of meaningless struggle, and he also intuits the waste and the agony in a fragmentary, futile, unknowing way.

Only the glamor-stricken person yields to the belief that he alone can find the path; to do so is to delay. When the pupil is ready, the teacher does appear. Woe unto him who dallies by the way.

The ready novice recognizes his teacher by *the works* he sees the teacher do. If his heart is selfless, his heart will tell him whether the works of the teacher are united to the service of the Real. Should any amount of self-glamour remain in his self-esteem — due to something yet unresolved in his egotistical karmic retention — he may attract first a false teaching or teacher, that he may be scourged with the demoting fires of the ego. Or, he may become his own karmic obstacle, if he expects to retain something of the glamor, while yet being instructed in the spiritual life. Such persons invoke heavy inner and outer disciplines, attracting the extreme karmic initiatory confrontations. All of these must be cleansed and made right so that the *true* underlying desire may at last be mechanized as a perfected instrument for the light.

Thousands of grapes must go into the press to produce a wine for the sacrament. Thousands of tasks must be undertaken to countermand the unfinished and faulty acts of the past. The teacher representing the way to the door, and the cherubim angels guarding the door to the sacred way of wisdom, watch over, guide, strengthen and reinforce the one who would truly rise in the light.

In the Western world of higher instruction, the hand of the teacher may be first recognized in a book placed in one's hand, pointing the way to, or giving an answer to, a prominent anxiety or problem. Following this, in its natural course comes a specific teaching fulfilling the novitiary requirements for transposing the more orthodox and intellectual concepts of the past. The third aspect in progression instruction begins when the inner teacher appears. He may appear as a holy person in the physical world, or he may appear only in certain aspects of meditation, and he may also be experienced as a voice and a presence during night-flight or dreams. It is certain that when the teacher appears, a unique type of telepathy enters into the thoughts of the novitiate heretofore not experienced in his mind.

JESUS AS THE GURU OF THE GURUS

Jesus is the first and supreme avatar for the world. All who have reached higher self-genesis consciously enter the door to instruction through Jesus.

Even though it may outwardly seem that a self-genesis ego is united in instruction to an eastern guru, Jesus is the Mediator and true mediative light for all guru instruction. The greater guru line is headed by Jesus, and more and more it may be seen that Rishi instructors seek to identify themselves with Jesus. In some manner all religions puzzle over the magnificent enigma in Jesus, intuiting Him to be the One who contains the Way, the Truth, and the Life.

To cling to guru eastern instruction through love or bhakti instruction endears an initiate to Jesus. To finally open the heart buds in loving is similar to a flowing stream irresistibly drawn toward the source of love, Jesus. The Jesus heart is a magnet drawing all inwardly toward the soul-winged way of irresistible love. All teachers, gurus, and saints know Him who loves all.

The Rishi systems of instruction teach one how to fulfill self salvation. The Jesus instruction prepares one to take part in world salvation. To pray for a teacher never fails to produce a teacher or a guru. To each one comes the teacher perfectly and closely aligned with the seeking and the call. A true guru, in teaching, never fails to point toward the One higher and beyond. This is that One called Jesus. Blessed is the one who comes in the name of the Lord.

The Master's Apprentice

Until a person shows himself to be willing to use ethically the psychic forces of his nature, he must receive instruction from the lesser teachings rather than from the greater Masters and finally Christ.

The mighty Rishis' ethic, as established by the guru-line, is: no one comes under the instruction of the Masters until he is willing to accept the discipline enabling him to master the sub-charged psychical energies and fires possessing his lesser thoughts, emotions, and will.

Under the Master's supervision the first probationary steps in initiation consist of stilling the unruly facets of the psychic nature. Self-responsibility, self-reliance and self-control are the result of subduing the unruly energy and forces as experienced in the psychic life.

Thousands of lives make an initiate, millions of years a Master. The Masters, living in the eternal aspect of time, never grow impatient with their proteges. Sometimes the Master appears in meditative vision; or in crisis times of initiation the eyes of the Master may be seen, speaking a tender message, giving a counsel of strength and love. For there is no greater love outside of Christ than the love of the Master for his disciple. Beyond even the love of a mother, the Master loves, understands, and guides.

When the novitiate first enters the Master's stream of telepathy, he flows and goes with the direction of the stream of the Master's creative design for his proteges. If one is obediently inclined and disciplined, blessings will increase day by day. If he happens to have a resisting mind, blessings will become widely spaced until certain lessons are learned. To him who has stamina and an appreciative heart, there will come a certain grace-bearing strength.

To be an apprentice of the Masters is a blessing of holiness. Under the Masters, physical eyesight gradually becomes spiritual seership; hearing of gravity tones becomes a rapture of responding to heavenly music.

The Master knows what and how much the initiate can absorb. The initiate will endure all phases of initiation with the help of his Master and the angels until he has gained a spiritual strength equal to the agony experienced in and through greater initiation trials.

THE GATES AND THE DOOR TO INITIATION

The spiritual disciple seeks to become an initiate; the initiate seeks to become an adept. Once the hand is on the plow he looks not back, and in time he will experience the great or sacred initiation whereby he will become more than a dove mystic or an eagle initiate. By the spiritual law of ascension, he will become a transcended avatar.

The divine avatar chain of illumination is inconceivable to the mind of the lesser initiate. The dove initiate or mystic-heart initiation of love pertains to feeling and the emotions. The eagle initiate relates to the use of mental powers as received from communicable levels of telepathic mediation. Mind initiation unites the initiate with certain powers of imaging, enabling him to use some degree of de-manifestation and manifestation.

All teacher-gurus are *gates* to the sacred initiations. Christ Jesus is the *door* to the divine Father of this eternity system. The Father's indwelling center is fixed within the Divine Thalamus located in the upper portion of the back of the skull or head. When one speaks the words of Jesus, ". . . the Father that dwelleth in me, he doeth the works," he opens the Divine Thalamus, and the Father takes command of the creative process of imaging in the initiate's mind. To keep

this envisioning reality in one's thoughts is to enter into communion with the Father within — and thereafter, thought
and visioning images become as one.

There is no sudden attainment of spiritual power or powers.
All initiates must cross the bridge of discipline into the gates
of evolvement to finally reach the door and become one with
Him who came to unite all with the heavenly Father.
Spiritual acceleration may be attained in only one manner:
one must remain with heart, mind, and soul continually
fixed upon God.

Meditation opens the *gates*. Through extended communion
the *door* opens. The power to go in and out of the door is a
walk of light. All in the light will go in and out with blessings,
and thus serve Him who has made all.

XVIII

SUGGESTIBLE DIRECTIVES TO COMMAND AND CONTROL THE UNRULY PSYCHIC CURRENTS IN THE LOWER MIND

How to Use Your Aura

The aura, or the field of energy around the etheric and physical bodies, is a defense mechanism against the noise, the force, and the unrefined energies received from the outer cosmic life, and is also a depository reflector for all of the interior and inward life of a person.

The initiate uses his auric energy field to transpose and to expand the light generated by the akasic fire of his soul. This light begins with the higher mind, the higher will — and is sent into the aura as a form of utmost desire to give light to darkness.

Light gathered within the auric field overflowing spiritually into the lives of others is sometimes spoken of as holy magnetism. Spiritual light in the aura has the power to draw persons or conditions to an initiate and also has the power to flow over into the lives of all whom he contacts.

The inner life of the initiate, when regularly observing spiritual rhythms, prepares him to sustain the auric light without variance. He can become an effulgent presence literally giving off the life and the light of the spirit.

To have a magnetic aura influencing the lives of others one must have earned the influencing techniques through having access to unique resources of soul power. The auric field is charged with living life force in one who is invigorated with living ideas, living desires. The aura, when powerful, can become a condenser for telepathic sending. The in-and-out telepathic flow of the auric field, being a sending and receiving process, all intelligible telepathic sending is screened out onto the auric field, thrusting forth into the agreeing minds of those whose auric fields are receptive to the sender.

One can only be receptive to the benefits from the higher telepathic wave lengths of the soul, spirit, and mind when his own auric field is sympathetic to what is being sent. In the case of a damaged aura caused by wrong use of the influencing suggestible arts, one gives off from the soil levels of the negative; thus one receives the depressing suggestible telepathies from the aura of a person who has a low-grade demagnetized aura.

The student and initiate learns to keep his aura flooded with love. The more love outpictured on the aura, the more radiance, the more joy, the more healing. One cannot artificially manufacture or force the auric picture of love. Love is a living force generated by a heart filled with superconscious love. The heart and the aura can do mighty works through the emanation of a radiant selfless love. Love's presence in the aura cleanses the aura of anyone touching the vicinity of the aura. All are cleansed in the purifying fire of love in the auric proximity of love.

Use the aura each day as an antenna and as a sender to send the light generated by love. The more love sending from the aura, the more the soul will expand its work of revealing, instructing, and healing. When the auric field is short-circuited by over-accumulation of debris, of self-doubt, of anxiety, or of unbelief in God, the soul becomes as a lung system without oxygen. One must keep the auric-field currents open and outward so that soul-power can be reflected and activated upon the auric screen.

Remain aware of the aura as an actual bracer against the harsh blows of the external world. Keep the aura spiritually alive by uniting with your own healing, sending, suggestible spiritual power in your aura.

Observe regular periods of spiritual stillness so that your aura may recondition and maintain its balance. Refuse to permit alien negative thoughts and emotions to color or add to any soil remaining in your aura. Learn to define what thoughts or feelings stem from yourself. Refuse to become an auric dumping ground for the soiled emotions and thoughts of others. Live through your own emotions, your own desires. Rout out false sentimentality and weakening dependence upon floating ideas of the past which brought only sorrow and confusion. Stay tuned in to the divinity of your soul. To maintain positive auric flow start always inward in your thinking and feeling. God first in your thoughts will determine that your aura is a healing sender of the pure and the good.

The flow of life current from the soul when locked-in to unknowing produces but partial knowing, living, and being. With receptive mediation, with mantramic speaking, one frees the locked-in powers of the soul, producing energies, vitalities, and joy. The auric field, when flowing outward with radiance, is the Presence manifested. *Use your aura to be free as a presence for God.*

SUGGESTIBLE EXERCISE AND MEDITATION

The most suggestible time of the day begins at dusk or sundown. The etheric body is from this time onward less charged with kinetic psychic fire. The Masters teach their disciples to take advantage of this spiritual inward drawing tide by deliberately entering into a mood of union with the spiritual presences. These presences are the angels, advanced initiates living in the world, gurus, teachers, Masters, the greater Elect or inward Masters and, finally, Jesus, the Archangels and the Father.

The body of the day is weary at each day's ending, weary of contesting, of aggression, of work burdens and of the endless round of earth glamour. The soul sun or light rises at dusk as the physical sun goes down, and the irresistible fire of the immortal self can be seen by the light of the soul.

Meditation at dusk should be a time of quiet, of peace, of health, of joy. It should be deeply desired in this time to make union with the One. Looking upon the gift-blessings given by the Divine Companions as a natural support in this time will give to the one meditating a feeling of enrichment and perfection.

If one is fortunate enough to be close to Nature during meditation, he should make himself at one with the life force pulsating in Nature. He should use the companion power of meditation — visualization — to see and feel the pulsating heart beat in the root of a plant or flower. He should feel the winged bird's heart beat beating in unison with the hum of the universe. In his visualization he should let Nature bless him and cradle him. He should become the plant, the flower, the bird, the sky, and thus he will clairsentiently prepare his mood for meditation.

Meditation begins with the heart. One should think of his heart as the sacred castle or a cathedral or a vast tryst place or a pranic mirror, that he can feel, see, know and thus widen his true perspective of love.

Heart openness is necessary as a first step in meditation. In the left ventricle of the heart is the sacred atom called the Atma by the Eastern teachers. Centered in the sacred atom is a microscopic blue flame of eternal akasic fire. This flame is the spark of God in man, or the eternal particle of spirit which never dies.

When visualization and union with Nature has been made and the heart has acknowledged itself to be a receptacle for love where the spiritual powers of love unite, one encounters God and feels with a love warming in his whole being the flame of God within the heart.

The blue flame in the heart is a moving flame, moving with contraction and expansion motion, working directly with the pulsation point of the soul over the crown of the head.

When one has touched the reality of love in the heart as a moving life force, the blue flame in the heart automatically begins to rise upward toward the pulsation point of the soul. In meditation upon the blue flame in the heart, one begins by breathing upward softly and gently without tension, counting inwardly, slowly to the count of six. With the upward count of six the blue flame rises and unites with the pulsation point of the soul. The breath is then held for a slow count of eight.

During the time of the waiting for the count of eight, the higher mind unites with the soul. One contacts the causal body or higher side of the etheric body.

When the causal body is contacted, one begins to exhale slowly to the count of eight. On exhaling he visualizes drawing downward and outward the golden rays of the higher mind into his heart. These rays are brighter than the sun. As they touch the heart, they become small golden spheres. As the breath exhales to the count of eight, the one meditating visualizes the golden spheres floating out and out into his environment, into the world and into the universe.

He should visualize and see the golden spheres coming from the dynamo blue-flame center of his heart. He should see the moving, pulsating power of his soul. He should know that his higher mind is involved in his sending of love into the world.

The raising of the blue flame into the soul's pulsation and the sending of the rays of the higher mind is a freeing process for the one who meditates, that he may unite his heart, soul and higher mind with all life in earth and in heaven.

This exercise in meditation should be used before *total receptive meditation*. One should bring the blue flame of the heart upward to make union with the soul's pulsation not more than three times. He should avoid tension in his breathing. He should be careful to eliminate all force or pressure in his desiring to send the golden spheres of his mind and heart into the world. Following this visualizing process and meditation, it is suggested that the one meditating will continue to meditate without emphasis upon the breath. He should release his breathing impulses to what the soul desires in his breathing.

The soul of man works in waves. The higher mind of man works in rays. When one breathes in and holds his breath, he unites with cosmic prana. In holding the breath, one literally touches *eternal spiritual substance*.

When one exhales or breathes out consciously during meditation, the life force or pranic substance he has gathered while holding his breath contains healing. He should be aware on breathing upward that he is reaching for this pranic healing substance, and he should be aware on exhaling or breathing out that he is sending selflessly to the world God's healing substance which is using him as a directing agent of healing love.

Should there be any condition in his own physical body in need of healing, he can when exhaling direct this pranic, outgoing healing life force into any portion of his own body needing health. He can also send this pranic healing life force through inoffensive loving intent into the etheric body of anyone he would seek to heal. Precaution: He should avoid sending this pranic healing indiscriminately. Only after he has prepared his heart by making union with his soul and higher mind should he seek to use this pranic life force. He should also abstain from *telling any man* or person that he has used this life-force transfusion healing technique. "See thou tell no man," said Jesus. Jesus knew that the power of pranic transfusion must be between the soul and God.

Receptive meditation should always be preceded by a visualizing preparatory suggestible exercise as the blue-flame exercise just given. In receptive meditation, one having made union with his heart, his soul and his higher mind has stilled the processes of his lower mind and he has polarized, taken command of and stilled the rampant psychic energies in the etheric body and in the astral core; from this, intense quiet enters into his being. His higher self becomes the Watcher overlooking the processes of his meditation.

In *receptive meditation* one moves into wave lengths of consciousness beyond the phenomena of psychic excitation. One makes no effort to see anything special or to interpret anything seen or heard during receptive meditation. To do so is to activate the intellect and set in motion the analytical aspects of the lower mind.

Receptive meditation is a practice of listening, of absorption and of union. Precaution: One should not extend receptive meditation for lengthy periods until he has learned how to organize and still the processes of his lower mind. He can only do this through preparation visualization exercises. One should seek always to experience meditation *consciously*.

The time limit of meditation when grace is present is determined by either the Guardian Protector Angel watching over one's soul powers or by the Master, teacher or guru.

When one is unready for extended meditation, some form of intrusion will take possession of the mind, such as thoughts concerning things that must be done, or things that one will do. When this occurs frequently, one will come to know that he has been monitored and censored in his meditation, and he should make a covenant thereafter that he will respond and be obedient to guidance and also more dedicated to Awareness.

The spiritual art of *Awareness* begins with concentration, attentiveness and contemplation. The lesser mind is similar to a restless animal. It is unruly, acknowledging no master. The lesser mind will do everything it can to place an obstacle between the one meditating and his higher mind. The lesser mind is a stubborn mind filled with hate, lust, pride, envy, covetousness. The lesser mind is a run-away combination of psychic energy forces. One subdues the lesser mind through attentiveness, contemplation and meditation.

The only true mind man possesses is his higher mind. This is the mind of creation. The Overlord of this mind is the Higher Self. The Higher Self when given free rein through the power of meditation will take command of the psychic forces in the lesser mind and transpose them into spiritual powers.

The spiritual art of meditation is attentive listening, attentive observing, plus receptive absorption of increased light.

Meditation is a light experience supported by the exercise of love's extending.

The physical time element in the Western disciple is his enemy. The practice of meditation will bend time, rearrange time and extend time, so that one will turn to the rhythmic supplementing inner time flow given through meditation.

To still the little mind one must firmly *take hold and let her not go—through love.* The lesser mind is similar to an animal desiring to be stroked. One should through suggestible soul-therapy stroke the resisting lesser mind with gentle assurances that it is worthwhile and has a place — however, never letting the lesser mind believe that it can have its own mind and own way.

One can speak to the lesser mind as he would to a hyperkinetic child, but he must especially make the lesser mind aware that it must work with the higher mind as a team worker or a partner.

Self-suggestible healing begins before one is getting ready to fall into sleep. To have a better day for the coming day one should give orders to the lesser mind, giving to it a clear outline of the basic skeletal pattern for the next day. To do this, one first addresses the *lesser etheric body* in tones of love. Lying on the right side of his physical body, he visualizes himself as looking inward into the etheric body. He sees this body of ether as a pranic duplicate of his physical body. He sees it in a golden pranic light, warm with life force. He begins to send love transfusions and reassuring reinforcements into the etheric body. He addresses it in this manner, "You are a wonderful body, containing life force, life restoring and life vitality. I see in you regeneration for my health, vitality for my efforts and unrestricted peace for my creation."

With this procedure one should feel a glorious warmth responding in the etheric body. After one has given the etheric body the love praise to relax it to the receptivity of the night's sleep and prepared it for dream experience of the night, he next turns to the lower mind and gives it instructions for the following day. Thus, he will say to it, "Tomorrow we will be outgoing. We will not be afraid of personal obligations or contacts. We will not procrastinate tomorrow. We will go directly towards discharging our responsibilities. We will eagerly do all of the things presented to us. We will accept any frustration knowing it to be discipline, but we will correct the cause of frustration if it comes from our being at fault. We will use our higher instincts to preserve our physical body and to care for it. We will not permit any habit to stand between us and what we really want to do. We are determined tomorrow that we will not be impulsive, greedy, selfish or pushy. We will utilize all of our good assets and use them as well as the day and the circumstances of the day will allow. We will acknowledge that we are not the one who is running the show. We will extend every sense into common sense and spiritual knowing."

After one has spoken to the lesser mind in suggestible soul-therapy, he will then *speak a mantram before sleep*. The speaking of a before-sleep mantram will enable him to have dream cognition of the night wherein he will meet the inward Master and receive instruction that he might better fulfill the coming day for the peace of his soul.

If he has failed to make peace with the lesser mind before sleep, he will have lower Quelle dream experience and enter into exhausting sleep sub-astral chimeras in the night. His dreams will devitalize him rather than refresh him.

If he has made peace with his lower mind and will accept what his conscience will tell him in the night, he will experience corrective dreams.

If sleep is to him a reality of the extension of his soul and spiritual nature, he will meet the Master in the night, and he will be given the third vitality, through which he can sustain and create on the following day.

Each day's awakening will find him eager and enthusiastic, awaiting the day's sunlight with joy. Having been replenished by the soul light of the night, his soul-sheath shall be luminous throughout the day, lighting his way.

On turning the emotions inward so as to suggestibly quicken the etheric body to its highest velocity of action, one should avoid love in the sense of self-love or a Narcissan love. One should take care that he does not call forth even the smallest portion of egotism and of pride. He should use his suggestible addressing to the lesser etheric body with soft mental speaking tones. Speaking aloud is not necessary. His praising should be the inward audible sound speaking. Such self-suggestion exercise is to be used only for one's self alone, not to be used under any condition upon the etheric body of another person.

One should be careful in his suggestible directives to his lesser mind that he will give no command having any form of desire for the getting of money and for the attaining of any form of physical success. All suggestible directives to the lesser mind should be that it might become a more flexible instrument to the events of the coming day and that the former defeatism attitudes of the lower mind might be transformed into willing, flexible allies of the higher mind.

If one has the inclination to have revengeful thoughts, his lower mind is heated with a wasplike stinging ability. Suggestible directives to such a mind will cool the energy fields supporting thoughts of hate, passion and overtension.

A contemplative exercise to be used for cooling the heat of passion and hate in the lower mind will be a contributing help. One should use it before retiring. Sitting on a chair in perfect quiet, he should begin this exercise by visualizing a red rose in the center of his heart. The rose is the flower of forgivingness. When used in contemplation before retiring and before the use of the suggestible directives, one will still and calm the tensions of the mind, will and heart.

By holding the visualization of a red rose in the center of the heart, visualizing its root, its stem, its leaf, its bud, and finally its flower, its velvety softness, its color — and with absolute attentiveness holding the vision of the rose softly in the heart's forgiving love — automatically one begins to relax aggressive and retaliative feelings. At the conclusion of this contemplation rose exercise, one should breathe softly from the diaphragm upward for the count of six. He should hold his breath for eight, exhaling eight. On exhaling, he should feel that the fragrance of the rose is going out gently through his nostrils, saturating the room, healing the fear atmosphere of his mind and emotions. He should repeat this gentle breathing exercise for seven times. On the last or seventh breath he should send the love of his heart wherever it desires to go. There should be no thought upon any particular person, letting love have its own winged choice of selection and direction.

THE AFFIRMING ANGELS

Believing shifts the life currents into health. Believing directs the mind currents into divine thinking. Believing inspires the soul-life currents to produce exquisite formulas for creation. Believing gives range, breadth, and freedom to the angelic suggestible flow, that life, mind, and soul may work without distraction. To be encompassed by the dear angelic assurances, to believe in their constant fortifying is to harmonize, to heal, and to bless. When one believes that he is divinely created for a very special way and purpose, the affirming angels sound their yea, yea, yeas. Then, one's thoughts move upward into wave currents of sublime joy. When one joins his own yea, yea, yea affirming to the angelic affirming, at this moment that which is sounded as true, that which is beheld of the right is done; it is manifested instantly, quickly. God — the first, the One — is the pinnacle for lifted beliefs. Believe on Him, on His power. Cease not in believing.

SUGGESTIBLE EXERCISE FOR THE HEALING OF OTHERS

One who desires to spiritually heal the sick should avoid intruding upon the will of another person. The spiritual scientist recognizes first of all the right of every person to experience for himself. Therefore he avoids intruding his will, which is colored by his own opinions and judgments as to the cause and need of healing. Knowing the angels to be the most totally selfless suggestible ministers to the healing needs of man, he uses a unique and miraculous technique to give surcease and help to suffering, confusion, and sorrow. This technique of suggestible healing' is called Mediative Healing.

MEDIATIVE HEALING TECHNIQUE

1. Mediative healing begins by prayer on the knees.

2. After prayer, one should be seated. He should prepare to become a mediative channel for healing by speaking a *before-meditation mantram*.

   Example: Before-Meditation Mantram

   I pray that I shall have wisdom, reverence, and ethic into the good way of healing, and that my mind may be illumined with new skills, new words, new healing tasks. May I move with the times, aware of the need through which men suffer under the burden of the world.

3. Gently close the eyes. Hold love in the heart (ten seconds).

4. Visualize Light stilling the thoughts on the level of the brow (ten seconds).

5. Raise the Light to the crown of the head; hold the Light steadily, and then visualize the person or persons to be healed. Each person should be held in the Light singly. (This portion of the Mediative Healing Technique should not extend longer than five minutes.)

6. While holding each person in the Light, speak an *Angel to Angel Mantram.*

Example: Angel to Angel Mantram

Beloved, my angel speaks unto thy angel.
If it is the Will of the Father,
May you be healed in the name of the Christ.

7. Conclude by speaking an *after-meditation mantram.*

Example: After-Meditation Mantram

O Lord, Carpenter of human hearts, extend
my roof of heart comforts; see into my house-
hold of love; teach me how to live in Thy gen-
erous unending love.

8. Optional: prayer on the knees. With complete conviction and faith, give thanks to the Father.

For best results, this Mediative Suggestible healing exercise should be used at sundown.

GLOSSARY

AKASIA — A supernal spiritual-life substance used by consciousness. The akasic light is soul-light. The color of akasia is indigo blue and is seen often in visions during meditation. Ether is the coagulating life substance. Prana is the energizing life substance in ether. Akasia is a light *consciousness* animating substance. Akasia substance is used in the highest form of spiritual telepathy. The more highly evolved one is, the more akasia he has in his mental and soul-light. One breathes in pranic energy to renew life force. One meditates to increase akasic light in his mind.

AKASIC RECORDS — Records of former lives.

ARCHETONE — The Word under command of the Holy Spirit used in conjunction with all great archetypes. When the archetone sounds, the archetype comes alive with whatever compulsion is ripe or ready to be manifested. Thus an archetype remains dormant until the archetone sounds. The Holy Ghost working with the Will of God sounds the archetone, that the great ideas or new impulse for man may enter the world or fall into the mind of man in timing to the Will of God.

ARCHETYPE — Original or divine blueprint for the mind and life processes in the earth. The greater archetypes work first as the unmanifest or as the Word yet to be made flesh. These spiritual creative divine archetypal compulsions move in tides into the world through the minds of men. In each great archetype is an archetone. The Holy Spirit sounds within the archetone when the divine Word is ready to enter into the mind and life of man.

ASTRAL — Star or planetary reflections. The astral is a unique, unceasing, fermenting, mirroring and moving action producing in man a state of emotion, mood and inductive feeling and thinking.

ASTRAL BODY — Emotional body.

ASTRAL CORE — An ovoid shaped envelope of astral fire kept in balance by nadi points or sound vortices located along the spinal system. The nadis act as absorption points receiving the sound and vibratory currents from the planets. The astral core represents the emotional body. The planetary fire playing upon the spinal system is distributed and generated by the assistance of the glands and the nadi points. Thus, the nervous system is protected in the etheric and physical bodies from being the recipient of direct vibrational force playing upon the spinal canal. When the astral core is unprotected, the glandular system goes out of balance, and the emphasis is an overcharge of psychic energy in the etheric body and in the lesser mind. One protects himself from the unruly charge of the astral-core fire through mantrams, contemplation, meditation, prayer and selfless service.

ASTRAL WORLD — The astral world is supported by the magnetic belt around the earth. The higher astral world is the First Heaven. The lower astral world relates to man's subconscious mind in death and in life. The grotesque level of the astral world reflects the sin-body of the earth. The four lower planes of the astral world are the recipients of the lower vibrations and energies of the planetary light. This sub-planetary energy produces a chimera mirage-like effect upon the emotions of man in life and in death, producing glamor and mesmeric effects upon the lower mind and senses of man. The astral world in the Bible is called "the serpent." Man commands the astral world by the use of his higher will and higher mind.

AURA — The energy field around the body.

CENTER Q — Same as Quelle.

CO-ATOM — To be co-atom to any person, one must be on the same wave length of energy emanating from a sacred atom, as to be co-atom to Jesus one must have an open circuit in his own heart's sacred atom to the heart of Jesus. To be co-atom to a teacher or a Master, one must have a wave-length open circuit or a degree of light in his mental atoms to the mental atoms of his teacher or Master. In this way he is telepathically communicable to the mind and thoughts of his Master and teacher, and thus receives a continued flow of instruction. One can develop his own capacity in co-atom association through meditation and through thoughts of oneness with all life as given of God. When two persons have instant recognition of one another, and absolute congeniality, they are co-atom to one another. This can only occur when one has been with the other person in many lives where relationships have proved to be harmonious. When God prepares to use a person for a greater work, He first sends to the one chosen a teacher or Master; secondly, He sends to him a co-atom person in the world, that the work may be consummated and fulfilled.

COSMOS-GENESIS — After man has reached the perfected self-genesis stage of evolvement, he will become a cosmos-genesis man. His emotional body will be fully developed and he will be at one with the love atoms of Jesus, the Lord of Love. All great Bodhisattvas of the East had reached full development of their emotional bodies, and thus gave to man the bhakti love instruction. John the Beloved, the disciple of Jesus, had a perfected emotional body and therefore was the closest disciple to the heart of Jesus.

EFFLUVIA — An intelligible animating reflecting side of ether through which one is informed. Seership would be impossible without the effluvia chemical action in ether. Effluvia reflects what is, and is an instrument for all pictorial life, living and dead. Clairsentient psychics are familiar with effluvia's chameleon-like and versatile action. Everything a man touches leaves a revealing effluvia through which a psychic may extend his senses to gain knowledge of persons or objects. Effluvia is not a permanent substance, lasting only from sundown to sundown. Ether remains in environments; however, with time the effluvia is withdrawn. One therefore can be aware of ether imprints long after a person has ceased to inhabit an environment. But if effluvia is absent, he cannot penetrate the most intimate details concerning a person or an environment.

EGO — The higher individuality supported by the higher thoughts of past lives and of the present life.

EMOTIONAL BODY — The emotional body and the astral body are one and the same. In the less evolved, the emotions work primitively. The emotional body is an ovoid sphere of feeling. The shape of the emotional body determines that every positive or negative feeling shall return to the one who feels it, also that the desires of a person shall inevitably be manifested. The emotional body and the astral core work as hand in glove. The astral fiery core keeps alive and supports the feelings within the emotions and desires.

ENTITY — An earthbound-dead person lingering in the lower astral planes.

ETERNITY SYSTEM — Any system having a sun, earth and planets. There are countless eternity systems in the universe. All are born and die as man is born and dies.

ETHER — The life substance supporting all life, called "prana" in the East, and called by some "bioplasma" in the West. Ether is a coagulating semi-gelatile and semi-fluid substance. Ether is quasi-tangible. It can be photographed. Ether supports electric and magnetic action and other forms of energy yet to be discovered by man.

ETHERIC BODY — The double of the physical body. It is made of ether or prana. Its life substance is supported by the sun. The lower aspect of the etheric body supports the life in the physical body and the life of the lower mind. The higher aspect of the etheric body supports the spiritual and higher mental life. The higher etheric body survives death. The lower etheric body dissolves with the physical body.

FAMILY-ATOM — An etheric encasement psychically charged. Father, mother, and children in a family-atom are held together by the psychical charge or lines of force which have attracted them to one another. The low charge of psychic energy in a family-atom keeps alive the soul-debts memory between each person born in the family. The soul-grace of the persons born in the family-atom is watched over by a family-atom Guardian Angel. If grace is abundant, all souls in a family-atom progress. If the family-atom is heavily laden with karma, the result is suffering and sacrifice, that all may eventually evolve in a cluster of human souls.

FAMILY-GENESIS—Persons dependent upon ancestral myth inheritance as expressed through a mother and father in a family-atom. Family-genesis impulses seek to build a society patterned after ancestral heritage. From the family-atom compulsion comes the building of churches, the building of societies and education.

GURU — Teacher.

HIERARCH — The Elohim, the host or the zodiacal Overlords assisting this earth or eternity system in its development. Hierarchy uses the power of imaging or making. Sending their rays into the sun and the earth, they assist the Father and the Christ in the creation of mankind. Each Hierarch Overlord is a zodiacal prototype or blueprint for man, such as Aries, Taurus, etc.

HUMAN-GENESIS — Same as Family-genesis.

INITIATE — An ego who has followed a spiritual path in previous lives and is in a state of being initiated into greater illumination and spiritual power in this life, that he might better serve the world.

KARMA — The law of cause and effect or sowing and reaping.

LOGOS — The audible sound of the Holy Ghost speaking through inspiration, illumination and revelation. The center of logos is between the eyebrows.

LUNAR BRAIN — The abdominal automatic primitive brain supporting the instinctual life. The center of clairsentience situated in the solar plexus.

LUNAR PSYCHIC — One who is engrossed psychically with his emotions and sees all through emotions and feelings. He is dependent upon the astral lunar reflective light for his psychic powers. The lower lunar psychic is unable to interpret what he sees. The higher lunar psychic sees in part.

MANTRAM — The sounding of word-combinings to dissolve karma, tension, and fear. A mantram contains molecular energy particles of light. A mantram spoken with love and absolute belief is a freeing way.

MEDIATION — Mediation is the most unselfish and unclaiming means of spiritual serving through which one remains impersonally involved with the karma of those whom he would heal or help.

MEDIATOR — One who makes himself a divine artery or channel for the light. A mediator asks for no rewards for his mediative prayers and suggestible helps. He only asks to remain a perfect instrument, that the power and Will of God may flow through him supporting, healing, and lifting. When the mediator is sincere and wholly dedicated, he is free from the karma of those whom he would heal and help. He avoids boastfulness of his healing works. He asks no personal or physical rewards for his healing helps, knowing himself to be but a channel through whom God sends and heals. The highest technique used by a mediator is his use of Angel-to-Angel

Mantrams, as he knows on his releasing the one whom he would help to the angels' suggestible helps, that the angel taking charge of the one to be healed knows with an exact and precise wisdom what can be done and what will be done. Thus in the angelic mediative helps miracles occur as it is left to God to reveal to the angels what is the right and just way for the healing to come.

MENTAL BODY — A composite field of light. The higher mind expresses itself in the mental body through three mental atoms. The lower aspect of the mental body, called the lesser mind, is dependent upon the psychic energy coils of force inherited from past lives, from ancestral mental habits. The lower mind serves the physical senses, using instincts from tribal-genesis memory and ancestral memory. It is the work of all spiritual aspirants to still the more atavistic aspects of the lower mind or lesser mind and make of it a complementing additive partner to the higher self and the higher mind. The higher mind seeks to clear the field, that it may come forth as a supernal instrument in creation. In all selfless works of creation, the higher mind is in command.

NEUTRAL FIELD — A non-decisive mental atmosphere inviting entity possession. A neutral field is the product of many lives. One builds a neutral mental field by refusing to participate in the responsible issues of life. A neutral-field mind is described in the Bible as being "lukewarm." It is said that persons having such minds are "spewed out" and of little use to God. Mediumistic powers in the hands of a neutral-field person are sometimes pure, sometimes impure, as both the dark and the light can be housed at one time in a neutral-field mind.

PRANA — Life-force energy. Prana is the higher energy level of ether working simultaneously with the molding and shaping action of the effluvia in the ether. The energy in high prana has yet to be analyzed by science. One contacts prana through breathing. Prana life-force may be unlocked and freed into the etheric body through cosmic exercises, yoga, breathing, speaking of mantrams.

PRO-GENESIS — When men have become like Jesus, as promised in I John 3:1-3, they will be Pro-genesis men with cosmic powers of manifestation. They will do all things, as did Jesus. Following Pro-genesis will be All-genesis in which all mankind will be at one with our Father which art in heaven. And finally, men will become the sons of light with hierarchy powers. This period is called One-genesis.

QUELLE — The subconscious seated at the base of the skull. Quelle also has a higher aspect, called the higher unconscious.

RISHIS — Ancient sages, wise men, and teachers of the East.

SELF-GENESIS — The individualistic person concerned with his own evolvement. In lesser self-genesis he is engrossed with his own self-interest; in higher self-genesis he recognizes the right of every man to become an identity and to relate himself to the Cause of his being, or God.

SOLAR INITIATE — He is united to the informing principle. In his psi powers he is a scientist working with the Spirit of Truth.

SOLAR PSYCHIC — Same as solar initiate.

SOUL-MEDALLION — A pulsating vortex of supernal light in constant movement around the head of man, keeping alive his soul impulses and mental creative compulsions.

The soul's medallion works in conjunction with the heart beat in expansion and contraction. In the uttermost upper point of the soul's medallion directly above the skull is a pulsating vibratory action. This pulsating action becomes the heart beat for the spiritual body after death. The soul's medallion records on its outer rim man's negative actions. This is called the vibratory hum. The vibratory hum of the soul's medallion is reflected into the lesser mind. Each time a person meditates he must clear the field of the vibratory hum and slow it down.

SOUL-SHEATH — A rim of incandescent light around the physical body. This light flows from the light of the soul's medallion and is built from grace and purity.

STELE — The starry point between the eyebrows, or the center of command through which the higher consciousness moves forth into the world.

TRIBAL-GENESIS — Nomadic segments or clusters of people who have interlocking blood ties sealed into tribal encasements. Dependent upon primitive etheric laws, tribal-genesis persons live close to the tribal consciousness and taboos of their forefathers.

WORLD SOUL — The combined lower and higher subconscious impulses of all sentient and consciousness life of the earth united with the love of God, under command of Him who is the Regent of all souls of the earth — Jesus.

OTHER BOOKS
by ANN REE COLTON

THE JESUS STORY $7.95
 A miracle book in timing to the need for miracles.

THE HUMAN SPIRIT $6.50
 A scientific, spiritual, and healing book on the creation,
 purpose and destiny of man.

PROPHET FOR THE ARCHANGELS $5.95
 The life story of Ann Ree Colton
 (co-author, Jonathan Murro).

THE SOUL AND THE ETHIC $5.50
 A profound book on the soul and on the ethical use of soul
 power.

THE KING $5.00
 From the personal, hieroglyphic journal of Ann Ree Colton.

DRAUGHTS OF REMEMBRANCE $3.50
 An extraordinary book on the subject of reincarnation.

MEN IN WHITE APPAREL $3.50
 A book of vital revelations about death and the life after
 death.

THE VENERABLE ONE $3.50
 An initiatory book for those who love Nature and who would
 unveil Nature's secrets.

VISION FOR THE FUTURE $3.75
 A prophetic book to comfort men in a perilous time.

THE LIVELY ORACLES $3.75
 A prophetic book on world events.

ISLANDS OF LIGHT $3.95
 A book of initiation with an underlying prophetic theme.

PRECEPTS FOR THE YOUNG $1.25
 Appreciated by the adult . . . inspiring to the child . . . and
 beneficial to the family.

VISION ON A BATTLEFIELD $ .50
 An unusual story about war.

SONGS OF MIRTH, REVERENCE AND FAITH $1.50
 Songs to be enjoyed by persons of all ages—from the
 youngest child to the adult with a childlike heart.

HOME-STUDY LESSONS
 Monthly Home-Study lessons for adults. Lessons are also available
 for children and young adults.

ARC PUBLISHING CO.
P.O. Box 1138 Glendale, California 91209

362

INDEX